You're Never Too Old to Surf!
A Seniors' Guide to Safe Internet Use

Vicki L. Sauter

Library of Congress Control Number: 2015900881
CreateSpace Independent Publishing Platform, North Charleston, SC

ISBN-13: 978-1506163857
ISBN-10: 1506163858

Cover design by: Karen Kelly of St. Louis, Missouri
Interior Design by: Računalo Associates of St. Louis, Missouri

Contents

Preface

This book is for you if you have ever wanted to harness the power of the Internet, but haven't been quite sure what that means or how to do it. It is intended for the parents, grandparents and great-grandparents who want to use the wide range of tools that are available today on the Internet, from simply surfing the web to buying online, using email, blogs and even social networking sites. You may have sought guidance from your child or grandchild only to be annoyed at their exasperated response to your questions. Or, you may have tried it on your own and gotten frustrated with the tools, or had some problem result from that use (or know someone who did). You may be using the Internet, but just not feel very confident in what you are doing. If you fall in any of those categories, I wrote this book for YOU! Of course, if you are the child or grandchild and are having trouble explaining things to your parent or grandparent, this book could help you too.

I want to share information with you. I have distilled more than 40 years of experience without the techno-babble, but with an emphasis on the important issues. I think I have a different approach than other books because I am doing it from the beginning, avoiding jargon, and tying the efforts to things you already do and understand. I learned from my experience with explaining the Internet to my own mother that she would only "get it" when she could relate the experience to something she already knew. As I explained to her, and you will see in the book, an ISP is essentially a telephone exchange, and a URL is used the same as a street address. She could relate to the need for locks on her doors and windows, and that could be used to explain the various kinds of computer security needed for safe use of the Internet. A blog is nothing more than a diary where those reading it actually admit it and leave comments. In other words, I could explain this "Internet thing" as long as I related it back to the things she knew and understood in the physical world.

I had a second learning experience before I began this book; it was set in a swimming pool. I had a bad knee for years and needed to exercise in a pool to avoid further injury, so I joined a water aerobics class. Most such classes, I have learned, are populated by women over 65, so I was always the "kid" in the class. I did not talk much about my background because people tend to be put off both by professors and "computer people." But, it did slowly leak out that I was both. Thereafter people began to ask me questions about their computers. It is challenging, to say the least, to answer questions about computers when you are in a pool, there is no computer around, and your listeners do not really have much background from which to explain their problems. From this I learned to ask questions and explain fairly complicated problems and options in the simplest way I could. Here too I relied upon the tool of referring back to the physical world to explain how the electronics work.

This book uses the approach that I used with my mother and with the ladies in the pool. It is technically correct and complete, but it does not use the normal jargon in the explanation. I have tried, instead to make the book "chatty" in an effort to engage the reader and keep his/her attention long enough to convey the concept. Further, I have tried to explain all aspects of the computer using physical analogies and practical solutions. The result is, I believe, an interesting, easy-to-read book that explains internet activities, what kinds of activities they might want to consider, and a "how to" manual to make it happen.

I want to help navigate the Internet as things change and evolve too. So, I have set up a blog that has small discussions of whatever is impacting Internet use. You can read the blog at **http://internetuseforseniors.wordpress.com/**. You can ask questions to any posting, and learn more. This is another feature that is different about this book when compared to others.

This book has been a labor of love. I want to thank my friends and family for their support, encouragement and patience. I want to thank the following people who answered my silly questions about their Internet use to help me move this book along: Bob Abrams, Susan Albin, Celeste Amitin, David Bird, Jim Breaugh, M.A. Bushman, Christine Bullen, James Campbell, Mira Carlson, Carol Cohn, Lee Cox, John Cunningham, Marilyn Daegele, Dick Deckro, Mimi Duncan, Ed Fischer, Mary Forsyth, Bruce Fowler, Jane Garvey, M.J. Goerke, Deb Graslaub, Judi Guzior, John Hall, Vicki Harring, Dean Hartley, Carol Heineck, Anne Hopkins, Ken Hunt, Sue Hurst, Art Hurter, Barb Kalnes, Kris Kerth, Ann Koby, Maureen Kruszynski, Don Lewis, Larry Madeo, Silvia Madeo, Leslye Madden, Chris May, Carol Jean McCarthy, Dan McCollum, Rae Mohrman, Al Martinich, Joe Martinich, Tony Martinich, JoAnne Meachum, Ken Monroe, Peter Mueller, John Myre, Bob Nauss, Dick Navarro, Craig Nelson, Pat Niehaus, Mike Nolen, Margaret O'Connor, Tom O'Hanlon, Maggie O'Toole, Paul Pratte, Jimi Quick, Loie Riehl, Wayne Reidlinger, Carolyn Reineke, David Ronen, Paul Roth, Randy Robinson, Nancy Rubenstein, Bob Samples, Susan Sanchez, Bill Sauter, Linnea Sauter, Roger Sauter, Spencer Sauter, Wayne Sauter, Debi Scarpelli, Joe Schofer, Alan Shenberg, Phyllis Siegel, Art Smialek, Mimi Smith, Carolyn Sumner, Rosie Talarzyk, Frank Trippi, Roseann Vonesh, Helen Wall, Tim Walsh, Larry Westermeyer, Mel Whapham, Jean Wiering, Wayne Winter, and Eric Wolman. Anyone whose name I forgot, I thank you too. I am grateful to the following people who read parts of this book and helped to make it more readable and meaningful: Marilyn Daegele, Joe

Martinich, Loie Riehl, Tim Walsh, and Mel Whapham. I am grateful to Karen Walsh for her technical support in creating this book.

I want to thank Karen Kelly, Artist-in-Residence at the Framin' Place for capturing the spirit of my book with the cover art.

The people who really deserve thanks are my family. My husband, Joseph Martinich, has been with me every step of the way -- not only with this book, but in my entire career. He is supportive and an excellent editor! I sincerely doubt that I could have done any of it without him. My son, Michael Martinich-Sauter, has demonstrated infinite patience with his mother. More important, he has inspired me to look at every topic differently and more creatively. I am most grateful he has shared his wisdom with me. Finally, I want to acknowledge the sage Lady Alexandra (a.k.a. Allie -- the dog), who made me laugh when I really needed it, and whose courage made me appreciate everything more.

The Author

Vicki Sauter received her Ph.D. in systems engineering at Northwestern University, and has been a Professor of Information Systems at University of Missouri – St. Louis for over 35 years. She is a baby boomer with over 40 years of experience using and programming computers. She has published many academic papers and two books (John Wiley publisher). Sauter initially used email using BITNet (a predecessor to the Internet) in the 1980s. Her first attempts to put information on the Internet used Gopher, the predecessor to the World Wide Web (now known simply as the Web). She chaired the university's committee to create its first web presence, and has been active in developing and using the web to share information since then (see http://www.umsl.edu/~sauterv). Sauter's first purchase online was in 1997, and she has used Facebook since 2005. Said differently, Vicki Sauter has been using and teaching the tools since they were invented, and so she has a great deal of experience to share, about the how and why to use the Internet, and how to use it safely.

What is the Internet?

What do people mean when they refer to "the Internet"? The term is used extensively in the media, in business settings, and in everyday life, but few people know, with any degree of clarity, exactly what it is. The Internet, often simply called the Net, is simply a group of connected computers that exist around the world. Some of these computers belong to individuals such as you. Some of them belong to businesses, such as General Motors, news organizations, such as the *New York Times,* universities, research centers, or governmental agencies, including the White House. They exist not only exist across the United States, but also in China, Argentina, France, Zambia, Malta, Tuvalu, and most other countries of the world.

The Net is nothing but connections of computers that make it convenient for computers to communicate; much like the Interstate highway system is nothing but high-speed road connections between cities and towns in the United States. The Net is a high-speed pathway by which information travels from one computer to another, just as the Interstates provide paths by which vehicles travel. By itself, the Net is as boring as driving through central Illinois. But the beauty of the Internet lies in the fact that people can share information and interests. The Net can allow you to talk to people all over the world, to develop a discussion or support group, to pursue a hobby, to explore a question that has bothered you, play games, go shopping and more. The Internet has made possible a range of opportunities by which people link together that would have been unimaginable a few decades ago.

It is important to realize that *no one* owns the Internet. While connected through the Internet, computers and their users are *independent*. The computers are maintained to different standards of accuracy and currency, and exist for different purposes; the users are bound by different laws, and guided by different ethical standards. Some computers house information to educate people or sell products. Others, unfortunately, exist to support theft, fraud, kidnaping and other malicious ends. The Internet is a powerful platform both for doing good things and for doing bad things. Unethical or illegal operations exist, not by any inherent shortcoming of the technology, but because some users are moved by nefarious tendencies.   Part of learning about the Net is learning how to surf *safely* and avoid these traps.

How Are the Computers Connected?
When you first think about it, you imagine a lot of cables and cords going from

your computer to lots of other computers. Then, you look outside and see that is clearly not the case. So, how are all of these computers connected? The connections of the computers are much like the connections of traditional land-line telephones. The analogy is easier to understand if you can remember back to when there were named, neighborhood telephone exchanges. There was a local office into which telephones of a certain neighborhood connected. When I was growing up, our telephone number was COlumbus 1-3442, so we were connected to the Columbus exchange. The Columbus exchange had connections to all of the other exchanges in Chicago (and then ultimately the country). When I wanted to make a telephone call to MAnsfield 6-1987, I would link to the Columbus exchange (by picking up the receiver), and then use its connection to the Mansfield exchange which would, in turn, allow access to the specific number I was calling. In other words, I linked to the Columbus exchange, my friend linked to the Mansfield exchange; since the Columbus exchange and Mansfield exchanges were connected, we could talk.

The computers connect in much the same way. Your computer connects to something called an Internet Service Provider (ISP). This might be your local cable or telephone company, a university or company or some other provider. These providers, in turn, have connections to other providers. So, when you want to connect to another computer, you connect to your ISP, and use its connection to another ISP which will connect directly to the desired computer. This is shown below.

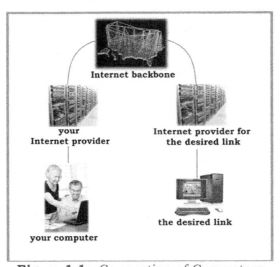

Figure 1.1: Connection of Computers

So, do you want to know what the Net "looks like," and how all those computers are really connected? As you might guess, this is very hard to describe because currently there are almost three billion Internet users worldwide. But, there are people who attempt to map the connections and study them. One group is the Opte Project, which created a variety of maps to describe the internet. The one below was created in 2005, and is one of the best visualizations of the Internet I have found.

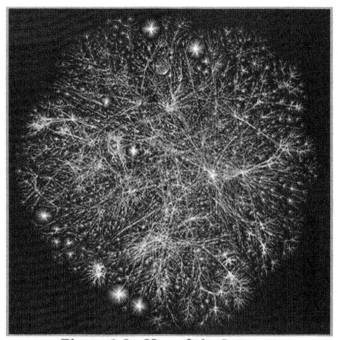

Figure 1.2: Map of the Internet

You can think of the map in Figure 1.2 as many Figure 1.1 images put on top of each other.

Another way to visualize the Internet is to consider the ISP's that provide Internet access, and the amount of access they provide. Some nodes, such as Google.com, would be shown as very large because the vast majority of users access them. Other nodes, like a vintage doll shop, are small because only a small percentage of the users on the Internet access them. If you view them as a map, as Google did with their "Internet Map" shown on the next page, you can get a wider view of what is available. You can move around the map, and zoom in and out, to see the biggest and the tiniest nodes.

Google's Internet map allows you to search for a particular node (such as ancestry.com) and view related nodes. In addition if you click on the node, you can get more information about the node as shown in Figure 1.3.

A variety of computers are connected to each of these nodes. The principal data routes, called the Internet backbone, connect to many major nodes which, in turn, are connected to smaller and smaller nodes, which are eventually connected to individual computers. To get from one place to another, you must hop among these nodes. The key to making the Internet work is that the computers know how to make those hops; so for us, movement is automatic. It is a lot like the root structure for some of daylilies that try to overrun my garden!

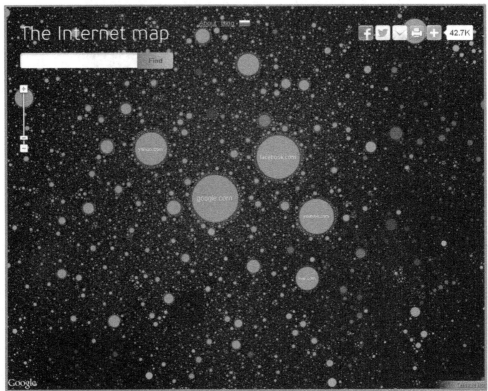

Figure 1.3: Google's Map of the Internet
http://internet-map.net/

Having these nodes makes it easier to find specific information. Each of those computers has a unique address, much like each of our homes has an address. To "people," my office is at 226 ESH, Building 10, 8001 Natural Bridge Rd., University of Missouri-St. Louis, St. Louis, MO 63121-4400 USA. To find me, a person would first need to find a map of the USA, then Missouri, and then St. Louis so as to be able to arrive here. Once in St. Louis, the person would need to locate Natural Bridge Road on a map of the metropolitan area, and travel to 8001, which would put them on the campus of the University of Missouri-St. Louis. The person would need to locate a map of the campus, and locate Building 10, and then move to office 26 on the second floor. We do it every day, and it seems quite natural.

Computers know nothing about locating my physical location because they have a different addressing system. Computers are more interested in the address of my computer, which is called an Internet Protocol Address (generally referred to as an IP Address). Computers locate my computer using the address of my Office, which is 134.124.22.17.

Finding Your Own IP Address

Generally you will not need to know your own IP address. The computer broadcasts it to other computers, and that is what is important. If you wish to know your IP address, you can get it from your computer. *How* to do that depends on your operating system. A quick way to find it, however, is to check sites such as,
http://whatismyipaddress.com or
http://www.lawrencegoetz.com/programs/ipinfo/

You may get information on your ISP or just the address. Remember though, these services exist to sell you things. Be careful what buttons you push!

To find me, they would need to locate node 134.124, which is a unique identifier for the University of Missouri - St. Louis. The campus has many networks on which to connect computers. The 22nd one happens to connect the computers on my floor in my building. I was the 17th office that was connected. So, a map of just part of the University of Missouri-St. Louis component of the Internet resembles Figure 1.4. It is easy to see how this could get as large and complicated as Figure 1.2 quickly.

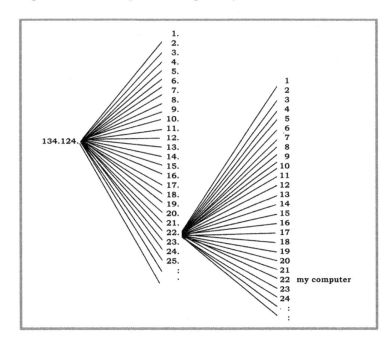

Figure 1.4:
Graphical Representation of a Small Part of the Internet

Every computer on the Internet has a unique IP address, such as this. People

Google Maps

When getting a physical location these days, many users go to the computer. One popular site for maps is http://maps.google.com. Google has mapped the world allowing users to find locations and to visualize what it would be like to be at that location. If you were to type in "Express Scripts Hall", "UMSL" on maps.google.com, you would get directly to my building (and not need to go through the process described to the left. In addition, you could even see a photo of my building (shown below).

generally do not need to know what it is, but, other computers need to know it to know where to send information. Sometimes we use the "official address," which will always be a four-part number separated by periods (stops) as with my address. While this is good for computers, people are not good at remembering numbers such as these. So, we frequently use aliases. My computer is also known as giverny.umsl.edu.

This says that my computer is in an educational institution (because of the .edu), specifically the University of Missouri - St. Louis (UMSL), and that my computer is listed as "Giverny." This is much easier for me to remember. But, unfortunately, it is not easy for the computer to remember (it likes numbers better). So, there is a general address book that is replicated many times over the network, called the Domain Name System (DNS). It translates these people-friendly names into the IP addresses so the computer can locate the correct place to send information. The ISP's keep this "address book" called a "DNS server" so they can find any address anywhere in the world. You, therefore, do not need to do anything but type in the people-friendly address. The ISP does the rest.

There is an interesting trivia note with addresses that I need to share. Computers in all countries other than the United States require a country code at the end of their addresses. So, for example, addresses in Canada will end in .ca; addresses in the United Kingdom will end in .uk; addresses in Namibia will end in .na; addresses in Japan will end in .jp; and so forth.

You might ask why this is so, and why the United States does not need to use a country code designation. There actually is a precedent for this: postage stamps. The concept of the postage stamp began in the United Kingdom, and was in use there before being adopted by other countries around the world. So, their stamps never had the name of the country recorded. When other countries began to use postage stamps, they needed to state the name of the country to differentiate their stamps from those in the United Kingdom. Even today, every country must designate its name on its stamps – except for the United Kingdom. Likewise, the Internet, including domain names, was in use in the United States before it was adopted by other countries. Hence, the names in other countries needed to distinguish themselves from the United States.

In the United States, computer addresses generally end with what is called the "domain type," intended to differentiate the kind of organization with which a computer is affiliated. It is not a perfect system, but at least there is an attempt to help users understand what kind of organization they are viewing.

Common Domain Names in the United States

.com	Commercial Organization
.edu	Educational Institution (usually higher education)
.gov	Government body
.int	Organizations Created by International Treaty
.mil	Military site
.museum	Museums

However, it is about to get more confusing because ICANN (the group that assigns names) is in the process of creating new domains, some using alphabets other than those we see today.

Why Does the Net Exist?

By now, you probably are asking, *why* does the Net exist? If you ask the "younger generation" this question, they will probably say they could not exist without it. But, we have, and quite well, thank you. So, from where did it come? As with Velcro, Tang, athletic shoes, enriched baby food, and pool purification systems, the Net traces its existence to the U.S. Space Program. The beginnings of the Net can be traced back to the US Government's response to the launching of Sputnik in the 1950s. The Defense Department created a network of computers called the Advanced Research Projects Agency, more commonly called ARPAnet, to facilitate research projects that were distributed across several locations. Later, universities founded a similar project to link computers for research collaboration called BITnet (Because It's Time). In the 1980s, the National Science Foundation used ARPAnet and BITnet to link supercomputers. Most research institutions and universities were connected, but it was not until programs were created to make it easy to use that the Net came to life for other uses. Once it was established people have continued to find new ways to connect with each other and to share their interests.

The Internet of Things

You might have heard a news report discussing the Internet of "Things" or perhaps the Internet of "Everything" and wondered about it. A short definition is the wireless connection of everyday objects to each other and to the internet. This might include everything from your toaster to the inventory used by or created by your company. The goal is to measure the performance of objects and respond to it via the computer. You may have seen commercials whereby people turn lights on or off, secure doors or alarms, and even start the morning coffee remotely by using their smart phone. This is possible because those items each have an electronic tag that is linked to information about your home, which you access via a program on your smartphone via the internet. In the future, we will not only collect data about the safety of our homes, but also the productivity of our food supply. Sensors in the field can measure weather conditions to trigger irrigation use automatically. Or, the sensors can check the food to determine if it is ready for harvest. Or small intelligent fetal monitors can maintain a record of progress and alert doctors as problematic conditions are detected.

This is All so New – Or is It?

Over the last ten to fifteen years, we have all heard a lot of hype about what the Internet is, what it promises, and the strange things that can happen there. It all seems very futuristic to think of the Information Highway, as if we are finally inventing something *new* in the way that we communicate. As with most things, though, this is not new; we have been there before with what the Victorians called the "Highway of Thought."

As a self-proclaimed computer geek, I was surprised one day when I saw the book *The Victorian Internet*[1], because I had never heard of such a thing. The book illuminates the features common to the nineteenth century and the Internet of today: hype, skepticism, hackers, on-line romances and weddings, chat-rooms, flame wars, information overload, predictions of imminent world peace, and so on. In the preface to the book,[1] when discussing how people reacted to the telegraph, Standage states, "For some people, they tap a deep vein of optimism, while others find in them new potential ways to commit crime, initiate romance, or make a fast buck – age-old human tendencies that are all too often blamed on the technologies themselves."

---

1 Standage, Tom, *The Victorian Internet,* New York: Walker and Company, 1998.

This fascinating book traces telegraphy (and the Internet) back to 1791 with the Chappe brothers who used black and white panels, telescopes and codebooks to send messages between distant towns. He then goes on to discuss how early-on the telegraph was seen as "more of a conjuring trick than a means of communication" (as was the Internet) and the development of a new electronic jargon. Unfortunately, he also finds instances of people exploiting information imbalances and stolen secrets. He found examples of "online" love, marriages over the wires, "chat rooms", naming conventions, capacity problems and their solutions and even online meetings. For someone who has been involved with the Internet for a very long time, the parallels were amazing and revealing.

Projection of the Impact of Telegraphs
(and later of the Internet)

The different nationalities and races of men will stand, as it were, in the presence of one another. They will know one another better. They will act and react upon each other. They may be moved by common sympathies and swayed by common interests. Thus the electric spark is the true Promethean fire which is to kindle human hearts. Men then will learn that they are brethren, and that it is not less their interest than their duty to cultivate goodwill and peace throughout the earth.[2]

Why do I share them with you? These parallels demonstrate an important truth about the Internet – it is not the technology that drives what is done, it is the people who drive what is done. So, as you consider the use of the Internet and read this book, keep in mind what *you* want to do, and how this tool can help you build. The computer and the Internet are nothing more than tools that can help you communicate, learn more, join communities, shop, play games and more. Today's tools make it easier for us to do those things without needing to know exactly how the tool works and without doing a lot of seemingly unnecessary things. This means you do not need to learn about how the computer works just to use it (you can if you want, but you don't need to). Further, you don't need to use all of the capabilities of the Internet – just those that help you. This book is intended to help you accomplish what you want to do. Period.

So, what do you want to do? The World Wide Web represents a vast array of services that will be discussed in the remainder of this book. It will highlight not only what you can do, but also how to do those things *safely*.

---

2 This is an excerpt from a speech by David Dudly Field, called "The Telegraph." It was given at a dinner in honor of Samuel F.B. Morse in New York City, December 27, 1863. It can be found in the book, Reed, Thomas B., *Modern Eloquence: Vol II, After-Dinner Speeches E-O,* Chicago: George L. Shuman & Co., 1903. Project Guttenberg Release, July 13, 2006.

The World Wide Web

The easiest way to describe the World Wide Web ("the Web") is that it is a library. There are lots and lots of different kinds of documents sitting "out there" on computers around the world being maintained by different people. All together they make up the Web.

Think about walking into your local library. There are reference books, magazines, novels, nonfiction and more. Some are well written, some are very good; and some seem odd, and you wonder why your library bought them. In addition, most libraries include a collection of newspapers, magazines and other periodicals, as well as videos, DVDs, music, and some government documents for citizens to browse.

All libraries have reference librarians, those magical people who expertly find just what you want, be it a particular book, references to some historical event, statistics, or your great grandfather's birth certificate. These people can help you find something specific, or teach you how to use the library, or provide summaries of information to help you investigate topics effectively.

Most libraries also have an announcements bulletin board and a place where local and not-for-profit organizations can place fliers so that people can learn about what is happening in their neighborhoods. Sometimes people post "opinion statements" to share, or requests for help.

In addition, your library probably sponsors book clubs. These groups select a genre of books, and select a particular book to discuss each month. They meet at regular times, talk about the book and then decide what to discuss next time.

The library may sponsor other group discussions, such as young people's groups, or people between jobs or whatever topic is of interest to the local community. A quick look at my local library's offerings include sessions on Russian quilts, a career center workshop for job hunters, knitting and crocheting, introduction to genealogy, travelog Austria, tax assistance, and several needlework and crafting sessions. All of the descriptions encourage citizens to bring a friend, or make new friends there.

The Web is all of this and more. There are documents, periodicals, places to learn things, places to discuss things, places to voice your opinion, experts, clubs and more. It is similar to a library – but it is very different from a library. It is similar because there is a vast amount of information that is available to anyone – and most of it is available for free. The Web, like a library, includes so much more than references. It includes places for people to meet, ways of communicating, ways of sharing opinions, programs that accomplish some specific task and probably many things you may not yet have considered.

The scope of this library is enormous. No one knows with certainty how many webpages exist because people put them up and take them down as they feel the need. One estimate is that there are over 600 billion items on the Web today. That's over 100 items per person alive. And, the number of web pages available is growing exponentially. At your computer, you can access an amazing variety of music and video, an evolving encyclopedia, weather forecasts, help wanted ads, satellite images of any place on Earth, up-to-the-minute news from around the world, tax forms, TV guides, road maps with driving directions, real-time stock quotes, telephone numbers, real estate listings with virtual walk-throughs, pictures of just about anything, sports scores, places to buy almost anything, records of political contributions, library catalogs, appliance manuals, live traffic reports, archives to major newspapers, and more. So, the Web is a *very large* library!

But, there are a few very important differences. The first of these is that *anyone* can post whatever they want on the Web and no one will stop them (usually). This differs from what we see in books, newspapers and magazines, where an editor decides if the substance of the content is credible, well written and worthy of

Happy Birthday World Wide Web

During the opening ceremony for the London Olympics in 2012, Danny Boyle closed his musical segment, by celebrating the 21st birthday of the World Wide Web. The focus moved to the creator of WWW, Sir Tim Berners-Lee sitting at a computer. From that computer, he tweeted the following.

Tim Berners-Lee
@timberners_lee   Follow

This is for everyone #london2012 #oneweb #openingceremony @webfoundation @w3c

← Reply ⇄ Retweet ★ Favorite

10,113   1,739
RETWEETS   FAVORITES

2:08 PM - 27 Jul 12 via Twitter for iPhone · Embed this Tweet sharing. On the Web, there generally is no editing, no overview and no one who decides that something is bad to include. Readers need to consider things with a grain of salt, until they know of the writer's credibility and credentials.

Second, the Web is alive. What was available yesterday may not be available today, or if it is, it may have changed. Documents are not like much-loved novels that read the same way today as hundreds of years ago. People can, and do, update documents daily (or even more often), or replace them with something different. So, it may be difficult to find items that you have seen before, even if you remember where you have seen them.

Third, in many ways, the Web is anonymous. People need not identify themselves when posting pages (or as we shall see later, sending email or talking in a chat room). People can, and do, disguise themselves both for reasonable purposes as well as for nefarious ones. The user needs to have the same concerns for safety on the Web as they would in the "real world" and perhaps more.

What IS a Webpage?

If you have never been online, then you are probably wondering what is a "webpage"? A webpage is simply information arranged and saved on a computer that serves it up so that everyone can see it around the world. When people have many webpages, the first of them generally is referred to as a "homepage," to indicate the starting point of a particular site. On the next page is part of my homepage, located at http://www.umsl.edu/~sauterv.

You can see that my homepage has some basic information about me and what I do. In addition, I have some photos and quotes. This page provides some background about me, my teaching, my research, and other activities. But, not all webpages look like this one. For example, Figure 2.2 shows the homepage of a secondary school library.

This page has different kinds of information because it has a different purpose. The goal is not to provide overview information about the school, but rather to provide quick access to the online sources the students might need to complete class projects. So, the focus and structure are different – it simply provides a menu with which to access further resources. It is a research tool that makes using the electronic library easier.

Vicki L. Sauter

Professor of Information Systems   College of Business Administration   University of Missouri - St. Louis

We are what we repeatedly do. Excellence, then is not an act, but a habit.

-Aristotle

view all quotes in database

You are never too old to be all you can possibly be!

Research and Writing
Teaching

My Streetlight Collection

Advanced IS Laboratory
IS Advisory Board
Grace's Place
Mentoring Program
Imagine IT! and *Xtreme IT!*

Joe   Michael   Allie

Northwestern University
Ella Flagg Young School

IS Area News
Technology News

Why IS
IS Curriculum

IS Alumni

AIS Resources
UMSL Library
Syster's Links

ITS
Technology Help
Internet Links

Learn More!

My Blog
Old Blogs

SEARCH

Vicki Sauter joined the faculty of the <u>College of Business Administration</u> in 1979 after receiving her Ph.D. in systems engineering from <u>Northwestern University</u>, and serves currently as Professor of <u>Information Systems</u> at <u>UM-St. Louis</u>. Her <u>research interests</u> began with decision support systems, especially in the model-management area. You can view her book, *<u>Decision Support Systems for Business Intelligence</u>*. Currently Professor Sauter is working in the area of systems analysis with a focus on the improvement of methodologies. In addition, she is conducting research in the role of women in the information systems profession.

Professor Sauter <u>teaches classes</u> primarily in Systems Analysis, at the undergraduate, graduate and doctoral levels. She also teaches decision support systems and web development.

Dr. Sauter's book has just published a new book, *<u>Street Lights of the World</u>*, the ultimate visual guide to this often overlooked architectural accessory. She is also working on a new book, *You are Never Too Old to Surf*. You can read the <u>proposal</u>.

Currently Dr. Sauter is working on three research projects. One continues her systems engineering work by examining the importance of Swimlane Diagrams to the interaction of analysts and users. Her second research project is examining the relative satisfaction of IT professionals in ISO Certified and CMMI rated organizations, compared to the organizations that do not have either ISO or CMMI credentials. This ultimately will also examine the impact on maintaining women IT professionals. The third project currently is stalled, but interesting. It is a social-linguistic examination of decision making styles.

Professor Sauter serves on the Board of <u>Craft Alliance</u> and on the Board of the Restoration Committee of Bonhomme's Old Stone Church. She also volunteers her technological skills at the <u>Stamper Library</u> of John Burroughs School. Professor Sauter is also one of the volunteers working on rehabilitating the garden in front of ESH. You can check out our plan and the progress <u>here</u>.

Celebrate!

INFORMS Online   IFORS

Photos   Gateways

Vicki Sauter's Blog

- Giving Tuesday
- Grace's Place: A Gallery that Remembers
- Life

HEADLINES BY FEEDBURNER

Proud Wildcat

🔲 SHARE

AUDE ET EFFICE

Life is what happens when you are busy making other plans!   -John Lennon

Information Systems Area -- 226 CCB
College of Business Administration
One University Blvd. (m/c 22)
St. Louis, Missouri 63121-4400
+1 314.516.6281

Figure 2.1: My Webpage
http://www.umsl.edu/~sauterv

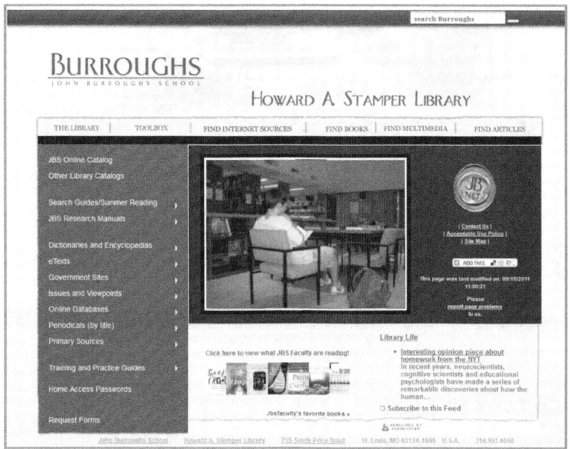

Figure 2.1: The Homepage of a Secondary School
http://library.jburroughs.org

So, a webpage could display *anything*. What makes it a webpage is in the how and where information is stored and served so that it can be read by anyone. We will discuss how the pages "work" in just a few pages.

Figure 2.2: A Car Dealership Homepage
http://www.wgsis.com

Who Makes Webpages?

It is said that on the Web, "content is KING." That is to say that while the aesthetics of the page are important, people surf to find information. But how does all of this information get out there? Some of it is produced by companies or not-for-profit organizations. For example, descriptions of items in a store are generally provided by the store. Corporate earnings statements are produced by the accounting departments of those corporations. Information about pending bills and voting records is provided by the US Congress (as well as many state legislatures). Publishers have provided online sources to complement their book and periodical selections. Not-for-profit organizations provide information about their programs, services and location.

On the other hand, much of the information is provided by volunteers too. One of the biggest groups of volunteers providing information on the Web is in the area of genealogy. Dedicated genealogists transcribe cemetery records, ships' records, and old books or magazines. For example, www.rootsweb.com depends on volunteers to provide this free genealogy site. The result is a huge repository of information that any genealogist can share. These dedicated individuals have provided information to one another for years; the Web gives greater access to that information. Recently you have seen increases in the number of professional websites supplementing the volunteer-based sites.

Similarly, people develop web pages because of a passion and/or interest. For example, for over twenty years, I have collected photographs of streetlights, such as the one shown in Figure 2.4. With the internet, I can display those photographs for those individuals who are interested in viewing them. Not surprisingly, the group of interested people is not large, and there could be no business case for making this information available. However, it is there on the web because it is of interest to me; surprisingly, people do often contact me after viewing them, even offering new photos.

Streetlight from Istanbul, Turkey

These streetlights were photographed by Silvia Madeo while vacationing in Summer, 2012.

Figure 2.3: Example from my Streetlights Webpages; **http://bit.ly/rtCuJb**

Likewise, since my elementary school class (from decades ago) decided to start meeting, we created a website about the school and our class. No one would pay to put this information online, yet it is there because we want to find the remainder of our classmates. Not only has this provided a mechanism for sharing photos and information, it has attracted individuals from the class whom we have not been able to locate.

Even the success of the Web at this scale was impossible. But if we have learned anything in the past decade, it is the plausibility of the impossible. What we all failed to see was how much of this new world would be manufactured by users, not corporate interests.

Linking unleashes involvement and interactivity at levels once thought unfashionable or impossible. It transforms reading into navigating and enlarges small actions into powerful forces. The electricity of participation nudges ordinary folks to invest huge hunks of energy and time into making free encyclopedias, creating public tutorials for changing a flat tire, or cataloging the votes in the Senate. More and more of the Web runs in this mode. One study found that only 40 percent of the Web is commercial. The rest runs on duty or passion.

-Kevin Kelly
WiredMagazine

Even commercial sites take advantage of volunteers to create content. Amazon.com, the world's largest bookstore, allows volunteers to write reviews of books that are available for sale. In addition, volunteers create lists of recommended books for potential customers. On eBay.com, a well-known auction site, customers are asked to rate the individuals or stores from which they make purchases to help guide future customers' purchases. These ratings are, of course, done on a volunteer basis.

Webpages are special because they exist on the Internet. Any computer anyplace in the world that has a connection to the Internet and the appropriate software (we will discuss this later) can view the page and it will look the same. This is because webpages are primarily written using a special computer language called "hypertext markup language" (html, for short).

How do Webpages Work?

A part of the html used to create the webpage in Figure 2.3 is shown in the box on the following page. As you can see from a quick look at the box, this html is difficult for most people to understand. *Fortunately,* people do not need to understand what it says. It is only necessary for the computer to understand what it means.

The computer reads this special language using a program located on your computer called a "browser." The browser reads the cryptic information such as the box below and translates it into the words, figures and navigation you see on a webpage. Most people will use Chrome, Firefox, Safari, or Internet

Explorer as their browser. There are other options, however, including those that only work on mobile devices (such as smart phones and tablets).

Example of How Web Pages are Built

```
<body bgcolor="#E3E5DA" background="main/graphics/background.jpg"
text="#000000" link="#000000" alink="#000000" vlink="#000000">

<map name="image-map2">
        <area shape="rect" coords="0,0,78,78" href="index.html">
        <area shape="rect" coords="79,0,408,45" href="index.html">
        <area shape="rect" coords="79,45,189,83"
        href="inventory.html">
        <area shape="rect" coords="189,45,288,83" href="inventoryisu.html">
        <area shape="rect" coords="288,45, 408,83" href="inventorysuz.html">
</map>

<table width=80% bgcolor="black" align=center cellspacing=10 cellpadding=10
border>
        <tr><td>
        <table border=2 width=100% align=center bgcolor="#8F989A" cellpadding=3
        >
        <tr><td bgcolor="#8F989A" width=40%>
        <img src="main/graphics/top_logo2.jpg" alt="Webster Groves Subaru-
        Isuzu-Suzuki" border=0 usemap="#image-map2" width="409"
        height="87"></td>
                <td rowspan=2 width=60%><table border=0 width=100%
                height=100%><tr><td>
                        <h3><i><center>
                        <font color="#E3E5DA">G.A. IMPORTS, INC.</i><br>
                        <font size=-1>Est. 1963</font></center>
                        <br>
                <table align=center>
                <tr>    <td><center>
                        <img src="main/graphics/gray_space.jpg" width="23"
height="20">
                        </td>
                        <td><center><a href="main/new.html">
                        <img src="main/graphics/button_new1.jpg" alt="new cars"
                        border=0 width="48" height="47"></a><p>
```

How do I Surf?

OK, so what is "surfing the Web"? Surfing refers to moving around the Web by moving from one webpage to another webpage. Rather than riding a wave, you are riding the information highway. Rather than relying on the tides to direct the movement of the water, you are relying on the interconnections of webpages. This interconnection is not random; it is a linking of concepts from one document to another document. For example, on my webpage, I link various sources of information. Since most of my life revolves around the University, I link to webpages for my department and college, classes I teach, research I do and activities in which I am involved. So, for example, if you want to know about my department's computer museum, mentoring program or advisory board and do not know where their webpages are you can go to them by clicking on the links from my home page. I also have found some inspiring writings, such as graduation speeches, songs and quotes to which I have links. You can link directly to National Geographic, several companies, the National Cyber Security Alliance, National Mathematics Awareness organization, and Wikipedia! Indirectly, you can also get to the *New York Times, Chicago Tribune,* and the *Washington Post;* my webpage links to some listings of articles about research issues and those pages link to those three newspapers (among others). I also keep listings of sites I like on several topics that are linked from my homepage. These lists will take you to many other organizations.

Origins of Surfing

The word "surfing" is from the Hawaiian: he'e nalu, meaning "wave-sliding." Historically, it referred to the popular recreational activity and sport in which individuals are propelled across the water by the force of waves, while standing on an almost flat, wide board.

Whose Idea Was This?

Computing pioneer Vannevar Bush was the first to propose the idea of hyperlinked pages – in 1945! But it took a while for the idea to catch on and for the computing power to allow it.

So, on my homepage, there are things called hyperlinks (or sometimes just links). These are connectors to other webpages. Earlier we discussed that webpages are written in a special programming language. Within that language there is a capability to tell the browser (the program that controls the viewing of the webpage) that when a hyperlink is clicked with a mouse that the browser should transfer to another location on the Web. Often hyperlinks are identified as underlined words, and sometimes might be displayed in a different color than the rest of the text. If you return to Figure 2.1, you will see information about my previous book, *Streetlights of the World*, and about this book. Each of the underlined words in this list will take you to another webpage, so each of them is a hyperlink. But, those are not the only hyperlinks. You will also see the icons for LinkedIn, Facebook and other so called social media websites (we will discuss social media later). Each of those are hyperlinks too. Picture hyperlinks generally are not underlined, although they may appear with a colored border. Generally you know a hyperlink because when you move the mouse pointer over the image, the arrowhead will change to a hand with a finger pointing that appears on top of the image from my webpage, such as that shown in Figure 2.5.

Figure 2.4: An Image that is linked to a Webpage

One way you can surf on the web is to click on the text or the image and that will cause you to jump to a new site on the Web.

The process of surfing, then, is just to follow the links on pages to new pages. This process of surfing allows you to explore what is available on the web and sometimes to find surprising treasures. For example, you can "surf the links" from my webpage to find a sculpture of Napoleon in a frock coat that you can purchase. How? Start at my home page:

- http://www.umsl.edu/~sauterv
- Look at the menu on the right side of the screen (on the green background) and select (click on) "Gateways."
- That link takes you to another of my pages, which provides links to pages in some of my areas of interest. Select the link labeled "Art" which appears in the second group under "Hobbies and Other Interests."
- That link takes you to a page with some of my favorite art links. Select the one for the Louvre Museum, and you will leave my pages, and even the United States, and now be on the home page of the Musée Louvre (the one translated into English).

- There are many interesting things to peruse at the museum, but scroll down a page (on the left you will see "practical information) to the "Online Shop."
- You can see a number of categories of items generally available in a museum gift shop on the left. Select the link to "Sculpture" (the last one above the shopping bag).
- If you scroll through these sculptures to Page 3, you will see a bust of Louis IV (assuming they have not changed their offerings of late). You could at this point, purchase the sculpture and have them ship it back to the United States!

Where Do I Go Next?

Just to review, you must start by opening a browser. We discussed several in the last section, but some of the most popular are Firefox, Chrome, Safari, and Internet Explorer. The term "to open a browser" simply means that you start the program. If you have an icon, click on the icon to start it. Otherwise you will have to locate the program through the menu on your computer. Where do you go from there? Well, almost anywhere! But, here is how you might do it.

> The first person to try to build out the concept was a computer scientist named Ted Nelson. He was the founding designer of the first hypertext project, *Project Xanadu,* in 1960. Unfortunately, he had little success making it work on a reasonable scale. By 1984 he was certain that *every document in the world should be a footnote to some other document, and computers could make the links between them visible and permanent.*
>
> -Kevin Kelly
> *Wired Magazine*

There are lots of ways to find a webpage. The most basic approach is to type in the web address. Webpage "addresses" are called URL's (universal resource locator). Just as we discussed in Chapter 1 that every computer has a unique address, every webpage on the Web has a unique address. That address tells us the computer on which the page is stored, and where on the computer we can find it.

Addresses on the Web begin with "http://" That stands for "hypertext transfer protocol." The computer needs to know that because it needs to understand how to "read" the webpage, but you don't need to know that. You just need to know it starts with "http://"

This is followed by the domain name. Domains are simply the host of the organization at which the web page exists. Most companies try to get a domain name that is close to the way that people think about them. So, Sears, for example, has the domain "sears.com," Kodak has "kodak.com," the White House has "whitehouse.gov," the Humane Society has "humanesociety.org," the Missouri Botanical Gardens has "mobot.org," and the U.S. Army has "army.mil." Notice that the domain is made up of the name of the organization and the type of organization, separated by a period (full stop). These types of organizations relate back to those we discussed in Chapter 1.

It is important to take care with the domain type designation. Similarity of site names, such as domain.com and domain.org, does *not* imply they are owned and/or operated by the same organization. For example, "whitehouse.gov" is the domain name for the United States White House. On the other hand, "whitehouse.com" takes one to a pornography site.

Sometimes you will see the domain name preceded with "www" and sometimes you will see it preceded by something else. What precedes the domain name is some indicator of the actual machine on which the webpage is kept. Most organizations name that machine by its conventional name, "www," and that will usually work. Some organizations, such as the U.S. Army, though, have multiple machines and different parts of their website are stored on these different machines. In order to get your request to the correct page, the links need to track the machine as well as the page. So, as you surf through the Army's site, you may notice the website changing to www4.army.mil or www3.army.mil.

However, sometimes site designers provide aliases to specific parts of the website to make them easier to find. So, for example, while www.umsl.edu will take you to the main webpage of my university, the MIS department can be accessed directly with mis.umsl.edu. The computer knows they are the same site, but this is shorter and more convenient for us to remember than the full address, "http://www.umsl.edu/divisions/business/mis/index.html."

Search Engines

Up until this point, we have identified two ways to surf: knowing the address (and thus going there directly) and going surfing by following links on pages and seeing where they lead. But what if you do not know the URL or address of the page you want, but you want to get there directly. What if you do not know even where to find the information you want. How do you even know it is there? The answer to the last question is that the information is probably there somewhere. The scope of the Web today is hard to fathom. The total number of Web pages, exceeds 600 billion.

The answer to the first question is that you use a search engine. Are you picturing going to your car and looking under the hood? That engine powers your car and gets you where you want to go. A search engine is similar, but it has nothing to do with your car. A search engine helps you "go" on the Web where you want to go. In fact, about 85% of surfing is done through some search engine. It is a program available at a website that finds other web pages that match a word or a phrase that you provide. "Google" (www.google.com), is the world's most popular general search engine. There are other general search engines as shown to the right.

Popular General Search Engines

Anzwers	http://www.anzwers.com.au
Ask	http://www.ask.com
Bing	http://www.bing.com
Dogpile	http://www.dogpile.com
Google	http://www.google.com
ix quick	http://www.ixquick.com
Starting Point	http://www.stpt.com
Web Crawler	http://www.webcrawler.com
Yahoo!	http://www.yahoo.com

In addition, there are many specialized search engines. There are search engines that will only search in a particular country, or ones that search only particular topics, such as industrial products (Thomasnet.com), or the law (LexisNexis.com). There are job search engines, such as CareerBuilder.com and Monster.com, real estate search engines, such as Zillow.com, and even food search engines (Yummly.com). Other search engines only look at a particular type of data, such as

Shopping and Price Comparison Search Engines

Bizrate	http://www.bizrate.com/
Google Shopping	https://www.google.com/shopping
Kelkoo	http://www.kelkoo.com/
PriceGrabber	http://www.pricegrabber.com/
PriceRunner	http://www.pricerunner.co.uk/
Pronto.com	http://www.pronto.com/
Shopping.com	http://www.shopping.com/
ShopWiki	http://www.shopwiki.com/
Shopzilla	http://www.shopzilla.com/
TheFind.com	http://www.thefind.com/

maps (Maps.Google.com or MapQuest.com), or blogs (IceRocket.com), or multimedia items (YouTube.com or FindSounds.com.

Generally, I just use Google.com, unless I am looking for something quite specific. Google is easy to use. When you go to the Google website, you will find almost nothing on the page except a box. You type the word or words that describe the kind of information you want to find into the box and hit enter. Google will respond with possibilities almost instantaneously.

So, suppose you were interested in genealogy and wanted to see what the web had available for you. (Genealogy has the most pages on the Internet. If you are interested in the topic, you will find many useful sources on the web.) If you type the key word, "genealogy" in the box and press the button labeled "Google Search," you will see results similar to those in Figure 2.6.

Notice that Google reminds you of your search term at the top of the page. Then it gives you some information about your search. It tells you there are about 250,000,000 pages addressing genealogy on the web (yes, that is 25 million pages!). If you go through all the pages, you can see all of the information. For most of us, that would be overwhelming, and we will discuss how to reduce that list shortly.

If you look at the actual search results you will see that Google provides you with the name of the page, the description or first line of the page, and the URL. Each highlighted word (generally in blue) is a hypertext link. As we noted in the previous section, if you click on those links, the web will redirect you to that page automatically. In this way, you can surf the web simply by going down the list and clicking on the link to see what resources the search has located.

Not all pages displayed pages are there because of the popularity of a site. Notice the right column that is labeled "ads" and the first three links in the regular column that have the beige shading (also labeled "ads"). Those links appear to you because a company has paid to have them appear early in the list. The folks at Google have to pay the bills too. The provider pays a fee to Google, and then Google agrees to display the page either at the top of the links (in the shaded region) or on the right hand side of the page. These links *may* be very relevant sites that the provider wants to highlight. Or, they may only be addressing related topics. The fact that they are sponsored does not make them better or worse than other links; they are just not ordered in the same way as other pages.

The remaining links are identified by the search engine as relevant. Google, like other search engines, have programs (called web crawlers or spiders) that meticulously look through the Web each day for new pages. These pages are indexed automatically and provide the data for the search results it provides. This service is provided to the author of the web page for free. Eventually the web crawlers will find your page without you doing anything or paying anyone.

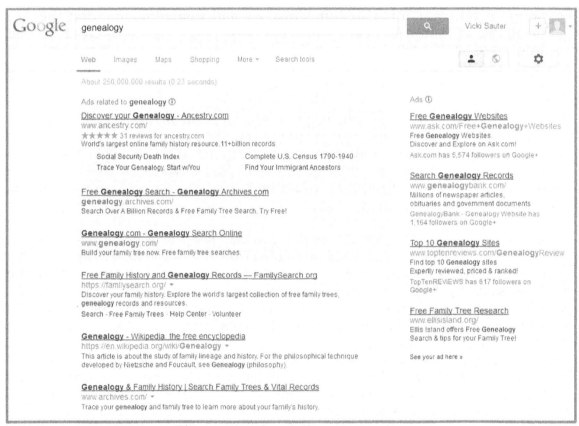

Figure 2.5: Google Search Results
http://www.google.com

Regardless of which search engine you use, the results of your query will be sequentially displayed based on their relevance and popularity. That is the engine will display pages it thinks are more relevant earlier in the results, and pages it thinks are less relevant later in the search. Different search engines will decide how relevant a page is in different ways. Some look at the number of times a particular term shows up in a webpage. Others look for the webpage's key words (that are invisible to the web surfer, but known to the computer) to determine its relevance. Still others look at those things *plus* a measure of a page's popularity. Google, for example, looks at not only the key words, but the number of relevant pages that link *to* a particular website. So, for example, if every website on genealogy has a link to a particular webpage, then Google will list that webpage first when a query about genealogy is performed. Their logic is that if all the other genealogy pages are pointing to that particular website, it must have useful information and links for genealogists, and hence should be listed first.

You can have some control over what is listed and in what order. Before the search results, there is a control bar that appears like Figure 2.7.

Figure 2.6: Google Control Bar

The default setting is for "web," so that is the option that is highlighted. You could also search only for images, maps, blogs, shopping options, or even recipes. That would narrow your search. Another way to narrow your search is to click "search tools" which gives you options about what time horizon and what physical locality you wish to search. I find limiting the time a page has been posted is often helpful, especially for news items.

Those options might not be appropriate for focusing your search. Another way to limit the number of pages identified is to increase the number of terms for which you search. Suppose we know we want to search not only for genealogy but also for a particular family name. So, we might list "Sauter genealogy" in the box to tell Google that we want both terms to be considered relevant. The result of that search is shown in Figure 2.8. Adding the last name "Sauter" means we have less than 1% of the original pages needing checking.

Well, although that search did provide a list of pages that have both terms, it probably has pages we did not expect. For example, if you scroll down, you will see the identification of a mathematics genealogy project (which shows how various mathematicians' work and education are linked together). That does not seem like it should belong. However, it does link the two words. In addition, it appears relatively high because Google will look first for pages that include Sauter and *then*, within those pages, for ones that also include genealogy. The first term you enter is more important than the second term.

The Google Doodle

Most times you visit Google.com, you are greeted with the colorful Google logo.

However, sometimes Google has someone sketch on their logo to celebrate an event that is happening currently (such as the World Cup) or historically (such as the birth of a famous person). The result is the Google Doodle. The celebration might be the first day of winter, or the Fabergé egg,

or Rozwell's 66th anniversary, or St. Patrick's Day,

or the birth of a scientist such as Petri or Schrödinger.

Note that when we reverse the terms, we get results shown in a different order, and perhaps including some different items, as shown in Figure 2.9.

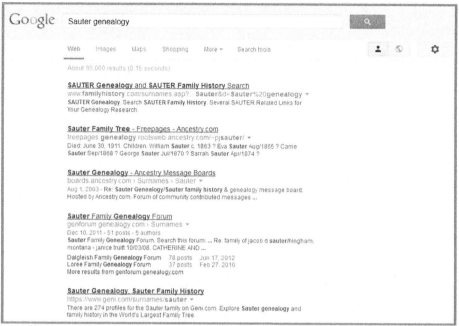

Figure 2.7: Google search using Sauter and Genealogy Terms
http://www.google.com

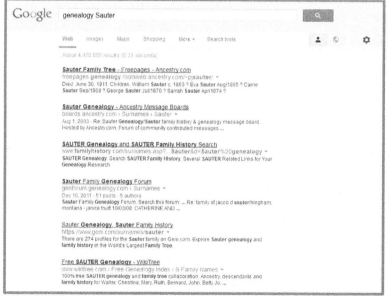

Figure 2.8: Google Search using Genealogy and Sauter as Terms
http://www.google.com

This search does not guarantee that the terms "Sauter" and "genealogy" will appear contiguously on the page; it just says you want both words to appear on the page. This can be a problem if your words are commonly used, or if using them together suggests a special meaning. So, Google (as well as other search engines) will allow you to put the term in quotes and it will search for the terms together. For example, if we search on "Sauter genealogy" (with that term in quotes), we will only identify sites where Sauter and genealogy appear together, hence we may get a different set of results than the first time.

Google allows you to specify other restrictions on the pages you obtain through their advanced search option. You get to the advanced search option by clicking the gear or asterisk item on the top right of the screen. The result, shown in Figure 2.10, allows you to specify what words need to appear, and how they appear together, as well as language, dates, domains and other factors. This will help you get to the page you want, faster because you have less total pages to search.

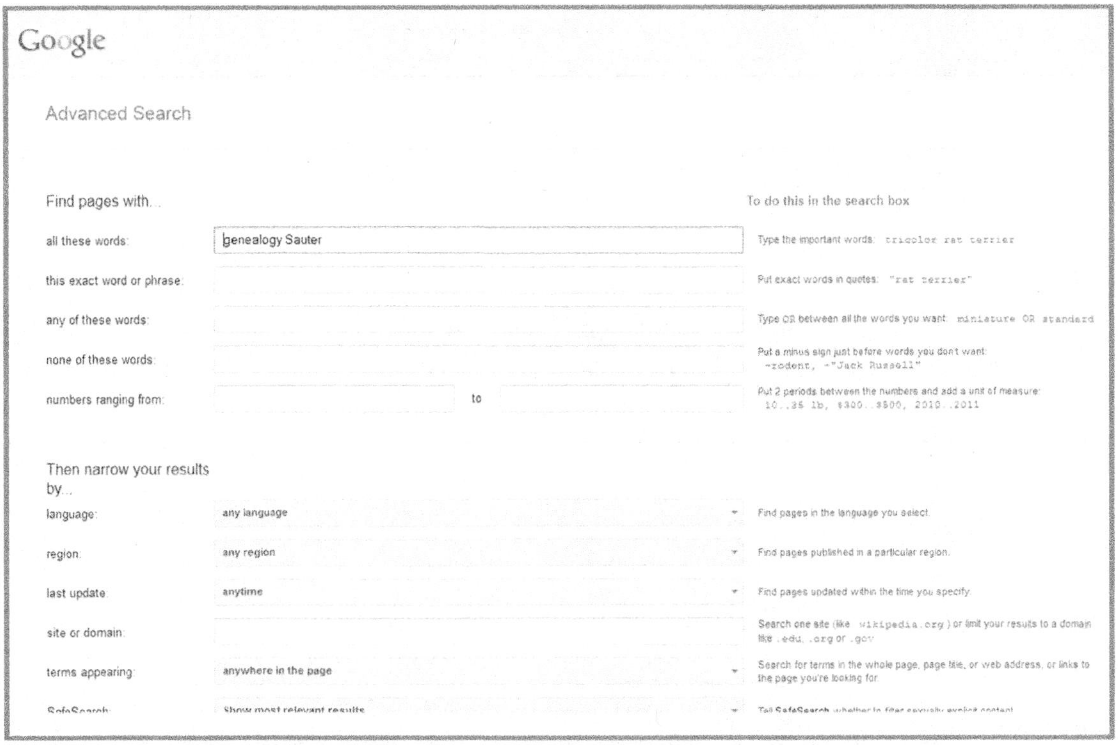

Figure 2.9: Google's Advanced Search Options
http://www.google.com

Google clearly is not the *only* search engine available on the Web, however it is by far the largest search engine accounting for approximately 66% of all searches done on the Internet. Yahoo and Microsoft rate as the second and third, most used search engine respectively, each with only about 15% of all searches. Why are Google, Yahoo and Microsoft more popular than the other search engines? A good search requires two things: a large number of pages in the index that are searched *and* a good mechanism for searching. Google has both the largest number of pages in the index, and an excellent method for searching. In fact, the engine behind Google is the same one behind searches in Yahoo (they lease from Google). Does that make Google the best? Certainly in many people's view it does. However, there may be better search engines for specific topics or specific types of searches. If you find one that is more comfortable for you, use it.

Bookmarks and Favorites

Suppose you have typed in an address, surfed from someone's webpage or searched to find the page you want. You know you are going to want to go back to the page from time to time, but you certainly do not want to take the path to the page that you used this time. Of course we have a solution to that, and it is called "Bookmarks" in Firefox and "Favorites" in Internet Explorer. As the name implies, this bookmark "saves" the address of the page you want to keep so that the next time you want to go to that page, you simply need to consult your bookmarks or favorites and you will go there directly. We will talk in the next chapter about how to set a bookmark or favorite. For the time being, let us suppose it has already been set from a previous visit. To access that page again, you again select "Bookmarks" (in Firefox) or "Favorites" (in Internet Explorer)

Wikipedia

Wikipedia (www.wikipedia.org) is a free, collaboratively edited encyclopedia launched in 2001. While anyone can write articles or edit existing articles, there is a team of editors who evaluate the significance of the topic. The result is over 30 million articles, including almost anything you can imagine. The quality of the articles is governed not only by a group of editors, but also by the population of users who can correct or comment on existing pages. A 2005 study in *Nature* found science articles to be approximately the same level of accuracy as those in Encyclopedia Britannica. Most articles also have references that can be checked to evaluate the article and/or to get more information. It is helpful for those nagging questions and for an overview of topics.

and simply select that item you previously added to your list. The mechanics of this will be shown in the next chapter.

So, what would be "good" bookmarks or favorites? That is a very personal decision. What makes them "good" is because *you* want to be able to find them quickly. Generally these are important pages, or pages you want to visit frequently, or pages that were hard to find and you want to be sure you can find them again. Often bookmarks and favorites include search engines (such as those shown earlier), newspapers or other periodicals, sites for hobbies, or sites that allow you to interact with friends or organizations. They are, therefore, as personal as your own surfing patterns.

I took a survey of 100 individuals who are aged over 50 and asked them about their favorite sites. I have included my own with the results of that survey in the list at the end of the chapter. This list is meant to provide you with ideas for things you can do on the web, not to limit you. So, surf on and find your own favorites.

Words of Warning
Getting information off of the web is easy and it can be fun. But, we all need to remember that the information we get from the web is only as good as the source that provides it. *Anyone* can have a webpage and can publish whatever he or she wants. It does not make it "true" just because it is on the web. No one edits the pages or decided what should or should not be posted. Nor can anyone ensure that everything on the Internet is what it appears. Some web pages have "malware" (which is short for malicious software) running on them that, as the name suggests, looks innocent but real Web searches that have been infected with "malware," may link you to an inappropriate source. Just because it has a company's logo, does not make it official. So, check the source and use your own good judgment before deciding to believe what you find on the web. We will discuss this more in later chapters.

In addition, no one decides what should *not* be on the web. This results in a wide range of materials available, some of which you may find quite objectionable. As you surf, you will learn how to avoid the sites you do not want to see. In the meanwhile, be cautious in your surfing activities.

Finally, it is important for you to know that your surfing behavior really is not "secret." When searching with most search engines, the company compiles

<table>
<tr><td colspan="2">Search Engines that
Do Not Keep Your Information</td></tr>
<tr><td>DuckDuckGo</td><td>duckduckgo.com</td></tr>
<tr><td>StartPage</td><td>www.startpage.com</td></tr>
<tr><td>Ixquick</td><td>ixquick.com</td></tr>
<tr><td>Blekko</td><td>blekko.com</td></tr>
</table>

your searches. They do not save the information by name, but rather by the address of your computer. So, someone could track all of your searches over time and learn about your interests and behaviors. In 2013, Edward Snowden divulged that the U.S. Government tracks electronic communications, including web searches, for a program called Prism. The large computer companies claim they did not participate, but there has been no verification by the U.S. Government of that fact. In other words, it is possible that your searches are being recorded and analyzed (along with your phone calls, emails, file transfers and more) to determine if you are a terrorist.

Since in 2011, most browsers allow users to select a "do not track" option (we will discuss setting options in the next chapter). If a user has selected this option, then when the browser finds the link you have requested, it will send a request to that link not to track you. However, users need to be aware that it is completely voluntary on the part of the companies to act on the request. In other words, the site might still track your searches despite your request not to be tracked. Browsers also allow a "private browsing" option. While this sounds as if users are protected, in fact that option simply keeps your search from being maintained in your user blog. The sites and your browser can still see, and track, what you are doing.

Websites that May Interest You

Art:

Artcyclopedia	www.artcyclopedia.com
Art Institute of Chicago	www.artic.edu
British Museum	www.britishmuseum.org
Craft Alliance	www.craftalliance.org
Fine Art Galleries	www.artpromote.com
Guggenheim Gallery	www.guggenheim.org
Hermitage Museum	www.hermitagemuseum.org
Metropolitan Museum of Art	www.metmuseum.org
MoMA	www.moma.com
Musée Louvre	www.louvre.fr
Museum Island (Berlin)	www.smb.museum
National Museum of African Art	africa.si.edu
National Gallery of Art	www.nga.gov
St. Louis Art Museum	www.slam.org
Smithsonian Museum	www.nmaa.si.edu
Spenmedia	www.spenmedia.com
Uffizi Museum	www.uffizi.firenze.it

Astrology:

Astrology.com	www.astrology.com
Dream Moods	www.dreammoods.com

Blogs:

Blog.com	www.blog.com
Blogger	www.blogger.com
Blog Index	www.theblogindex.net
Blogspot	www.blogspot.com
Google Directory	sites.google.com/site/blogsindex/web-directory
Wordpress Blog	www.wordpress.com

Charity:

Charity Navigator	www.charitynavigator.org
Charity Watch	www.charitywatch.org
Donors Choose	www.donorschoose.org
Market Day	www.marketday.com

Comics Sites:

Comics.com	www.gocomics.com
Piled Higher & Deeper	www.phdcomics.com
xkcd - A webcomic	www.xkcd.com
Washington Post	www.washingtonpost.com/comics
Yahoo! Comics	news.yahoo.com/comics

Electronic cards:

123 Greetings	www.123greetings.com
Blue Mountain	www.bluemountain.com
e-Cards	www.e-cards.com
Jacquie Lawson	www.jacquielawson.com
Southern e-Cards	www.dixierising.com

Classified:

Craig's List	www.craigslist.org

Computer News:

PC Magazine	www.pcmag.com
Cnet	www.cnet.com
Cnet TV	www.cnettv.com
ZdNet	www.zdnet.com

Cooking:

America's Test Kitchen	www.americastestkitchen.com
Epicurious	www.epicurious.com
Food Network	www.foodnetwork.com
Recipe Puppy	recipepuppy.com

Directories:

Area Code Directory	www.allareacodes.com
Country Codes	countrycode.org
Switchboard	www.switchboard.com
White Pages	www.whitepages.com
Yellow Pages	www.yellowpages.com
Zip Code Directory	www.zip-codes.com

Education:

American Universities	www.clas.ufl.edu/au
Chronicle of Higher Education	www.chronicle.com
Khan Academy	khanacademy.org
Life Explained on Film	www.videojug.com
Massively Online Courses	www.moocs.co
Ted.com	www.ted.com
Wikiversity	en.wikiversity.org

Employment Sources:

Monster	www.monster.com

Encyclopedias and Dictionaries:

Encyclopædia Britannica	www.britannica.com
Online Etymology Dictionary	www.etymonline.com
Merriam-Webster Dictionary	www.merriam-webster.com
Webopedia	www.webopedia.com
Wikipedia	www.wikipedia.com
Wikiquote	en.wikiquote.org
Wikisource	en.wikisource.org
Wikitionary	en.wiktionary.org
Your Dictionary	www.yourdictionary.com

Entertainment:

ABC	www.abc.com
Audible.com	www.audible.com
Book of the Month Club	www.bomc.com
Car Talk	www.cartalk.com
CBS	www.cbs.com
HBO	www.hbo.com
HULU	www.hulu.com
iTunes	www.itunes.com
National Public Radio	www.npr.org
NBC	www.nbc.com
YouTube	www.youtube.com

Environment:

Conserve	www.conserve.com
Conservation International	www.conservation.org
Freecycle	www.freecycle.org
Green Pages	www.eco-web.com
Nature Conservatory	www.nature.org

Finance:

Ameritrade	www.tdameritrade.com
Bank of America	www.bankofamerica.com
CITIBank	www.citi.com
Fidelity Investments	www.fidelity.com
NASDAQ	www.nasdaq.com
New York Stock Exchange	www.nyse.com
Charles Schwab	www.schwab.com
USBank	www.usbank.com
Vanguard	www.vanguard.com

Gardening:

American Horticultural Society	www.ahs.org
Garden Forever	www.gardenforever.com
Garden Guides	www.gardenguides.com
Garden Helper	www.thegardenhelper.com
iVillage Garden Web	www.gardenweb.com
Kid's Gardening	www.kidsgardening.org
MO Botanical Garden	www.mobot.org/gardeninghelp
Organic Gardening	www.organicgardening.com
Plant Information	www.chicago-botanic.org/plantinfo

Genealogy:

Ancestry.com	www.ancestry.com
Cyndi's List	www.cyndislist.com
Family Search	www.familysearch.org
Genealogy.com	www.genealogy.com
Migrations	www.migrations.org
Rootsweb	www.rootsweb.com
Social Security Death Index	ssdi.rootsweb.com

Government Sites:

Bureau of Land Management	www.blm.gov/nhp/browse.htm
Bureau of Prisons	www.bop.gov
Census	www.census.gov
IRS	www.irs.gov
Official Water Levels	waterdata.usgs.gov/ma/nwis/rt
Postal Service	www.usps.gov
Social Security Administration	www.ssa.gov
U.S. Senate	www.senate.gov
U.S. House of Representatives	www.house.gov
The White House	www.whitehouse.gov

Health and Fitness:

Center for Disease Control	www.cdc.gov
Mayo Clinic	www.mayoclinic.com
Mercola Health	www.mercola.com
Prevention	www.Prevention.com
WebMD	www.webmd.com

Knitting:

Knitting Magazine	www.knitty.com
Pattern Works	www.patternworks.com

Libraries and Facts: (see also Encyclopedias and Dictionaries)

AARP	www.aarp.org
Library of Congress	www.loc.gov
Old Farmer's Almanac	www.almanac.com
Public Libraries	www.publiclibraries.com
Refdesk	www.refdesk.com
Smithsonian Library	library.si.edu
St. Louis County Library	www.slcl.lib.mo.us
St. Louis Mercantile Library	mercantile.umsl.edu
UMSL Library	library.umsl.edu

Literature:

Classic Short Stories	classicshorts.com
Google Books	books.google.com
Literature Map	literature-map.com
Literature Network	www.online-literature.com
Timothy McSweeney	www.mcsweeneys.net
Nobel Prize in Literature	www.nobelprize.org/nobel_prizes/literature
Online Literature Library	www.literature.org
Read Julia	www.readjulia.com
Shakespearean Insult Generator	
	w.mainstrike.com/mstservices/handy/insult.html

Mail Sites:

Google Mail	mail.google.com
Yahoo Mail	mail.yahoo.com
Cox Webmail	webmail.east.cox.net

Maps and Directions:

Google	maps.google.com
Google Earth	earth.google.com
Mapquest	mapquest.com
Yahoo Maps	maps.yahoo.com

Movies:

AMC Theatres	www.amc.com
Hulu	www.hulu.com
Netflix	www.netflix.com

Museums: (see also "Art")

Anacostia Museum	anacostia.si.edu
Block Museum of Art	www.blockmuseum.northwestern.edu
City Museum	www.citymuseum.org
Egyptian Virtual Museum	www.touregypt.net/museum
Eugene Field House and Toy Museum	www.eugenefieldhouse.org/
Grace's Place	mis.umsl.edu/graceplace.html
Guggenheim Gallery	www.guggenheim.org
Holocaust Museum	www.ushmm.org
Museum of Science and Industry	www.msichicago.org
National Geographic	www.nationalgeographic.org
Newseum	www.newseum.org
Smithsonian Museum	www.si.edu
Soldiers' Memorial Military Museum	www.stlsoldiersmemorial.org
Spy Museum	www.spymuseum.org
St. Louis Art Museum	www.slam.org
St. Louis Science Center	www.slsc.org
Tech Museum of Innovation	www.thetech.org
Virtual Museum of the Civil War	www.civilwarvirtualmuseum.org

Music:

iTunes	www.itunes.com
I Heart Radio	www.iheart.com
King FM	www.king.org
Music Genome Project	www.pandora.com

Nature:

BBC Nature	www.bbc.co.uk/nature/
Online Guide to Snowflakes	www.snowcrystals.com
National Parks	www.nps.gov
PBS Nature	www.pbs.org/wnet/nature/
Science Daily	www.sciencedaily.com/news/plants_animals/nature

News:

BBC	www.bbc.com
CNN	www.cnn.com
Google News	news.google.com
Drudge Report	www.drudgereport.com
News Map	newsmap.jp
NBC News	www.nbc.com
News for Nerds	www.slashdot.org
News of the Weird	www.newsoftheweird.com
Yahoo News	news.yahoo.com

Newspapers:

The Boston Globe	www.bostonglobe.com
Chicago Tribune	www.chicagotribune.com
Cleveland Plain Dealer	www.plaindealer.com
The New York Times	www.newyorktimes.com
St. Louis Post Dispatch	www.stltoday.com
Seattle Times	www.seattletimes.com
USA Today	www.usatoday.com
The Wall Street Journal	www.wsj.com
The Washington Post	www.washingtonpost.com

Pet Rescue:

Animal Rescue Site	www.theanimalrescuesite.com
Humane Society	www.hsus.org
Pet Adoption	www.petfinder.com
Rescued Racers	www.rescuedracers.com
Stray Rescue of St. Louis	www.strayrescue.org

Real Estate Listings:

LoopNet	www.loopnet.com
Pad Mapper	padmapper.com
Zillow.com	www.zillow.com

Religion:

Al-Islam (Shi'ite)	www.al-islam.org
Episcopalian	www.episcopalchurch.org
Lutheran Church - ELCA	www.elca.org
Lutheran Church – MS	www.lcms.org
Lutheran Church – WELS	www.wels.net
Islam	www.islamreligion.com
Judaism 101	www.jewfaq.org
Presbyterian Church – USA	www.pcusa.org
Presbyterian Church of America	www.pcanet.org
Speaking of Faith	speakingoffaith.publicradio.org
The Holy See	www.vatican.va/phome_en.htm
United Methodist Church	www.umc.org

Rumors and Urban Legends:

Snopes	www.snopes.com
Urban Legends	urbanlegends.about.com

Sports:

Biking News	www.velonews.com
Bowl Guide	www.bcsfootball.org
College Football Research Center	www.cfrc.com
Daily Peloton	www.dailypeloton.com
DLB Racing	www.dlbracing.com
ESPN	www.espn.com
Fanball Fantasy Sports	www.fanball.com
Major League Baseball	www.mlb.com
Marathon Guide	www.marathonguide.com
New Hampshire Scooter Club	www.nh-scooters.com
NCAA	www.ncaa.com
National Football League	www.nfl.com
National Hockey League	www.nhl.com
Sports Car Club of America	www.scca.com
Sports Illustrated	www.si.com
Track Shark	www.trackshark.com

Stores:

Amazon	www.amazon.com
Art.com	www.art.com
Better Business Bureau	www.bbb.org
Café Press	www.cafepress.com
ebay (auction site)	www.ebay.com
Kelley Blue Book	www.kbb.com

Translators:

Google Translator	translate.google.com

Travel:

American Airlines	www.aa.com
Amtrack	www.amtrak.com
Greyhound Bus	www.greyhound.com
Hipmunk	www.hipmunk.com
Kayak	www.kayak.com
Megabus	us.megabus.com
Orbitz	www.orbitz.com
Trip Advisor	www.tripadvisor.com
Southwest Airlines	www.southwest.com
US Airways	www.usair.com
United Airlines	www.united.com
Cheap Tickets	www.cheaptickets.com
Expedia	www.expedia.com

Weather:

National Weather Service	www.crh.noaa.gov
The Weather Channel	www.weather.com

Woodworking

Wood Magazine	www.woodmagazine.com

The Mechanics of Surfing

Browsers

As we discussed in the previous chapter, webpages are everywhere. Some are located at companies or not-for-profit corporations, universities, and even on the home computer of some individuals. However, they are written in languages foreign to most of us, with locations that are difficult for us to understand. Fortunately, we have a special kind of program called "browsers" that can interpret those special languages and know how to interpret the location information. These browsers understand the commands to display text, images, sounds and more, as well as the commands on how to navigate from one page to the next.

What is nice about browsers is that you can download the one (or ones) you like to your computer and use them **for free**. Often new computers will come with a particular browser already installed on the computer. While it is convenient to use the browser that is already available, you do not need to do so; you can simply download another one if you wish. In 2013, there were approximately 50 different browsers available. Studies indicate that on average, 30% of users select Chrome, 20% of users select Internet Explorer, Firefox or Safari, *each*, and 10% of users select some other browser. Browsers provide slightly different features, and so appeal to different audiences.

The idea of a browser began at CERN (Conseil Européenne pour la Recherche Nucléaire or, in English, European Organization for Nuclear Research). This browser was created in 1990, and called WorldWideWeb. Soon thereafter, scientists at the National Center for Supercomputing Applications (NCSA) at University of Illinois developed a browser that could handle not only the text and navigation of the WorldWideWeb, but also graphics. This browser, released in 1993 and called Netscape, was quickly accepted as the "killer application of the Internet," and grew in popularity. Microsoft soon began marketing another browser called Internet Explorer (IE). In response, the developers working on Netscape began a different approach to developing a browser and expanded their product into one that is now known as Firefox. Apple later created a browser called Safari for their Macintosh machines. It is available on all computers now, and is particularly popular on iPad and other tablet computers. More recently, Google created a browser, and named it Chrome. By the latest measurements, Chrome is now the most popular browser in the world. All of these browsers complete the same tasks in approximately the same way.

Browser Icons

Internet Explorer   TheWorld   Opera
Safari   Mozilla Firefox   Netscape
Tencent Traveler   Maxthon   Chrome

What is the difference? That is a very difficult question to answer precisely. The differences vary depending on what version of the browser you use, what kind of computer you have, what version of the operating system and other things. But, people generally look at issues such as speed, ease of use, available features, security, and support when making a decision. For example, Firefox and Chrome loads web pages faster and use less computer memory than Internet Explorer, Opera, or Safari. That means you do not wait as long to see your webpages and you can open more programs and pages before your computer is overwhelmed.

In addition, Chrome integrates well with other Google tools and products. Internet Explorer, on the other hand, has good parental control functions, but its security functions are lacking. Firefox tends to adopt new features early and often leads the other browsers in its functionality.

Compatibility with industry standards developed for browsing are also important. While that sounds like technical stuff, and not of interest to you, it is important. Microsoft often elects to provide its own options and not necessarily to follow the industry standards in how its browser responds to codes in webpages. That means that IE will not always display a standards-based webpage as it was intended: the page may look odd, or may not display all of the information properly. Of course, it also means that any webpage that is written specifically for IE browsers will not display the webpage correctly in other browsers.

Security Issues Associated with Browsing

While Chapter 7 discusses security issues, it is important to note as we talk about browsing that any connection to a website has risks associated with it, and we all need to be on our guard. Some of the issues are:

Web pages can have software running on them that actually take control of your computer and cause programs to run that you do not intend. Some of those programs, called "malware," can steal information stored on your computer and monitor what you are doing on your computer. Other programs, called "trojans and viruses" can cause important programs not to function properly, can erase files, can even cause your computer not to run, and can even take control of your computer.

Web pages can also be involved in "phishing" activities. As the name suggests, the designers are trying to get you to share some confidential information, such as your bank account and/or passwords, so they can steal money or even your identity.

Software contained in the web pages can also identify your email address and subscribe you to thousands of mailing lists that will result in inappropriate and unwanted email called "spam." Finally, some webpages will use popup ads aggressively which, in turn, can make it difficult or even impossible to continue your browsing.

There are, however, easy ways to prevent these problems. We shall discuss them later in the chapter.

Today, most browsers have a privacy setting which allows a person to use the Internet incognito. When you use this option, no one tracks your browsing, and all saved information from the searches is eliminated at the end. This makes your life less transparent to others.

A related topic is the security of the browser software itself. As a user, you want a program that defends against nefarious attacks. These might include viruses that are intended to change how your computer works, spyware that tries to read and steal personal information (primarily financial) on your computer. The browser should also protect the user against phishing attempts. These are pages that appear to be legitimate sources that try to trick you into sharing personal information or passwords for the purpose of fraud. The top browsers do a good job in protecting users from these attacks.

Internet Explorer, however, tends to have more problems than the others. Because of its historic popularity and other issues, Internet Explorer attracts the attention of more hackers who try to exploit weaknesses and allow spyware, viruses, and phishing attacks. The browser often has more "holes" in the code that can be exploited. You can think of the code holes like you would cracks around your windows

Browser Maintenance

You will sometimes get messages from your system that it is time to update your browser. Should you? The answer is a clear yes! Browsers are simply pieces of software. The owners of the software work to update the software so that they allow the functionality built into newer webpages. They also update the software so that it is safer from the newest "hacks" or security breaches discussed earlier. So, always be sure you have the most recent version of the browser!

and doors. It is possible for *unwanted* air to seep into your home through those cracks. Likewise, malicious programs can sneak in through the holes in IE. This can leave your computer vulnerable to viruses and malware (that are discussed in Chapter 7).

In addition to interpreting the cryptic information of the webpages, the browsers provide usability and navigational tools through the incorporation of a "tool bar," which is simply a row of icons or images which, if clicked with a mouse, invoke frequently used commands in the browser. These days all of the browsers provide a rich set of tools.

Figure 3.1 shows the browser tool bars for Firefox, Chrome and Internet Explorer. They have similarities in their graphical symbols, but have very different looks. What they label, and where they locate their symbols are all dictated by what they believe creates the simplest user experience. To a large extent, which one is best is the one with which you have the most experience. I believe Firefox is the easiest one to use at the beginning because it has more words and menus.

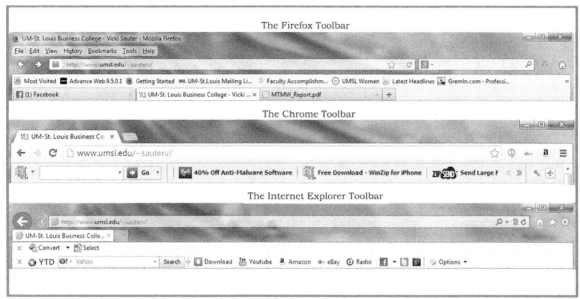

Figure 3.1: Browser Toolbars

You can see that each browser has similar graphical symbols and, as you might guess, they do similar functions. But, what are all of those functions?! Suppose you are working with a realtor to find a new house. The first thing you want to know is where you are. Each house has a street address. Similarly, each webpage has a web address so you can know what you are viewing at any particular time (we will talk more about addresses in a few pages). You find the address in the locator window (circled in Figure 3.2); the value shown is for my personal page, http://www.umsl.edu/~sauter. If you are like most of us, you look at many homes until you find the one you want to buy. So, suppose you are looking at a particular house that seems to be a good fit, but the realtor has one more that might be better. You look at the second house and decide you want to see the first house again. If the houses were web pages, you would use the "back" button as shown in Figure 3.2 to go and view the first house again. When you need to compare something to the second house, you press the "forward" button to view the second house again. In fact, you can use the back button and forward button to navigate among all of the pages (houses) you have seen to find the one you want. Unlike houses, webpages may change between visits to them.

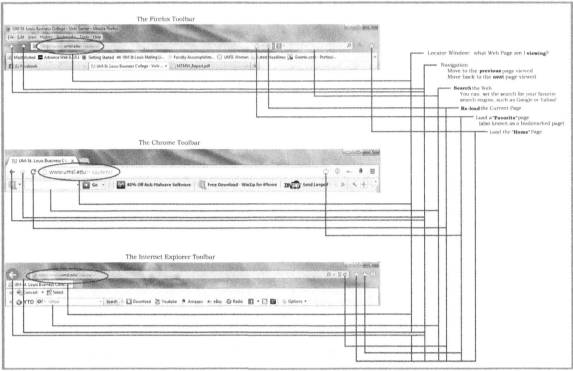

Figure 3.2: The Browser Toolbar – Labeled

If we think the page might have updated information (especially on news or sports pages), we press the "reload" button to see the most recent version of the page. Or, if we do not want to see the page, we might press the "stop" button. If we want to keep information about the page we might print it or we might want to bookmark it (also known as saving it as a favorite) so we can load it again easily. All of these buttons are noted in Figure 3.2.

Now that you have a browser, you are ready to begin the surfing described in Chapter 2. Once you get started, there is no limit to the kinds of information you can find on the World Wide Web. But, where should you start? Most of us start on a "homepage."

What is a Homepage?

We begin our surfing at "home;" this is your designated starting point. How do you know where "home" should be? Your homepage is the page at which your browser will start each time it is opened. If you have a web page, as I do, with links to pages you visit often, it could be your home page. Most people do not have their own web page though, and so they rely on another page to be their homepage. This page should be something you read often, or that has links to other pages you like to read.

Many people select news sources for their home page. Some of the common sites include: CNN's site (http://www.cnn.com), the *New York Times* (http://www.nytimes.com), CBS News (http://www.cbsnews.com), or BBC (http://www.bbc.com) because these sources provide headlines, links to articles and search capabilities. Other people prefer news sources closer to home. In Chicago, many people select the *Chicago Tribune*'s home page (http://www.chicagotribune.com) because it focuses on Chicago news and events, while people in Cleveland are more likely to select the page of the *Plain Dealer* (http://www.plaindealer.com/), and people in San Jose are more likely to select the *Mercury News* (http://www.mercurynews.com) because they focus on events local to their communities. Many sports fans start their web browsing at ESPN's site (http://espn.go.com) so they can get information about their favorite teams and sporting events.

Other people select what are called "portals" for their home pages. These portals may provide news, but they also provide links to a variety of other subjects that are of interest, such as movies, maps, weather, music, shopping, sports, health information, greeting cards, and even horoscopes and comics. In addition, the portals give you access to email accounts, search capabilities and other internet functions such as instant messaging and chat rooms. Yahoo's page (http://www.yahoo.com) is probably the most commonly selected portal, but, Google (http://www.google.com/ig) and Microsoft (http://www.msn.com) each have one too. In addition to the wide range of sources of information, most of these portals are customizable. That is, you can edit the page and decide what information should be available in what spot on the page each time you open it. So, I might want weather forecasts both at my home, and where we intend to vacation so I can plan both what to wear today and what to pack for the vacation. If I am active in maintaining my own investment portfolio, I might also locate a stock price window at the top of my homepage. Instead, I might have the sports scores or technology news high on my page so I see them each time I go to my home page. Some portals even allow you to adjust the colors on the page to make it seem more like your own.

Another source for a home page is that of organizations. Some members of AARP use the AARP page (http://www.aarp.org/) as a home page in order to see information that is of importance to them. Those who trade stocks and bonds might link to their broker, such as Ameritrade (http://www.tdameritrade.com/), or the New York Stock Exchange's site (http://www.nyse.com/). Others set their home page to the organization at which they work, or the one at which they study, or the one at which they worship.

There are specialized home pages based on interest. Grandma Betty (http://grandmabetty.com/) provides a portal for "baby boomers and seniors." EBay's site (http://www.ebay.com) is selected by those who spend significant time with the online auction site. The Sports Car Club of America (http://www.scca.com/) is a starting

The URL

The Universal Resource Locator (usually referred to as a URL) is the address of a website. For example, the URL of my webpage (see Chapter 2) is www.umsl.edu/~sauterv. Generally the URL gives us information about what organization is hosting a site (among other factors), and therefore a clue about whether or not the site is likely to have security problems. My URL indicates that it is hosted at University of Missouri – St. Louis with the "umsl.edu." By contrast, we know that the website www.gm.com is hosted by General Motors.

Be careful, though, because there are ways to disguise the real URL. Some of those ways are simply shortening services (such as TinyURL), but others disguise the location so you do not notice the malicious software (malware) the site is putting on your computer. Always be aware.

point for sports car enthusiasts, while collectors might start at the Collector's Connection (http://www.collectorsconnection.com/) and knitters might start at http://www.patternworks.com/. What is the *best* home page? There is no such thing as the best homepage to use. Best is what provides the information and links that are of importance to *you*. What is the most frequently selected home page? I tried to find this information and could not, so I took an informal poll of people I know who are over 50. I surveyed over 100 people from various aspects of my life – some were quite computer savvy, while others were just beginners. I have 92 responses; some individuals answered for multiple machines, while others did not answer at all. The results of this survey are shown in Table 1.

Table 1: Survey of Home Pages

Web Page Category	Specific Web Page	Number of Responses	Percentage
News Sources			21.74%
	www.msn.com	12	
	www.nytimes.com	3	
	finance.yahoo.com	1	
	www.slashdot.com	1	
	www.cnn.com	1	
	www.bbc.com	1	
	blackvoices.aol.com	1	
Portal Pages			21.74%
	www.yahoo.com	9	
	www.aol.com	9	
	broadband.zoomtown.com	1	
	www.charter.net	1	
	portal.wowway.net	1	
Search Pages			17.39%
	google.com	13	
	www.google.com/firefox	2	
	www.excite.com	1	
Place of Employment		11	11.96%
Browser Pages			9.78%
	www.apple.com/startpage	4	
	www.netscape.com	3	
	www.firefox.com	2	
Providers' Pages			7.61%
	att.yahoo.com	3	
	compuserve.com	1	
	netzero.com	1	
	www.adelphia.com	1	
	www.isp.com	1	
Blank Home Page		3	3.26%
Customized Home Page		3	3.26%

Changing your Homepage

It is relatively easy to change your starting point or homepage. How you do this depends on your browser. If you are using Firefox, you click on the "tools" menu and select options as shown in Figure 3.3.

Figure 3.3: Changing your Homepage with Firefox – Step 1

This will open another window (shown in Figure 3.4); you type in the address of the page you want as your home page as indicated by the arrow. If you happen to have the page you want as your home page open, you can just press the first button ("use current page"). Or, if you have the page bookmarked (we will discuss this later), you can select it by pressing the second button.

Figure 3.4: Changing your Homepage with Firefox – Step 2

A similar process is shown in Figures 3.5 and 3.6 for use with Internet Explorer. First, click on the "gear" icon in the upper right hand corner of the page (noted with an arrow). Select "Internet options" (also indicated with an arrow). This will cause Figure 3.6 to appear.

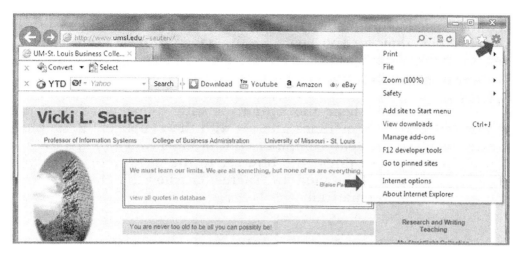

Figure 3.5: Changing your Homepage with Internet Explorer – Step 1

You will land automatically on the page of the "General" tab as shown. Type in the address for the page you wish to have as your homepage in the box marked with an arrow. Click the "OK" button at the bottom. How when you click on the "homepage" icon, you will go to that page.

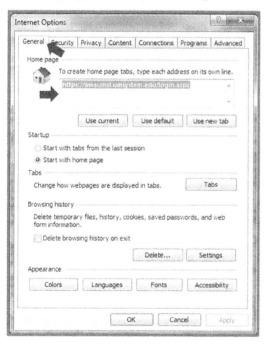

Figure 3.6: Changing your Homepage with Internet Explorer – Step 2

Plug-Ins

Plug-Ins are *not* scent-producing products, or anything new for which you need to find outlet space. Plug-Ins are free programs that work with your browser to allow capabilities that are not part of the main, browser program. They generally provide the ability to read special types of files, such as photographs, music, movies, and other multimedia files that may be incorporated into web pages. For example, many sites with just an audio feed require the RealPlayer plug-in so that you can hear the sound, or with "Shockwave" you can see special video effects and sometimes interact with the webpage. If the plug-in is not already installed on your computer, the browser will prompt the user to install it and often will re-direct the browser to the page from which you can download and then install the plug-in. Thereafter when the plug-in is required, the program will run automatically.

Cookies

Cookies are small bits of text that are stored on your computer by websites when you visit them. They may allow the website to identify you (actually your computer), track your browsing activities, and maintain specific information, such as site preferences or past purchases. Companies automatically gain access to relevant cookies whenever the user establishes a connection to them, usually in the form of Web requests.

For example, I read the *Chicago Tribune* on the web. When I read the paper online, the Tribune Company writes a small cookie to my computer indicating my preferences and interests. The string of characters, shown in Figure 3.7 next to "content," is unreadable by humans, but corresponds to something

> ## Cookies
>
> Third-party cookies are ones that are controlled by a domain different from the one in the location indicator. They should be blocked because they allow that organization to monitor your browsing.
>
> Supercookies are ones with an origin of a top level domain (such as .com). Their primary purpose is to introduce a hole in the security of the browsing session. They too should be blocked.

the *Tribune* computer understands. Then, the next time I go back to the site, the Tribune Company computer looks for that cookie (in a very specific spot) and adjusts my preferences according to what is stored in the cookie.

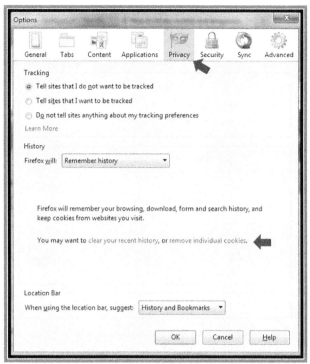

Figure 3.7: Chicago Tribune Cookies

So, are cookies good or bad? In some circumstances, cookies are very good because they make your browsing more efficient by allowing you to customize your browsing of a site and to have that customization maintained from visit to visit. Or, they can be used so that a vendor will default to parts of their store that are of the most interest to you. In other circumstances the cookies can be bad. Cookies can be used to track your browsing. This has become popular for advertising sites to view and set cookies so they can focus the ads to you more clearly. However, this also threatens the anonymity of your browsing behavior.

To protect your privacy, you can manage your cookies. However, how well you can manage your cookies depends on the browser you select. If you are using Firefox, you select "tools" and "internet options" from the menu across the top. What you will see is a box similar to that in Figure 3.8. Notice in the middle section there is an opportunity for you to view or delete all the cookies the computer has already stored.

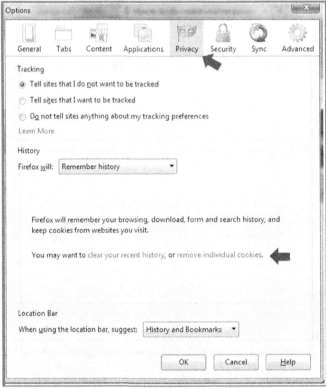

Figure 3.8: Locating Cookies with Firefox

If you are using Internet Explorer, you can select the "privacy tab" at the top of the screen and you will see a box with information such as that in Figure 3.9. This allows you to set a general security preferences for cookies. What is selected here is a "medium" policy that restricts the cookies based upon what is being stored. In particular, this policy blocks any personally identifiable information. You can select a variety of options from allowing all cookies to allowing no cookies (and not allowing the reading of any already available cookies). You can also override these options by specifying policies for individual sites that you either trust or do not trust. This is done by selecting the "advanced" button in Figure 3.9.

Figure 3.9: Setting Privacy Policies in Internet Explorer

In most browsers, you can select the "privacy" option to view and respond to the stored cookies. You can allow or not allow all cookies, you can clear the cookies, and you can view individual cookies.

Generally erasing cookies only impacts your efficiency in browsing. That means you must remember all of your passwords and select browsing options each time you go to a site. However, there are some sites that will not allow any functionality without being able to use cookies; in essence, you cannot browse some sites without allowing them to track you.

Bookmarks and Favorites

In the last chapter, we discussed a number of interesting websites to visit. Suppose you have typed in an address, surfed from someone's webpage or searched to find the page you want. You know you are going to want to go back to the page from time to time, but you certainly do not want to take the path to the page that you used this time. Of course we have a solution to that, and it is called "Bookmarks" in Firefox and Chrome, and "Favorites" in Internet Explorer. As the name implies, this bookmark "saves" the address of the page you want to keep so that the next time you want to go to that page, you simply need to consult your bookmarks or favorites and you will go there directly.

To access that page again, you again select "Bookmarks" or "Favorites" and simply select that item you previously added to your list. In most browsers, you set a bookmark by clicking on the yellow star next to the web address. That action causes the browser to write the web address into a saved file (generally called bookmarks.html or favorites.html) that can be accessed by that browser the next time you want to see the file. You do not need to keep track of the file or the name of the file because the browser does it for you.

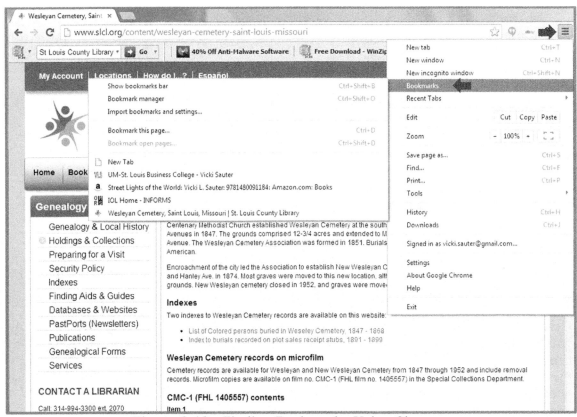

Figure 3.10: Finding Bookmarks Using Chrome

To return to the bookmarks, you must either go directly to the "bookmarks" tab (as in Firefox), or select it from options, as with the Chrome browser, shown on the previous page.

In most browsers, you can organize your bookmarks into groups called folders so you can find them easily. For example, my bookmarks are in folders to make it easier for me to find a particular bookmarked page. Pages are organized into categories, such as those I need for my classes, those for research topics, and others I need for administrative purposes. So, when I go to my bookmarks (in Firefox), I see a list like that in Figure 3.11.

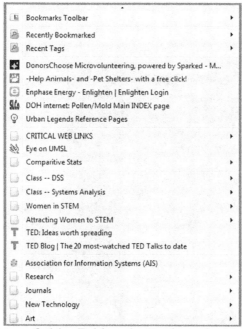

Figure 3.11: Folders in Bookmarks Menu

Putting the bookmark in a file is straightforward. Rather than simply saving a bookmark as shown earlier, you can save it to a particular folder (or create a new folder). You begin by selecting the page as one to be bookmarked. In Firefox, you can either move your mouse to select the Bookmark menu or right click somewhere on the page to bring up the Bookmark menu. Your page will then look like Figure 3.12.

Figure 3.12: Bookmarking a Page in Firefox

Rather than simply hitting "Done" (as you would do with simply saving the page in your list of Bookmarks), click on the down arrow that is circled above. This will result in a popup that appears like Figure 3.13. In this menu, you can select either one of the folders that is shown on the menu (which generally represent the most frequently used folders) or "choose" (see circled option) from options not on this screen or for a new folder. If you selected the "choose" option, you will now see a popup such as that in Figure 3.14. If you would like a new folder, select the "new folder" option (it is circled) and it will take you to the popup in Figure 3.15. Here you can give the newly created page a name and put your page in that folder. When you organize, you may also change the order of the bookmarks, or add dividing lines to the menu. While it seems like a lot of work to organize your bookmarks, you will soon find it makes using the bookmarks easier.

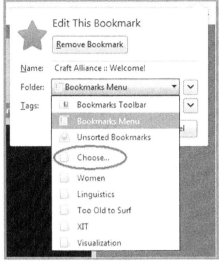

Figure 3.13: Saving a page to a Folder

Figure 3.14: Saving a page to a Folder

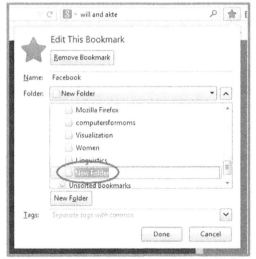

Figure 3.15: Saving a page to a Folder

Opening Multiple Websites at the Same Time

Suppose you are searching to purchase a product and you want to compare two vendors easily. Of course you could toggle back and forth between the two vendor's websites. Or, you could simply open both pages at the same time. There are two ways to accomplish this task.

The easiest thing to do is to open your browser again and to go to the new website. To do this, you can either click on the browser icon on your desktop a second time. Or you can use the "file" menu option to open a new window. After the user clicks, he or she will have two versions of the browser that work independently. The user may move back and forth between them to compare the two sites.

Most browsers have an additional option called "tabs." Tabs allow you to have only one browser window open, but at the same time to surf independently between the various pages and to move among them easily. In this way, it keeps your desktop more organized.

To access tabs, you simply click on the tab next to the one labeled with the page you are viewing currently. The image may look like an empty file folder or may have a "+" on it; the appropriate place to click is circled on the toolbars shown below.

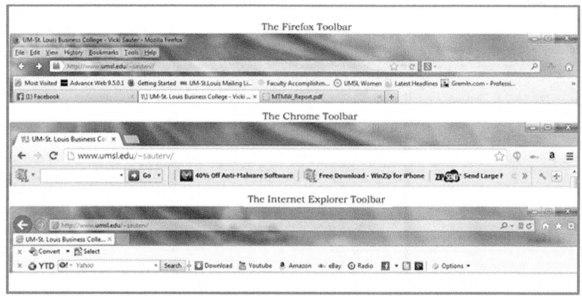

Figure 3.16: Opening Tabs

Once you have opened the new tab, your browser will appear as shown in Figure 3.17. The two tabs, similar to file folder tabs, are circled in this figure. The first page, represented by the tab on the left, is located at my homepage. The second page, represented by the tab on the right, is located at the webpage for Grace's Place, an online computer museum. You can move to my homepage simply by clicking on the left tab. What you do in one tab does not affect what you see when browsing the other tab. You can close either tab simply by clicking on the "x" on the right of each tab. Or, if you would like to close *all* of the tabs, you can click the "x" at the top right corner of the browser.

Having only one browser window open keeps your desktop neater. In addition, it makes it easier to maneuver between (or among) the webpages because you do not need to hunt for the correct version. Finally, it helps manage the computer's memory better because you are not opening unnecessary programs to get the job done.

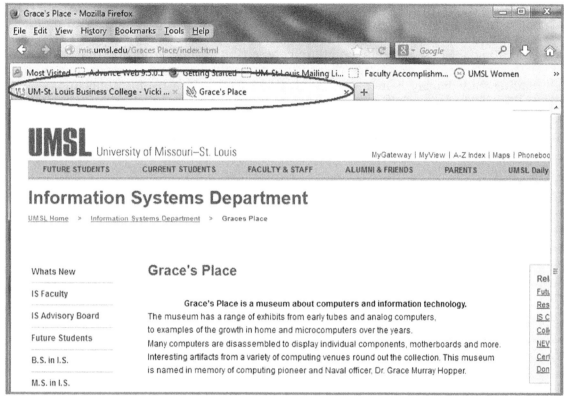

Figure 3.17: Browser with Multiple Tabs Open

Knowing how to navigate the browsers toolbars and functions is not enough for today's surfers. You need to know how to navigate specific web sites too. Chapter 4 introduces some common functions you will experience as you surf, and explains how to maneuver among them.

Can I Surf the Internet of Things?

As long as we are discussing surfing, let us spend a minute talking about how to access the "Internet of Things." The "Internet of Things" is a collection of objects with monitors that can communicate through electronic messaging, without human intervention. For example, my husband and I have solar panels on our home roof; the panels send signals to an application that allow us to monitor whether or not the panels are operational and, if so, how much electricity they are generating. These objects communicate on the same Internet that we surf. However, generally we access them via specific applications that not only take a reading, but display it in a useful form and feed it into useful applications. Of course, if you have their specific IP address, you can monitor the value itself, but then you will not get the additional applications.

Navigating Websites

Commercial Sites and Purchasing Online

One popular website today is Amazon.com; we will look at this site as a way of demonstrating common commercial sites. Amazon.com, which started as a single-product company (books), has now grown into a site at which you can purchase almost anything. Below is Amazon.com's homepage.

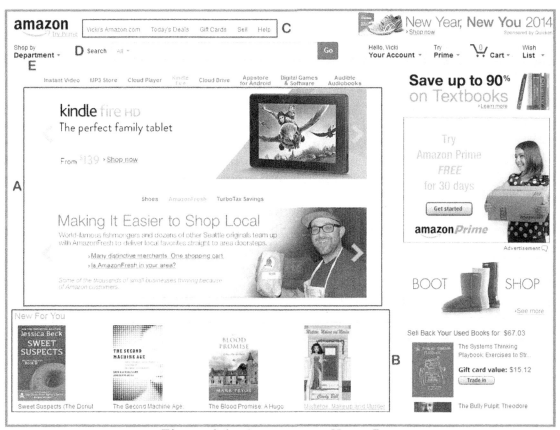

Figure 4.1: Amazon.com Home Page

The page has some general ads that it provides for everyone and then some ads that are targeted to a particular user. At the time of this writing, a significant amount of the page is dedicated to a set of revolving ads. These are featured advertisements that vary from session to session, but appear for everyone who comes to Amazon.com[1]. These ads have been boxed in Figure 4.1, and labeled "A".

Some people coming to Amazon.com either wants to see what new products are available, but they may be most interested in those that are similar to their previous purchases. For this reason, Amazon provides recommendations for each individual user. Notice there are some of these products shown lower on the page, labeled "New for You." These ads have been boxed in Figure 4.1 and labeled "B". They also have recommendations that reflect specific departments in which you have recently shopped if you were to scroll down further. In addition, there is a link to all recommendations, labeled (for my page) "Vicki's Amazon.com" This menu also takes you to the deals of the day, gift cards and help. This area has been boxed in Figure 4.1 and labeled "C".

Other people who come to Amazon.com seek specific items (or categories of items), such as a book by a particular author or a particular brand of kettle. For this reason, there is a search box high on the page; this is labeled "D." You simply type into the box what you want and press the "Go" button. For example, if you type in "Spiderman," you get a list with a figure, a computer game, an FX glove as well as other items.

Or, you can limit the items Amazon will suggest to categories that you know you want. For example, if you know that you want the movie or TV versions of Spiderman, you can type "Spiderman" into the box and specify a department using the drop down list on the left side of the box (in this case "Movies and TV"). That will limit the number of items you must look through.

You can also search Amazon by its departments. On the top left side of the page there is a drop down box labeled "Shop by Department," labeled "E" in Figure 4.1. If you click on the downward arrow, you can see all the ways of describing products at Amazon. If we select "Hardware," we will see a screen such as the one in Figure 4.2.

---

[1] The software used to run the site Amazon.com also runs many other websites. So you may have exactly the same experience at other sites. At the very least, you will have similar experiences and this explanation will help you navigate them.

There are four main sections to the page. The first section, on the left and labeled "A" is a list of the categories of merchandise that are included in the Hardware section. You can see general categories, such as "Door Hardware and Locks" as well as specific items, such as "Dead Bolts." This allows you to go directly to the product you want.

If you want to browse the Hardware section, you have two choices. The first category in the middle towards the top of the page, and labeled "B" includes "Featured Categories." These are the most frequently shopped Hardware items from all users who purchase hardware from Amazon.com. As you might expect, further down on the page, and labeled "C" is the category "Shop your Favorite Hardware Brands." Rather than providing the most frequently shopped item from all users, these are the ones either you specifically have purchased, or things Amazon.com has determined you would like based upon your past purchasing behavior. It can sometimes be a little mystifying as to why Amazon makes the suggestions it does. For example, one of the recommended vendors shown for me is "Chamberlin," which makes garage door openers and associated electronics. I do not even remember scanning Amazon.com for garage door openers, much less purchasing one from them. However, I must have searched in a way that suggests I may soon need a garage door opener (perhaps I should go and check my garage!). The final category of links, labeled "D" on Figure 4.2, are ads like you might see for any store.

As you move your cursor over the page shown in Figure 4.2, you will see the various options being highlighted. If you click on any of those, you go to that section. Another way you can tell exactly where you are on the web is to read the title posted on the tab. Although it is not showing in Figure 4.2, if you bring up the page, you will notice it says, "Amazon.com: Hardware: Nails Screws & Fasteners, Cabinet Hardware and More" If instead, you look at Figure 2.1 (in the second chapter), which is my webpage, you see it says "UM-St. Louis Business College – Vicki Sauter." Well-designed websites always use a title to help reassure you as to your location and to help you navigate the site.

Further, you will note that the "Hardware" is highlighted under the "Shop By Department" on the left end of the box labeled "E" in Figure 4.2. Immediately to the right you will see subcategories of things like "Top Sellers," "Door Hardware and Locks," "Garage Door Hardware," and others. These represent the primary sections of the store.

Above that section, and labeled F, is the search box discussed earlier. If you know what item, what type of item, or what brand of item you want, you can type it in the box and Amazon will respond with a listing of all items that match the description.

Figure 4.2: Hardware Home Page of Amazon.com

So, for example, if you type in "router," Amazon will show you 24 items of the 143 possible items in this department. On the right side of the page, you can show these items sorted by relevance, New and Popular, Price low to High, Price High to Low, and by the Average Customer Score.

Also in the top right section of the Amazon page, you see some links including "your account," "cart," and "Wish List." These are links that help you purchase items from the site and keep track of your items. We will discuss these after we discuss the other sections of the page.

Notice at the top of this section it says "Hello, Vicki." Amazon (as well as most commercial sites) keeps track of who you are, what products you view, and what products your purchase. Why? Ostensibly, they track your viewing and purchasing behavior so they can understand your interests, likes and dislikes so they can "serve" you better. Said differently, they would like to make recommendations about new products that you might consider purchasing and would like those recommendations to be as good as possible (so that you purchase more). The goal is to replicate a good salesperson in a small neighborhood store who always seems to know just what you want. For example, if you always purchase a particular author's work, then the vendor will track that pattern and will highlight a new book by that author when it is available. Or, if you enjoy mysteries by a particular author, and a similar author has a new book, Amazon might recommend the new book based on the similarity of the two writing styles.

The commercial sites take this level of recommendation one step further: not only do they consider *your* preferences when making the recommendations, they consider the preferences of people *like you*. Amazon analyzes your buying preferences and finds customers who seem to like the same kinds of books (as well as other items), and uses *their* purchasing behavior as a basis for recommendations to you. Suppose you like Eric Clapton music. If Amazon discovers that other people who enjoy Eric Clapton music, also tend to enjoy music by Neil Young, Bob Dylan and Jerry Lee Lewis, they might make recommendations for you, you might see music by Young, Dylan and Lewis – not because you have purchased these performers (or perhaps not even have heard their music), but because people with similar tastes enjoy them. So, you get the benefit of everyone's opinion without needing to talk to a large number of people.

Unlike your neighborhood bookstore, you don't need to worry about Amazon.com forgetting or hiring a new clerk. This purchase pattern and the associated recommendations, are updated every time you make a purchase or rate an item on their site, and are stored on a computer. Unfortunately, also unlike the neighborhood store, they do not track *why* you make specific purchases. So, I regularly get recommendations about sports books or baby toys because I purchase sports books for my son and toys as newborn gifts. I *might* be interested in these, but only occasionally; they certainly are not my first preference. Around holidays my purchasing behavior and preferences change substantially, but most online stores do not pick up these patterns to my choices. Not everyone wants to have their browsing behavior recorded or associated with their names. To avoid this, you can browse anonymously. Remember the beginning line, "Hello, Vicki?" Simply click this button and they will no longer associate the browsing with your name. Amazon always tracks purchases, but not all vendors require registration in order to purchase.

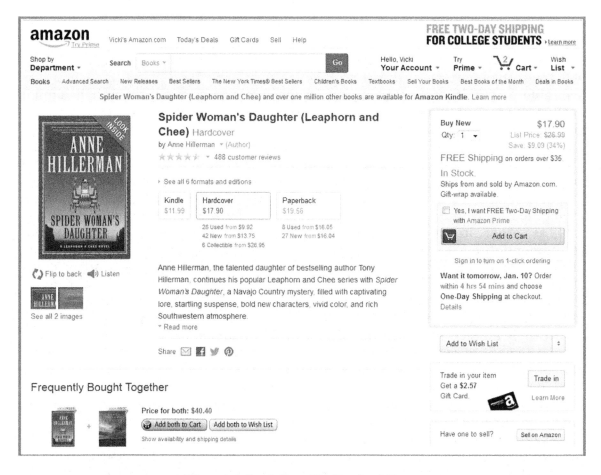

Figure 4.3: A Specific Product Page

Suppose though you do find an item you want to purchase. Consider Figure 4.3 which shows a book by Anne Hillerman, *Spider Woman's Daughter*. Amazon, like most vendors, gives you information about the availability and price of the item. This particular page is for the hardcover version of the book.

However, you can select the paperback version or the Kindle (electronic) version by clicking on those regions. In addition, Amazon provides you with a short summary of the book, and the rating by other customers. For some books, they provide a small number of pages the viewer can read.

If you scroll down on the page, you see publication details, information about related books, books that have often been purchased by people who like Anne Hillerman, and editorial reviews of the book as shown in Figure 4.4.

After the editorial reviews, you see customer reviews of the book. These are reviews are written by fellow customers. You too can rate the book by clicking the button labeled "Write a customer review." This button might appear at the top of the reviews, but always appears at the bottom of the reviews (as shown in Figure 4.5). If you click on it, you will see a screen such as that shown in Figure 4.6. The first task is to assign stars. You simply need to click on the farthest star to the right that you want to register. So, if you want to assign 5 stars as I did, you simply click on the far right star and all are clicked automatically. After you rate the book, Amazon provides a box in which you can write your comments. Your ranking will be merged with others who have ranked the book to result in the stars appearing immediately under the author's name. In addition, your rating and comments will then be available for everyone to read. Please note that these are listed with your name associated to them as shown in Figure 4.5.

In short, Amazon gives you a significant amount of information about the product and what others think about the product before you purchase the product.

The small shopping cart on the right side of Figure 4.3 is what you have currently identified that you want to purchase. Notice the number in the cart shows the number of items you have identified. You can review the contents of your cart at any time by clicking on the cart. It will reveal a page such as that shown in Figure 4.7. From this page you can increase or decrease quantities, identify the item as a gift, or proceed to checkout. Of course, Amazon always wants to remind you of items you have identified as desirable, but have not purchased. These are shown at the bottom of the screen under "Saved for Later." You can just click and add those to your order.

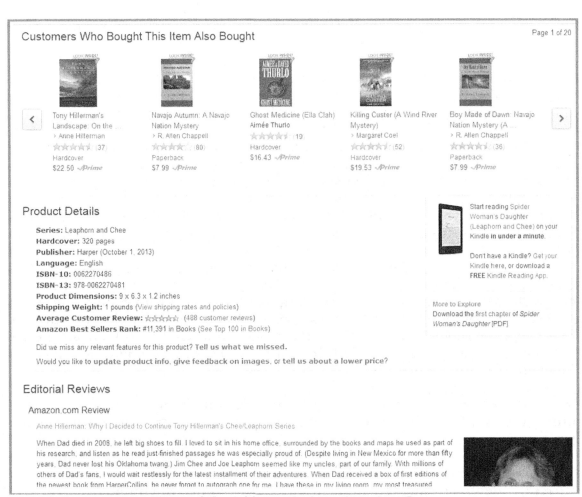

Figure 4.4: Additional View of Product Page

Figure 4.5: Final View of the Product Page

Figure 4.6: Registering Customer Rating

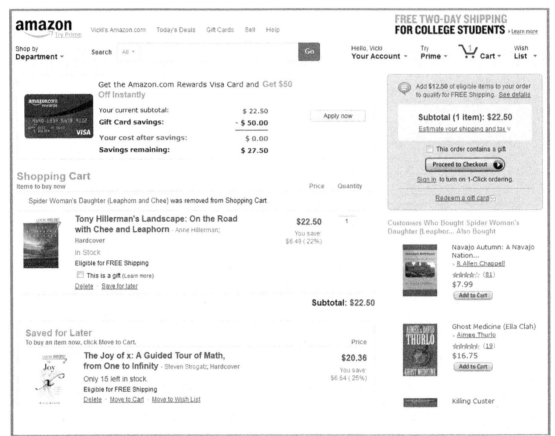

Figure 4.7: The Shopping Cart

Suppose you decide you want to purchase the book shown in Figure 4.3 as well. First return to the product page. Then simply press the yellow button with the shopping cart labeled "Add to Cart" on the right side of the page shown in Figure 4.3. This will bring you to a new page summarizing your order, additional advertising about financing and other books that you might like. This is shown in Figure 4.8.

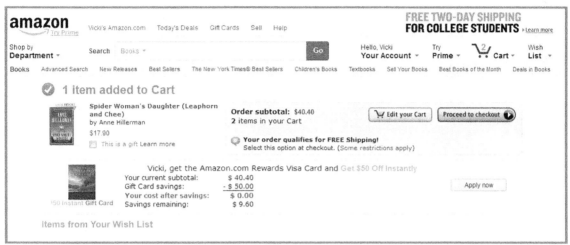

Figure 4.8: Purchasing an Item, Step 1

If you have an account, you will view a screen such as shown in Figure 4.9. Amazon will automatically complete your shipping information and your payment method that you have saved previously. As you can see, you can change your shipping address, your payment method or your billing address simply by selecting the word "change" next to what you want to change. For example, if you want to send the books to someone else as a gift, you would select the "change" near "Shipping address," and add that address. You would not, however, change the billing address because you have not moved.

If you do not have information saved, you will need to provide Amazon.com some financial information and you will see the screen shown in Figure 4.10. As you can see, you have the option of paying for your order with credit cards, debit cards, gift cards, an Amazon.com card, or using your checking account.

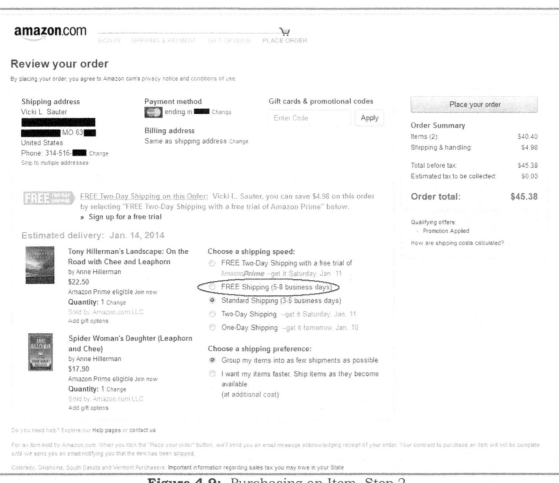

Figure 4.9: Purchasing an Item, Step 2

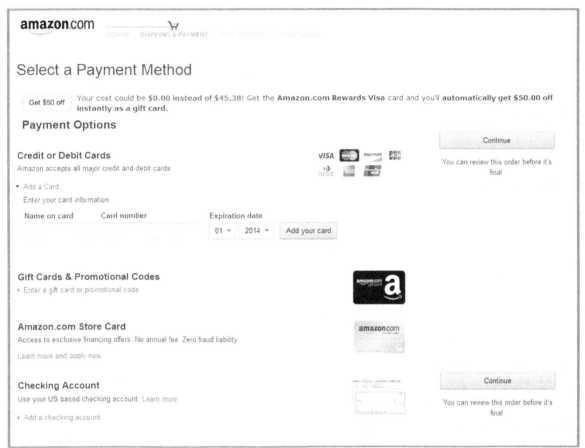

Figure 4.10: Entering Financial Information

Although some online stores allow you call in and provide your credit card information, Amazon does not. Is this safe? Many people feel uncomfortable about putting their credit card numbers on the Web. These same people have no trouble giving their credit cards to a food server to charge dinner. The fact is that putting your credit card on the Web is probably less risky than giving your credit card to a food server. When you use your account on the Web, someone must monitor and intercept your information as it passes from your computer to the vendor's computer. Clearly, this is quite possible. However with the number of messages and web pages that are sent, the odds of someone monitoring *your* surfing at just the right time are infinitesimal. However, the server has your card in his or her possession, generally in a secluded area, for several minutes. It is quite easy for that person to copy down your credit card number and security code (on the back) to steal it. Statistics show that servers, or store clerks, or other vendors steal the numbers at higher rates than people lose them on the Web. However, you must first ensure that the transaction is secure.

You will notice that the address section at the top will have changed from http:// .... to http**s**:// .... to indicate that the transaction is secure. So, what does that mean? This means that the store (in this case, Amazon.com) uses a set of programs that will decrease the likelihood that your personal information, including your credit card information, can be obtained by a third party. Just as it is possible to eavesdrop on a telephone conversation, it is possible to eavesdrop on a computer "conversation." That is, if the person has the right equipment, he or she could intercept your order, including your credit card data, without either you or the company knowing about it. Then the person could, of course, use that information to purchase with your credit card or even steal your identity. The security tells you, the user, that the company uses software to disguise your information in code so that even if someone eavesdrops on the transmission, he or she would not be able to understand the information, and therefore could not get your credit or personal information. This encoding and decoding process is much the same as was used during WWII for telegraph communications to avoid having the enemy understand the transmission. They similarly prevent eavesdropping, tampering, and message forgery.

While Amazon.com is well known, what if the site is not well known? How do you know that it is a store that is reliable and honest? There are two kinds of credentials you might consider to 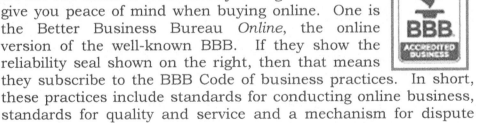 give you peace of mind when buying online. One is the Better Business Bureau *Online*, the online version of the well-known BBB. If they show the reliability seal shown on the right, then that means  they subscribe to the BBB Code of business practices. In short, these practices include standards for conducting online business, standards for quality and service and a mechanism for dispute resolution in the event that the consumer has difficulty with the company. If they also show the second symbol on the right, then they subscribe to the BBB*OnLine* Privacy program, which includes privacy standard-setting, verification, monitoring and review, consumer dispute resolution, compliance enforcement mechanism and educational components. In other words, the consumer can feel comfortable that the associated company is aware of privacy practices and tries to run its business so information is protected.

Another seal that has also become associated with safe and reliable websites is  from VeriSign. Like BBB, a VeriSign endorsement ensures that the company is following good business practices and protects data sent to them. VeriSign was recently acquired by Norton, and so you might see either Verisign or Norton (or both) to indicate security of the site. This company has provided guidance worldwide on the Internet since the mid-1990s, However, it also provides an electronic "certificate" that your browser can examine, and report to the user that the site is authentic, thereby providing an additional layer of security for the consumer. More recently, Thawte has begun providing security certificates to protect consumer sites, and some companies have adopted their security principles (similar to those of VeriSign). Its symbol also tells the user that the site is secure.

Now, let us return to purchasing those books! Go back to Figure 4.9 and assume you have entered your shipping, billing and payment information. You are not yet done. Amazon has indicated on Figure 4.8 (in the box) that your order was eligible for free shipping. While some vendors never have free shipping and others always have free shipping, most of the vendors have some intermediate policy. The policies generally involve a minimum order size, or a special time of the year, or some intermediary policy. The policy of Amazon.com is that they will give you free shipping if the order is over $35 (which this order is). However, Amazon, does not give that to you automatically. Notice in Figure 4.9 that the shipping speed chosen is "Standard." That costs you $4.98 for this order. To take advantage of the shipping offer, you need to change this to the "FREE Shipping" (as circled in Figure 4.9). Of course, you can also opt for Two-Day Shipping or One-Day Shipping, but those will cost more.

Once you have indicated the shipping speed, you select the button labeled, "Place your order" and you will get a confirmation screen such as the one in Figure 4.11. In addition, you will get a confirmation email from Amazon shortly.

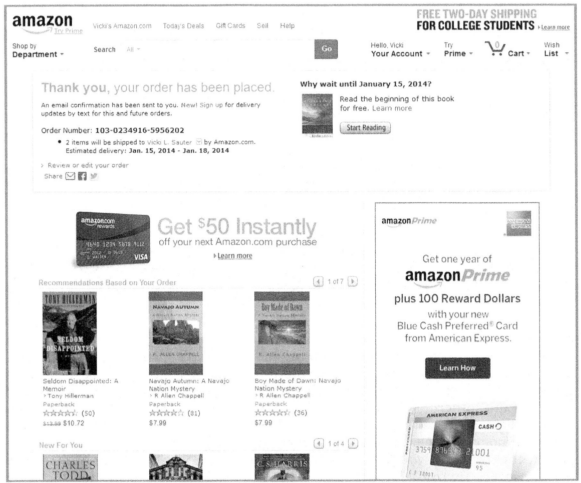

Figure 4.11: Confirmation of Order

As noted in the beginning, most sites have a process similar to that shown on Amazon for selecting items, filling the shopping cart and checking out. In fact, many of them use Amazon's system for their shopping experience. Even if the functions may look different at other sites, the basic operations will be the same.

Purchasing online from commercial sites are an important part of web use, but not the only use. In the next sections, we will visit other kinds of online sites and how one navigates them.

Click-Through Pages

The Greater Good Network (http://www.greatergood.com/) is a sponsored site on the Web. This site sponsors fundraising efforts in eight categories: hunger prevention, breast cancer prevention, animal care and protection, Veterans assistance programs, Autism treatment, Diabetes treatment, promotion of literacy, and preservation of the rainforest. Most sponsored sites work in the same fashion. Consider Figure 4.12, which is the Veterans assistance programs page on the Greater Good Network.

Figure 4.12: Veterans Assistance Page

Advertisers contribute to the cause of animal rescue in exchange for ads that appear on the site. Each time someone visits the page and clicks on the blue button labeled, the advertiser contributes money to the fund. The site returns 100% of sponsor ad dollars to the identified charity. So, it does not cost the visitor anything, but the charity benefits. Clearly, they advocate clicking each day.

The viewer is directed to a thank you page like the one in Figure 4.13. Notice the page tells you specifically how the money will be used; in this case it is to fund meals for homeless Veterans. The page notes that advertisers will donate additional funds if the viewer shares the page through their social media outlets. Advertisers will also provide additional funding if viewers click through to their page, if viewers sign petitions, and for other activities. Finally, the Greater Good Network provides an online store from which purchases help to fund support.

Each of these sites in the Greater Good Network has a "click through" program whereby visitors can help the cause simply by "clicking each day" and purchasing from the associated store. You can click through on one of the causes or all of the causes to help them address the associated charity. The network allows users to click once per cause per day (per computer). I try to go through the entire network first thing each morning to provide support for these worthy causes.

Figure 4.13: Response Page

These click-through sites are becoming a popular way for municipalities, groups, or even companies to run contests. For example, St. Louis recently sponsored the "Cakeway to the West," a competition for citizens to identify 250 iconic St. Louis attractions to receive fiberglass "birthday cakes" to help celebrate St. Louis' 250th birthday. These votes were calculated by the total number of clicks each attraction received; people could vote once per day.

eBay

When I was in college, Evanston Illinois sponsored the "World's Largest Garage Sale" each year.[2] As I recall, they blocked off one of the parking garages and leased booths to residents and others. The city provided the advertising, traffic control and probably arranged for food and facilities. Each year people lined up to find a bargain. Of course, each person's treasure was someone else's junk.

In September 1995, a programmer created the online equivalent of Evanston's garage sale, called AuctionWeb. According to About.com[3] a programmer

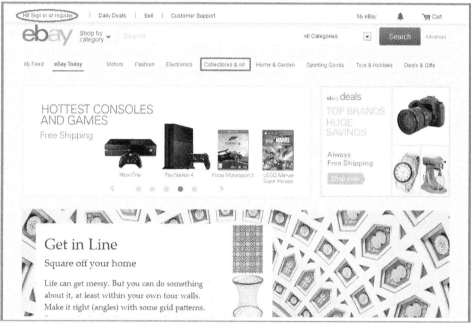

Figure 4.14: eBay's Home Page

launched his software by selling a *broken* laser pointer for $14.83. When he enquired, the purchaser noted that he collected broken laser pointers. One

---

[2] I have since seen other places claim to be the world's largest garage sale, so I am not sure Evanston's is, or even was, the largest. However, that is what they claimed!

[3] Hsiao, A., "How Did eBay Start?" *About.com*, http://ebay.about.com/od/ebaylifestyle/a/el_history.htm, undated, viewed June 12, 2007.

person's junk is indeed someone else's treasure!

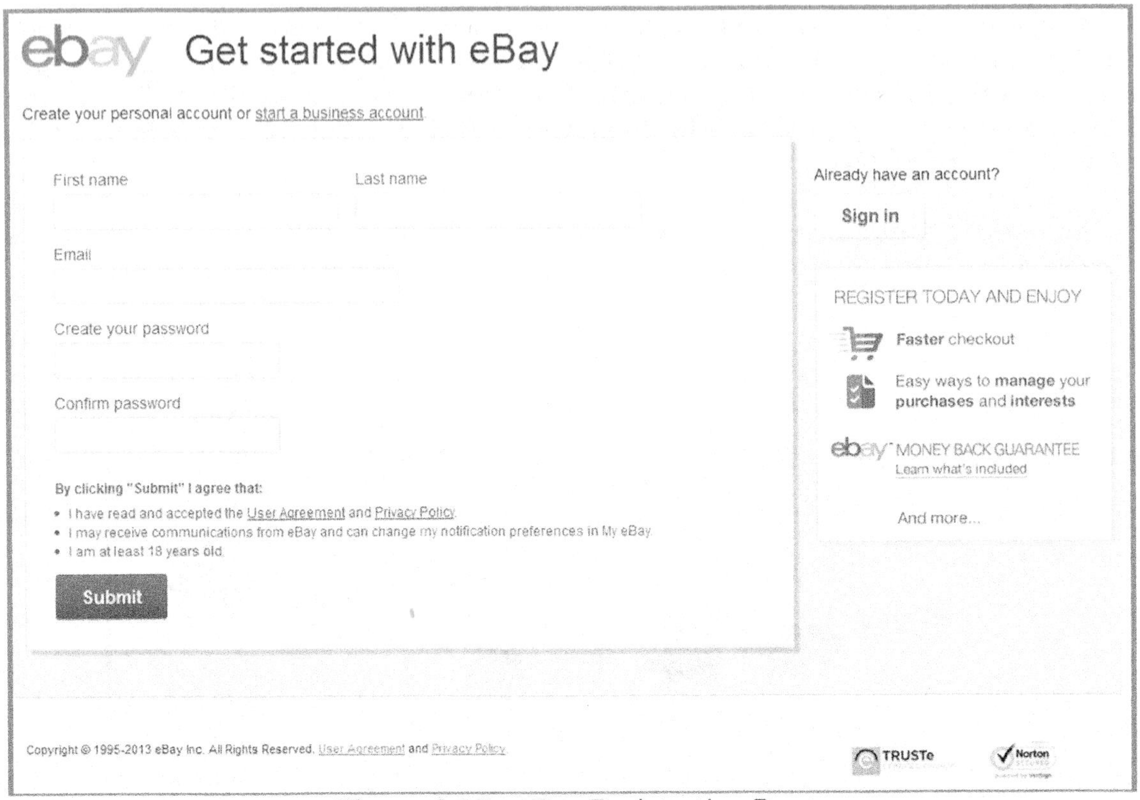

Figure 4.15: eBay Registration Page

After that time, Pierre Omidyar, the programmer, registered the name eBay (which was short for Echo Bay, the name of his consulting company) and the online auction site was born. eBay's mission is "to provide a global trading platform where practically anyone can trade practically anything." Originally the site provided an online garage sale forum. While that certainly is true about some of the sellers on eBay, it now also provides a forum for small businesses and close-out stores to market their items to the world. Almost anything you could want to buy can be found on eBay.

The first step to using eBay is to create an account. If you direct your browser to eBay's main page (www.ebay.com), you will view a page that resembles the one in Figure 4.14. Just above the eBay logo (circled in Figure 4.14) is the link to register as a user. Once you click on the link to register, you will see a page similar to Figure 4.15.

As you can see, the registration page collects the standard contact information. After you submit this information, eBay will create a user name for you which will display when you bid, buy or sell items on eBay. Throughout the system, eBay uses this ID instead of your name, email address or other personal information. Your bids on items will be displayed by your ID, your sale of items will be displayed by your ID, and email between you and other eBay members will be handled through the eBay form system.

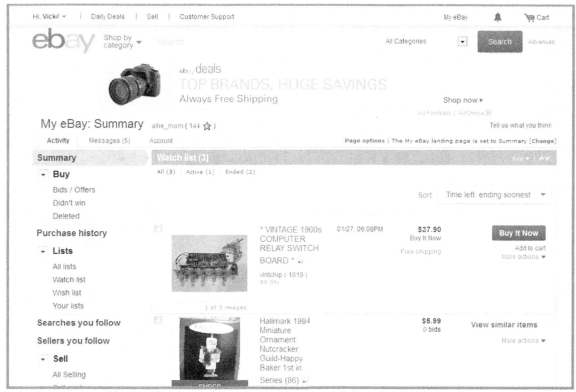

Figure 4.16: A Personalized Form of the eBay Home Page

So, once you have an ID, start looking for bargains! As with most sites, once you sign into the system, eBay will show you items that are similar to what you have purchased before. For example, when I sign in on the home page, instead of Figure 4.14, I get a page that shows what is on sale now similar to those items I have recently purchased. It is shown in Figure 4.16. I collect vintage computer parts and nutcrackers. You can see eBay has identified one from each category to show to me when I log in.

You can start with looking through eBay's categories, shown across the top. So, suppose you were interested in coin collecting. You would scroll across that menu on Figure 4.13 and click on "Collectibles and Art" (this category is boxed in Figure 4.13 to make it easier to find). This would take you to the page for this category, where you would find a section for coins (it is circled in Figure 4.17).

Figure 4.17: eBay's Collectibles and Art Page

Predictably, the Coin page offers first the most popular selections, and then you can view U.S. coins, then World Coins, and finally Coin Dealers. Suppose you were interested in Croatia, an Eastern European country on the Adriatic Sea. You would select "World Coins" and see a page such as the one in Figure 4.18.

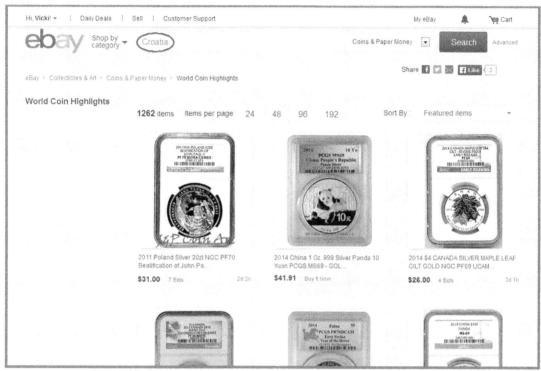

Figure 4.18: World Coin Page on eBay

You could scroll through all of the items available in world money. Or, you can go to the searchbox at the top and type in "Croatia" (this is circled in the image above). Then you will get a display of only Croatian money such as that shown in Figure 4.19. Notice on the left side of the screen (and boxed in Figure 4.19), there are categories of Croatian money you can view, including paper money, coins, medieval coins, ancient coins, and collection supplies. If you wish to look through all of the items, you can simply scroll down.

When viewing items on eBay, the default is to show items that are the closest to the search terms first, and to show them in a list. However, you can adjust both of those using the "sort" and "view" menus at the top right of the screen (they are circled). You can view the items by time (the auction that will end first, or the most recently listed item), by price (either by price with shipping highest or lowest, or just price highest), or by distance (nearest first). In terms of view, you can view a list, such as shown in Figure 4.19, a gallery, such as Figure 4.18, or customize your view.

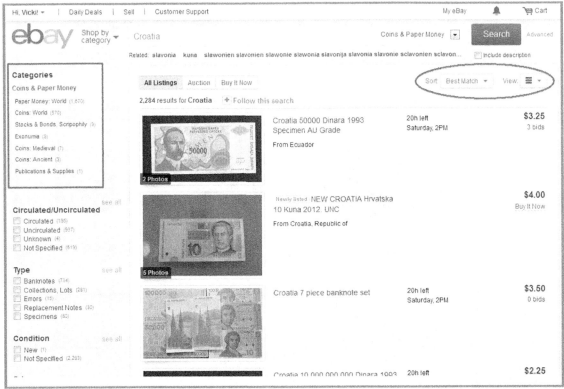

Figure 4.19: Croatian Money on eBay

Suppose you find an item that interests you. If you click on the photo or the description of the item, you get the details of the auction such as shown in Figure 4.20. You will note three major regions on the screen, as designated by the rectangles. The first area (the left side of the figure) shows the photo of the item; the second shows details about the auction, and the final shows details about the seller.

Consider the items in the second region. First, you see information about the bid and a button that allows you to place your bid (labeled "A"). We will return to this shortly. However, above that , and labeled "B" gives you clues about how likely you are to get your item. First, it tells you how long you have until the auction is over. Clearly, the more time until the auction ends, the more likely it is that someone else will bid against you. Further down, near the button for placing a bid (and labeled "C") is a number in brackets which gives you information about how many bids have been made on this item to date. In the case of the item in the image, there has been only one other bid. You would be able to click on the number and see an encrypted name of the people who have bid on the item. If it is the same name multiple times, you might guess the person is fairly determined to get the item. If, instead, it is a variety of people, then they might never return to re-bid on the item.

Shipping costs and location are labeled "D." Note the shipping is a cost above and beyond what you bid for the item. If it is shipping from another country, there could be delays in its arrival and you might have to sign for the item upon delivery.

Finally, in this second region, you have the ability to "watch this item" without committing to purchase (shown in area E). If you select this option, eBay will remind you of your interest when it gets close to the end of the auction, or whenever others bid.

Before you commit to purchasing, it is prudent to learn about the reliability of the seller. That information is in the third region of the page. You can see the user's name (it is his or her eBay id as we created earlier), and how many items that user has put up for auction in the past (in this case, it is 4), and the vast majority of the feedback on the user is positive. If you click on the seller's name you can learn how long this seller has been active (in this case, since July 15, 2013). You can also see there are icons to the right of the name that indicates "power seller" and "me." The "power seller" icon means, "the seller meets the criteria for being a PowerSeller---consistent volume sales, 98% total positive Feedback or better, eBay marketplace policy compliance, and an account in good financial standing. With this mark, you can be confident that you are transacting with an experienced eBay seller who has proven that they're

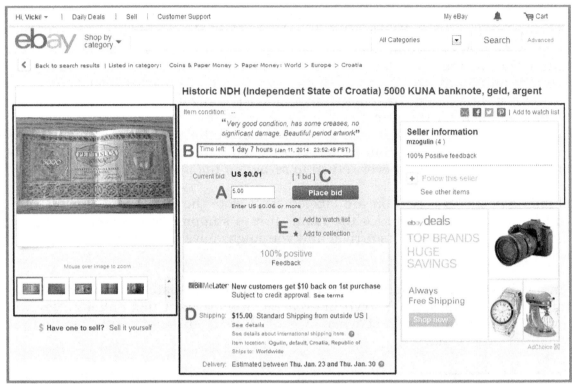

Figure 4.20: Specific Item Bid Page

committed to customer satisfaction."[4] The "me" icon means there is a page about the seller that gives you some specific information about his or her auction business and what other auction items that seller has available. Further down below the name is information about the seller's rating, and a link to the past feedback about the seller. If you click on the "Read feedback comments," you get information of what other purchasers have said. You can get the summary information as well as specific comments further down.

Suppose you have decided you like the item, you like the seller and you want to make a bid. Return to Figure 4.20. You would then click on the blue button in the middle region labeled "place bid." You will be prompted to sign in, which will require that you use the userid assigned earlier and your password. Notice that in Figure 4.20 that I put in a bid of $5.00. After confirming the bid, you will receive

---

[4] "Power Sellers," *eBay*, http://pages.ebay.com/services/buyandsell/welcome.html, Undated, Visited June 19, 2007.

a notice, such as that shown in Figure 4.21.

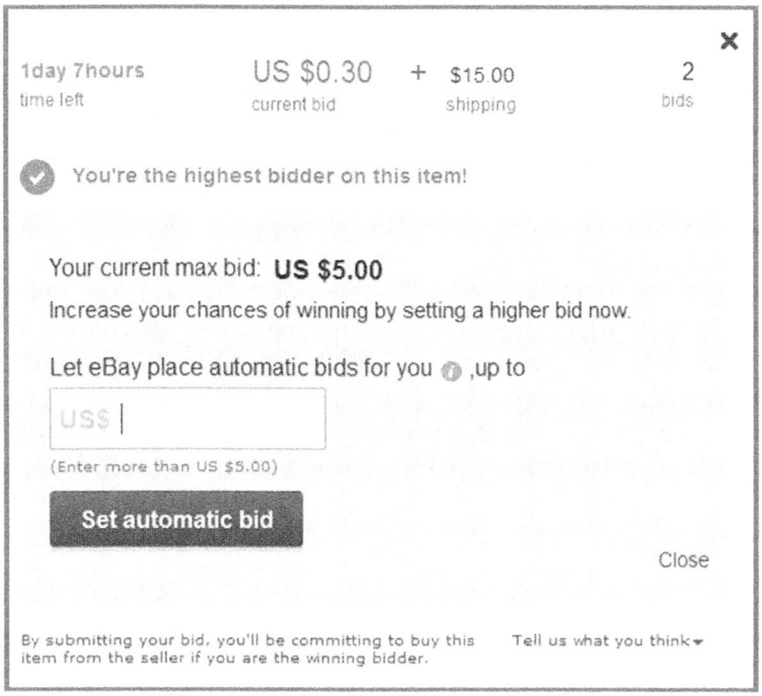

Figure 4.21: Confirmation Screen

While I put in a bid of $5.00, eBay only registered it high enough to outbid the previous user. So, at this time, users can only see that I have bid $0.30. If someone bids above $0.30, but below $5.00, eBay will automatically increment my bid above the other bid. When the bidding gets above $5.00, eBay will send a message and you can decide whether or not to bid again. So, in this case, I placed a maximum bid of $5.00.

If you are successful in your bid to purchase an item, you will receive an email at the end of the auction telling you that you are successful and prompting you to send payment. Sellers differ in what payment option they will allow, but almost all of them allow "PayPal." PayPal is a service owned by eBay that allows you to pay the seller without divulging financial information to that seller *and* while protecting the seller. It is an alternative to using checks and money orders, even when the seller (who is often another individual) cannot take credit cards. It is a global online payment solution, with millions of account members in hundreds of countries and regions around the world. In addition, PayPal has received many awards for technical excellence from the internet industry and the business community at large.

To use PayPal, you must, of course, create an account. In addition to the normal contact information, you must enter information about your banking account or credit card. Then, when you have won an auction, you click "pay with PayPal" and login to your account. If you verify that you want your account debited for the amount, two things happen. First, PayPal either sends an invoice to your credit card company or to your bank for the amount of the purchase. Second, PayPal credits the seller for the purchase price. In this way, you do not need to divulge the financial information to the seller, nor do you need to worry about having your credit card available at the end of an auction. The credit information is stored by PayPal and available anytime you need to use it. You can use PayPal for payments for non-eBay items too. In fact, you can send money to another individual (who also has a PayPal account) if you so need.

StumbleUpon
Another product that may be of interest is called StumbleUpon (http://www.stumbleupon.com). This product is being highlighted here both because it is interesting to use and because it interacts with your browser differently than a standard webpage. According to its own description, "StumbleUpon lets you "channel surf" the best-reviewed sites on the web. It is a collaborative surfing tool for finding and sharing great sites, which you might not have discovered otherwise.

StumbleUpon is a browser "discovery engine" that allows its users to locate and rate webpages and other resources available on the web. Not only can you go to the page to surf, you can "add-on" this program to your tool bar on most browsers. An add-on or plugin is simply another program that works with your browser to provide some specific functionality. (I will discuss add-ons and plug-ins below.) Since the plugin is written to work with a specific browser, you need to use the plugin that is appropriate for your browser and version of the browser.

The StumbleUpon program recommends webpages and allows you to rate those webpages. What is interesting about this product is *how* it recommends webpages. It uses your past ratings as well as ratings of other individuals with similar interests to make recommendations about pages. StumbleUpon claims to have over 25 million members, so you get lots of help from others to find new and wonderful websites.

If you just want to browse StumbleUpon, you can direct your browser to http://www.stumbleupon.com. You are faced with a very simple screen that asks you to login (in the top, right corner of the screen, and circled), shown in Figure 4.22. Although it invites you to use the page, in reality, it will not show you much until you log in. Of course, since the purpose of StumbleUpon is to learn what kinds of pages are of interest to you and share only interesting ones, it makes sense that it asks you to sign in. Once you have gone through this process, you see a screen such as the one shown in Figure 4.22.

Figure 4.22: The StumbleUpon Home Page

Figure 4.23: The result of a "Stumble"

The StumbleUpon menu is across the top. In the middle of the page is the main navigation area. In the circled region is a button, labeled "Stumble." If you select that button, the system will take you to another recommended page, which may or may not be similar, depending on how often you have used the system. To either side of the "Stumble" button are buttons to vote "thumbs down" (to the left) or "thumbs up" (to the right). If you vote negatively, the system will show you fewer pages such as the one shown, while voting positively will cause you to see more pages that you like. This voting allows you to influence your recommendations. You do not get any feedback, the vote simply is tallied and used as it recommends later pages.

Seeing the page is nice, but frequently, we want to save the page so we can show it to someone else, or to visit again. StumbleUpon takes care of those needs too. First, suppose you would like to share the page you found. Start by using the "word balloon" button, labeled "A." If you click on item A, you can view the comments that other viewers have left, and include your own comment. The "f" icon, labeled "B," is a pathway to a product called Facebook (we will discuss it in Chapter 6). Clicking on that image allows you to share the page and your comments on the page on your Facebook newsfeed. If you would like to share the comment, but you do not use Facebook (or that is not where you would like to share it), you can click on the image with the arrow, labeled "C." Using this function, the system allows you to email the page to one or more people by including their email addresses, or, as shown at the bottom, post it to LinkedIn, Twitter or Facebook (or all three of them); we will discuss those tools later in Chapter 6.

If you would just like to save the page, StumbleUpon helps you with that functionality too. You can do that two ways. The first is to give the page a "thumbs up," and check the pages you have liked (I will show how to do this below). The second is to click the "+" icon at the left of the page, and labeled "D" which allows you to create a list and save the page in it (and access it any time you are on StumbleUpon).

To access those pages, you want to look at your dashboard. To do this, click the downward arrow labeled "E," and you will see a menu box such as the one shown in Figure 4.24. We will come back to that menu, but first, click on the link at the bottom (and circled) labeled "Edit Interests." This will take you to Figure 4.25. This dashboard allows you to see how many pages you have viewed, how many you liked, and how many lists you have created. From this page, you can see the pages you liked, the lists you made. You can from there, view the pages, or share the pages, or continue "stumbling" from that point. Notice also on the chart on the far right of the dashboard called "StumbleDNA." This is a graphical representation of the categories of pages that you have "liked" during your "stumbling." My largest category (at 37%) was about computers. You can click on the other categories and find your preferences too. The categories are selected from fourteen standard categories, including health, commerce, hobbies, sports, and sci/tech. Your choices might surprise you!

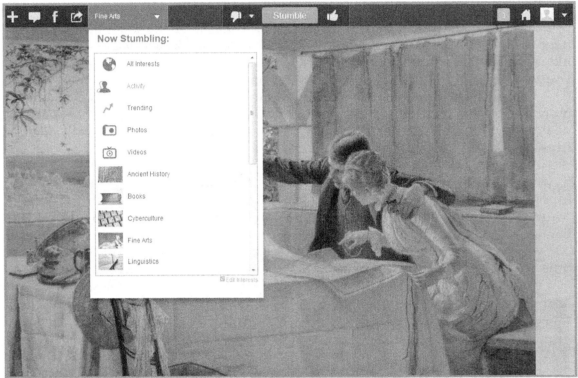

Figure 4.24: Changing the "Stumble"

Let us return to Figure 4.24 and the drop down menu. At the top of the page, to the left of the downward arrow, it says "Fine Arts." That means I am *currently* surfing among pages that have been identified as fine arts. You can tell that because of the art works that are showing up on the pages. Once I have pressed the down arrow, I can select another category, such as ancient history or books; these categories appear because of the pages that I liked (to which I gave a "thumbs up") in those categories. You can select "all categories," which allows StumbleUpon to select any random category. Or you can select particular categories as I did. There are some other options. First, you have the option of seeing only photos, or only videos by selecting those options. The photos (or videos) might come from any category, but you will only get pages in that format. An alternative is to look at the pages that are "trending." Trending pages are ones that a large number of people are liking; they can be in potentially any area. If more people "like" the page, share the page and talk about the page, it is said to be "trending." Some people just like to know what most other people are doing.

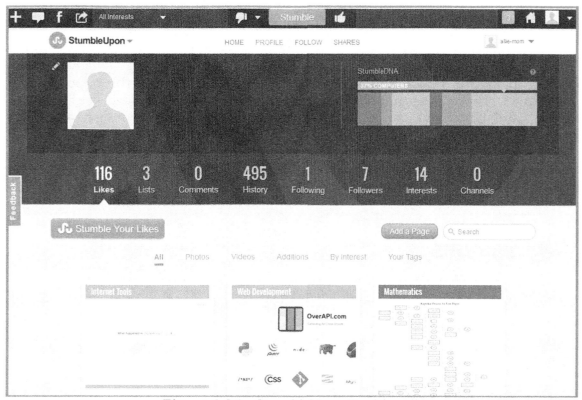

Figure 4.25: StumbleUpon Dashboard

The last three menu items in Figure 4.23, labeled F, G, and H (on the top right of the screen) are maintenance items for your StumbleUpon session. Clicking on Item F shows you messages that you have received. Item G takes you to your "home" site; on this site there will be several pages that are recommended to you. You can click on one and begin surfing, rate them, or, of course, share them. Finally Item H takes you to your settings for StumbleUpon, including your settings, profile, and the ability to logout.

I have described StumbleUpon as a webpage, but, there is another way to use the product, and that is as an "add-on." An add-on is simply a program that works with your browser to make a function easier to use. So, using StumbleUpon with the browser simply makes it easier to use. To find the add-on, you look to http://www.stumbleupon.com/downloads. It will direct you to the correct version depending on what browser you are using. Follow the instructions on the screen and you will have Firefox starting StumbleUpon as with any other button on your menu.

Some browsers, such as Firefox, have many products that are "add-ons" to the browser. If you select http://www.mozilla.org/add-ons, you get the screen shown in Figure 4.26. Notice, StumbleUpon is only one of the opportunities available. These programs give you more control over what you see, how you see it, and what you can do with the information. You can get alerts for activities, link your location to your surfing, link to your email, and add stock market quotes. Using the appearance link, you can change the colors and patterns in your browser, how your tabs appear on the screen, and how your bookmarks are kept. You can link your mail, and social networking sites to

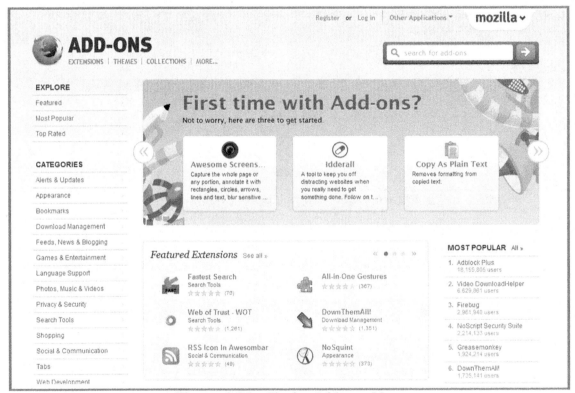

Figure 4.26: Firefox Add-ons Menu

your browser, change the language of the commands or get language translations of the pages, change how you download images and videos, find coupons, and shop. Finally, you can change how you browse, such as using search programs that do not track your activity. As long as you get the add-on from the page supported by your browser, then you know that it is safe and it will work with your browser. However, when you select an alternative browser, such as Chrome, Internet Explorer, or Safari, you will need to search their add-ons to find the functionality to work with that browser. Not all add-ons are available with all browsers, and sometimes even if the add-in is available for the browser, it may not work the same way or have all the same functionality as it does for another browser.

If you are looking for StumbleUpon, you can go to the searchbox at the top, right side of the screen, type in "StumbleUpon," and press the green arrow. You will then see a screen similar to that in Figure 4.27. You will note that StumbleUpon is the first one in the list. To the right of the description is a green button labeled "Add to Firefox." If you select that button, you will next see a warning message (as shown in Figure 4.28) that reminds you that it is only safe to download programs when you are sure they are legitimate. As said previously, as long as it comes from your browser's site, it is fine to download the program. Then press "Install Now" and StumbleUpon is added to your browser. When it is finished, you will see a new section has been added to your task bar as shown in Figure 4.29 (and circled). Of course, the first time you use it, it will ask for your account and password. You can let the browser store the account and password by not clicking the option for forgetting them when the browser is closed, or, if you do nothing, you can let the browser remember them. **The rule of thumb is that if you use a public computer, such as at a library, then make sure all of your passwords are forgotten at the end of your session.** However, if it is your own computer, it is probably ok allow StumbleUpon remember your password. After your password is entered, you can now "stumble" around the Internet and rate your pages just as you did with the internet version. If you click "Stumble" you get a page that might be of interest. You can rate it by using the "thumbs up" or "thumbs down" on the task bar. The program defaults to "all" for topics, but you can change those by pressing the down arrow and selecting some specific category of interest. If you do not currently follow the topic of interest, you can add that topic by selecting "update topics" from that drop down menu.

Figure 4.27: Results of the Search

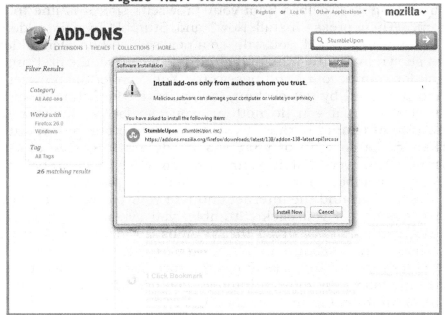

Figure 4.28: Warning about Downloads

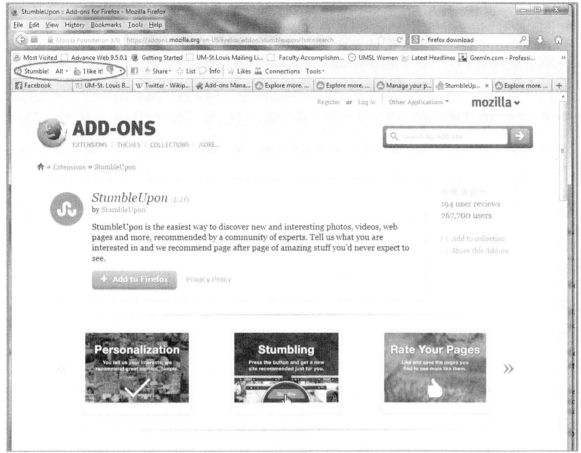

Figure 4.29: Using the Task Bar version of StumbleUpon

iTunes

In the 1960s and before, people carried transistor radios if they wanted music "on the go." I remember having a bright colored, boxy looking one with a wrist strap, that received only AM radio stations and sometimes had trouble with that. You got whatever was available at the time you wanted to listen. Quality was not very high.

Today, music "on the go" is, of course, more modern. Apple has sold hundreds of millions of iPods.[5] An iPod is a device that stores and plays digitally recorded music and videos. An iPod user can carry up to 20,000 songs (that is about hours of music!) on this device that is about 20% as large as an old transistor radio. Owners can listen to what they want when they want and where they want. When it has run down, the owner simply plugs the iPod into its charger (instead of replacing batteries). In addition to music, iPod users can watch movies or television shows or independently created shows on their iPod; these are called "Podcasts." These are similar to DVD's that you might rent at your local video store except that they come from the computer to the small device you can carry with you.

The music might have been bought as a CD and transferred to the iPod using the computer.[6] Or, the song might have been purchased individually, similar to the old 45's, and put on the device. The computer software that allows the user to move music to the iPod device, as well as to download and organize the music is called iTunes.

The program, iTunes, is a free download from Apple Inc., available at http://www.itunes.com. Unlike the other web applications we have discussed, iTunes is actually installed on your computer.

Even if you do not own an iPod (or other music device), you may want to use iTunes to allow you to organize music on your computer, listen to the music while you are using the computer and even create your own CDs that you can listen to elsewhere. After discussing how to acquire iTunes, we will discuss how to use its functionality.

To begin to use iTunes, you must download the software. You begin at the website, http://www.apple.com, from which I chose "iPod", as shown in Figure 4.30.

---

[5] The same music can be played on iPads and iPhones.
[6] In fact, there are even devices that can play those wonderful vinyl LP's and transfer the music to the computer.

Figure 4.30: The iPod Home Page

The main message that you get from this page is to purchase something, either an iPod, iTunes Radio, or some related tool. However, at the top of the page is button for downloading iTunes (marked by the arrow). If you press the button, it takes you to Figure 4.31.

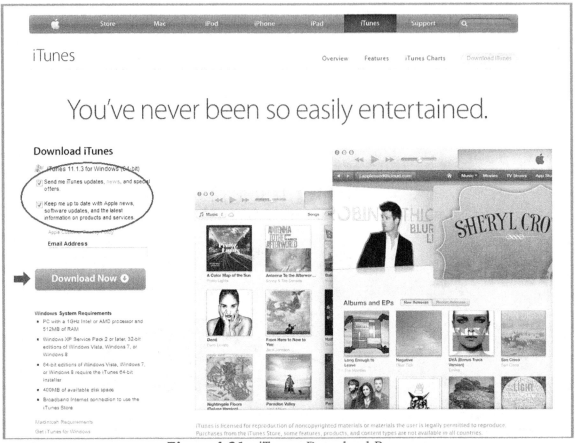

Figure 4.31: iTunes Download Page

The first questions with which you are faced are the options of how you would like to interact with iTunes, shown in the circled region. You can opt to receive iTunes news and special offers (the first checkbox) and/or Apple news (the second checkbox). If you wish to receive this information, you should leave them checked (the default), and provide your email address. If you do not wish to receive information from them, you must move your mouse to the boxes, and click them to uncheck the option. Then press the "download now" button, you will receive a popup message shown to the left. Select "save file"

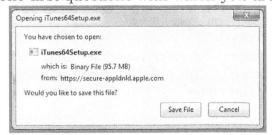

and then once you receive the message that it is downloaded, you will want to run the file by pressing "run" on the security warning as shown to the right.

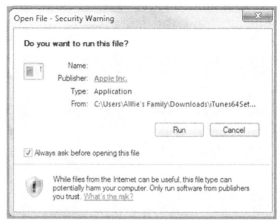

Once you have downloaded and installed iTunes, you can launch the program. You are faced with a screen such as the one in Figure 4.32. Notice that the page looks like it is a webpage even though it is running on your own computer. From this page, you can purchase music online that can be heard on your computer. That process is much like what we have seen before, so I will not go through it again.

Figure 4.32: iTunes Base Page

You can go from this general page to pages that offer music, movies, TV shows, podcasts and the store using the menu across the top. These give you the option to purchase from each of these media and download the title to your computer. Of course to accomplish this, you must first create an account. If you click "Account" on the menu (this is circled under "Quick Links"), the system will take you through various pages where you create a user id, provide information about yourself, share your credit card information and read the user agreement. Do not worry about the fact they ask for credit card information right away; the card is not charged until you purchase music.

Suppose you want to purchase music. Click on "Music" on the menu. You can click on the downward arrow next to music, or on the button labeled "all categories" under the term Music to see the various genres of music; you can select your preference by clicking the appropriate tab.

If you know what piece of music you want (or even what musician or group of musicians) and you simply need to search to see if it is available. In this case, you select type the name of the music or group in the search box at the top right and click on the magnifying glass. You may specify the artist, the composer, the title of the music, the album and/or the genre and press "search." In this figure, only "Water Music" was specified before the search button was clicked. You can see multiple versions of Handel's *Water Music* (my intention), but there are also other pieces by other composers and artists. To hear the piece and/or purchase the piece of music, you proceed as you did in the previous example.

Figure 4.33: iTunes Library Page

You can also go to your own items by selecting "Library," circled in Figure 4.33.

To play your music, click on a song and press the play button circled in the figure above. iTunes will continue to play songs listed after the one you selected until it runs out of music in your library. Alternatively, you can ask iTunes to "shuffle" the music so you do not hear it in the same order each time. Once it is shuffled, iTunes picks an apparently random song order for you.

Most people do not want to use their entire library when listening for music because they have multiple genres of music. For example, I do not want to listen to one movement of Handel's *Water Music* and then an early Beatle's song, followed by current music. So, iTunes provides playlists that allows you to group music together for listening and/or copying. To create a playlist, simply click on the file menu option and then "new playlist." This will create a new playlist on your left menu.

To copy a song from the library to the new playlist, open the library and highlight a song or list of songs. While highlighted, place your mouse over the songs and move it (drag it) to the new playlist, and then let go of the mouse.

Continue to move songs to the new playlist until all that you want is included there. To use the playlist, simply double click on it to open it. Click on a song to begin playing as discussed earlier. Or, you can burn (or make) a CD with all the music in the playlist. To burn the CD, click on File on the menu and move the mouse to "Burn Playlist to CD.". Then follow the instructions and you will have a CD with your own personal mix!

You have other options too. First, you might own some CD's you want to copy to your iTunes library. To accomplish this, load your audio CD into your CD/DVD player on your computer. In a moment, you should see an Audio CD icon on your menu (at the left) under "DEVICES." It should automatically begin to import the songs on that CD into your iTunes Library. iTunes will automatically retrieve as much information as is available about the music, including the title, time, artist, album and genre. If that information is not stored on the CD, iTunes will leave the position blank.

It is important for you to know that music purchased from iTunes can only be played on "authorized computers," and you may only have five computers authorized at any given time. In that way, Apple allows you to listen to the music on a variety of computers (at work, at home, on the laptop, etc.), while still protecting the artist's copyright and revenues. However, if you have created a CD as discussed above, you may take your music with you anywhere.

Photos
An important reason why people use the Internet is to share. For many of us, one of the most important thing to share is photos – of friends, of vacations and of children and grandchildren. Of course, you could create a webpage and share photos that way. However, that allows *anyone* to view the photos, and that may not be desirable, especially if the photos are of children or grandchildren.   Furthermore, even in this day of cameras and the internet, many of us want an actual photo that we can put in an album or in a frame, or carry with us. It turns out that the Internet provides multiple options for accomplishing these tasks.

Figure 4.34: SnapFish Home Page

Two popular websites for printing and sharing photographs are Snapfish.com and Walgreens.com. Snapfish, shown in Figure 4.34, is an entirely online service. After printing the photos, Snapfish will mail them to you (or to someone else). Others (to whom you give access) can also view and order photos. Walgreens also gives the opportunity to share the photos and to have prints mailed to you. In addition, Walgreens provides the additional opportunity of allowing you to pick up the prints in as little as an hour after uploading them to the site.

Since the two sites (and most other photography sites) work similarly, and since Walgreens photofinishing is more commonly used, we will walk through that one. Both, of course, require you to create an account first. Follow the online instructions to do so, and login. The following discussion requires that you have uploaded your photos to your computer.

You begin to use the Walgreens photo service on the main Walgreens page. Create an account and login to the site, and select "Photo," which will be the orange tab towards the left of the screen. You will then see the main Photo page, as shown in Figure 4.35.

You have many options available to you on this page. The page is created in a series of blocks. The top block allows you to select the kind of product you would like to order, from prints to books to wall décor and more! The middle section allows you to access photos you have already uploaded. Notice you can easily select the three most frequently created albums by clicking on them; if you want an album you created earlier, you must select "All Your Photos" directly under the "Order Prints" button. Below the section are links to administrative information, and to the right you get information about specials.

Generally the first thing you do is to upload your photos from your home computer. You do this by clicking the "upload photos" menu option circled in the middle of the window. This will bring you to a screen such as that shown in Figure 4.35, where you give your album a title, date and description. You can give any title (including the date) and no description if you would like.

Once the album is identified, the next step is to upload the photos. Click on the button identified with an arrow in Figure 4.36 and it will bring up a listing of files on your computer.   Using your mouse, you point the window to the directory that holds your photographs. Click (using the mouse) next to the photos you want to upload and the system will copy the photos from your computer to Walgreens processing lab. Depending on your internet connection, and the number of photos you have, this process can take some time. Fortunately, you will get information about how far your process has progressed, both in total and on individual photos.

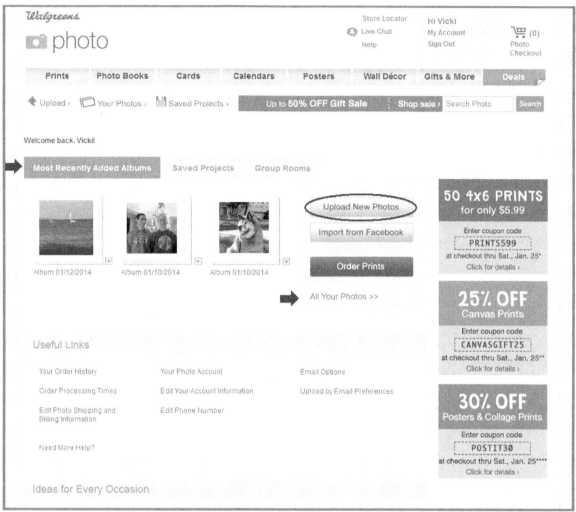

Figure 4.35: Walgreens Photo Page

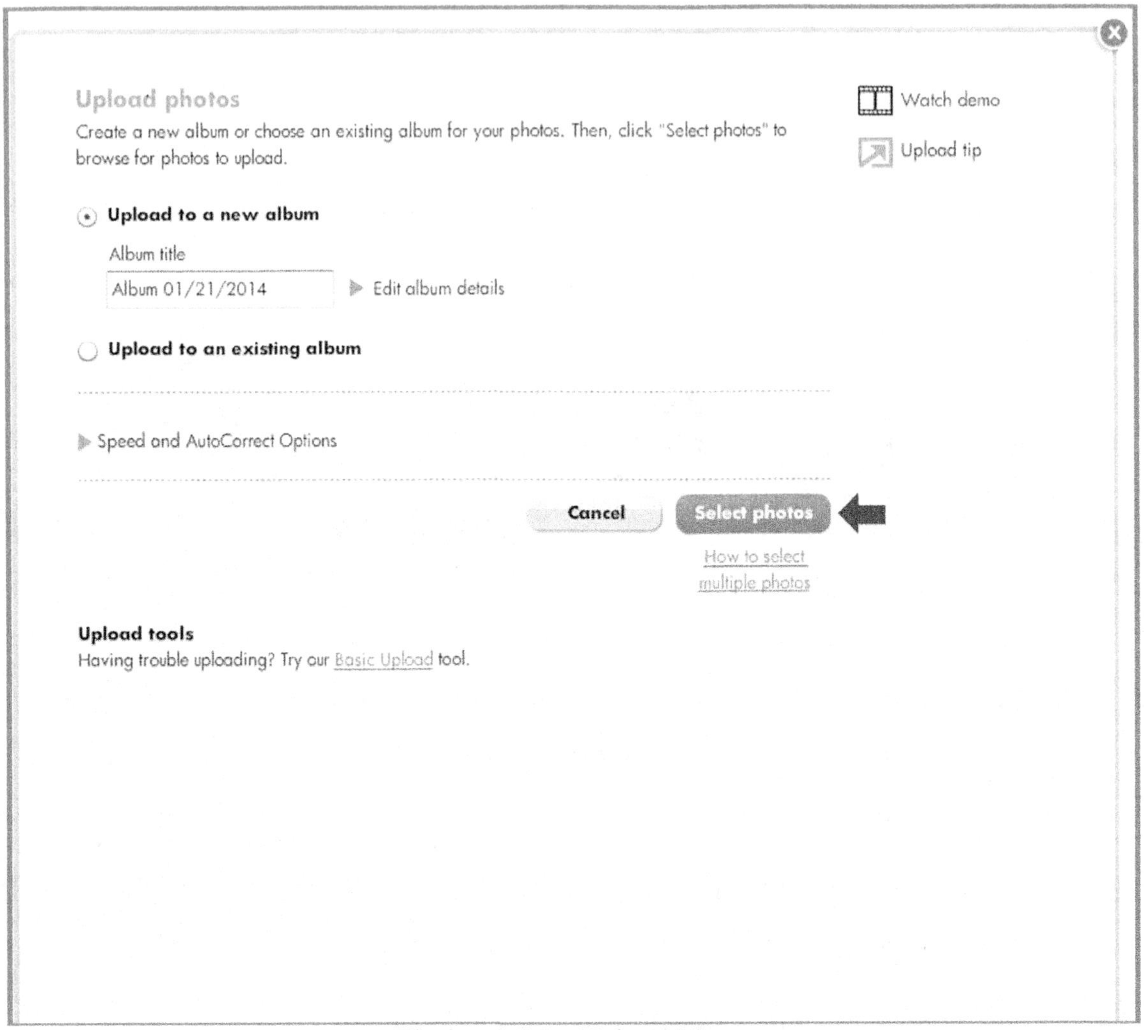

Figure 4.36: Upload Menu

Once the photos have uploaded into an album, you have choices. You can either upload more photos to your album, order the prints, or share the photos with other individuals. These options will be available as long as the photos are in the album on the site. Different photo finishing services provide varying amounts of time or conditions they will hold the photos for free. Some services store the photos for three months for free, but indefinitely if you pay a fee.

Walgreens will store the photos indefinitely as long as you purchase something once per year. Some services will limit the number of photos you can store at their site, while others provide no size limits. These are issues you should consider when selecting your photo finishing site. If you have elected to view your photos, you will see a page similar to the one in Figure 4.37.

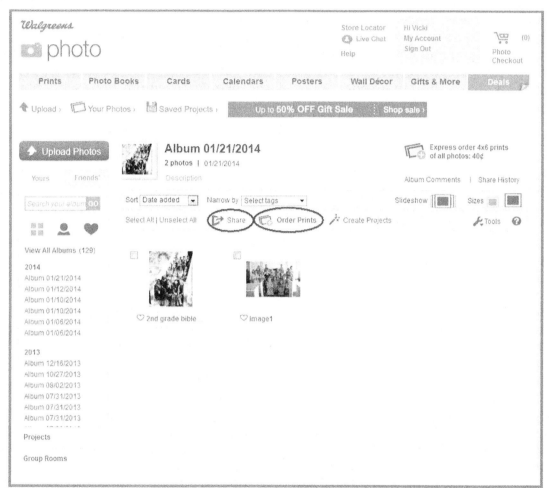

Figure 4.37: Focus on the Album

Suppose you want to share your album with friends and family. You want others to be able to see your photos and purchase prints if they are so inclined. For example, suppose you attended the birthday party of a grandchild and took photos. You might want to show those photos to other children, your siblings or friends. With the photo service, you can send them the link and they can view the photos and order prints of some (or all) of the photos if they wish. More important, people to whom you do not give permission can NOT see the photos. Hence you do not need to worry about strangers with questionable motives viewing your grandchildren's photos. To do this, start by clicking on the item "Share" circled in Figure 4.36. You will be given a screen on which you can type in the email addresses of all the people with whom you want to share the photos and even a short message so they know why they are receiving the photos. Most services will even provide you an electronic address book in which to share the email addresses of the people to whom you send photos frequently.

However, you might want prints of some or all of the photos you took. In that case, you select which photos you want to order, and select the option "Order prints" circled in Figure 4.36. The drop down box will let you order all the prints using 4x6 size, or allow you to select different sizes. That results in Figure 4.37.

There are two ways to indicate the size of photos you want. Towards the top of the page is a box labeled "Entire Order" (and noted with an arrow. Selecting that option allows you automatically to order the same number of the same size of all of the photos in your order. Notice, I have selected "1" next to the 4x6. If you look at the individual prints, they all have 1 4x6 selected. You can also vary the number and sizes of the photos you select next to the photograph. Look at the order for the first photograph. In addition to the 1 4x6 that was selected, I was able to put a "1" next to the 5x7 just for that photo (see arrow). In this way, you can get any combination you desire.

You also have some ability to impact how the photo is processed. Notice below each photo there is a "Crop/Rotate" option. This allows you to see how the photo will really look when it is printed. If you select Crop/Rotate, you get a screen with the photo shown in the sizes that you have selected as shown in Figure 38. Sometimes you will get very different perspectives on the photo depending on what size you select. Cropping and rotating allows you some control over it. For example, if you double click on the 4x6 image in Figure 4.38, you will see Figure 4.40.

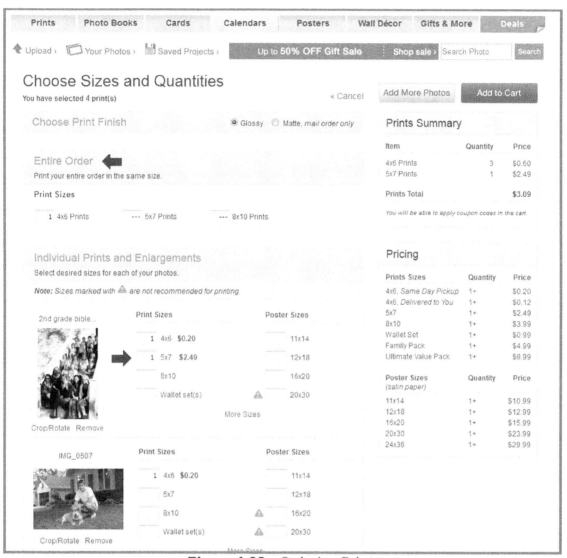

Figure 4.38: Ordering Prints

Figure 4.39: Selecting the Size to Crop

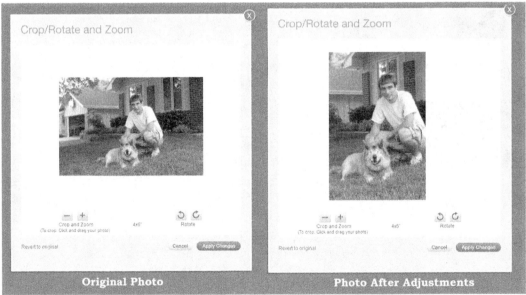

Figure 4.40: Cropping and Rotating Image

The window on the left is how the photo appeared immediately after double clicking on the image. It is, in fact, the original photo taken. But, you can use the Zoom (+) option and the Rotate option to focus on the subjects in the photo. The image on the right is how the photo looked after using the Zoom and Rotate options.

Different photo processing services vary in how they proceed at this point. Some services will give you the option of mailing the photos or picking them up at the store (if there is a physical store). Some will require a credit card for payment. If there are multiple stores, the service usually gives you the option of selecting a location at which to retrieve the photos. Walgreens allows you to select any Walgreens store (so you can send the photos to someone else and they can pick them up) and gives you the option of paying online or at the store.

Wikipedia

The last website that I will describe is Wikipedia. Generically, wiki's are applications that facilitate online collaboration. Using a wiki application, many people can add, modify or delete content on the Web. The name comes from a Hawaiian word meaning "quick." So, it is a quick and easy to use platform on which people can build a document together. Since it is on the Web, people do not need to be near one another or even know one another to share the technology. There are many wiki's on the web, and many uses of wikis.

The best known wiki, however, is Wikipedia (http://www.wikipedia.org). It is a collaboratively built encyclopedia available in almost 300 languages, available to all for free. Literally anyone can create and edit entries on the site, but everything is subject to evaluation by one or more Wikipedia editors for style, grammar and accuracy control. Pages that have controversial information are "protected" to prevent vandalism.

I know at this point you are probably shaking your head and asking why anyone would care about such a site. The reason is, *because it works*. The content in most Wikipedia articles is footnoted to provide its source. Editors watch changes to all pages, especially those likely to attract vandalism and/or inappropriate editing. The result is a document that provides stable, informative articles about a variety of topics. A study in *Nature* found the accuracy of Wikipedia entries on science pages was close to that of the *Encyclopedia Britannica*! It seems unbelievable, but it works.

Around the globe you are given the most commonly chosen languages in which to read Wikipedia, and the number of articles in each. Since Wikipedia was first a product in the United States, the most pages are in English, with articles of over four million topics! There are also over a million articles in Dutch, French, German, Italian, Polish, Russian, Spanish, and Swedish. As you scroll down the page, you see the range of languages and the number of pages in that language. This is pretty impressive, especially since volunteers write most of these pages!

Wikipedia is owned by a not-for-profit organization called Wikimedia. They use the same wiki technology and procedures to create a number of products, as shown below in Figure 4.41. You can find dictionaries, quotes, data, and more using Wikimedia products.

Figure 4.41: Wikimedia Products

As you can see from Figure 4.42, the Wikipedia home page is not difficult to use. Simply type in a word or phrase about which you want information, select the language of the encyclopedia you wish you use, and press the arrow key to begin the search. So, for example, you wanted to learn more about the city of Chicago, type in "Chicago," leave the default language of English and press the arrow key. The result of this search is shown in Figure 4.43.

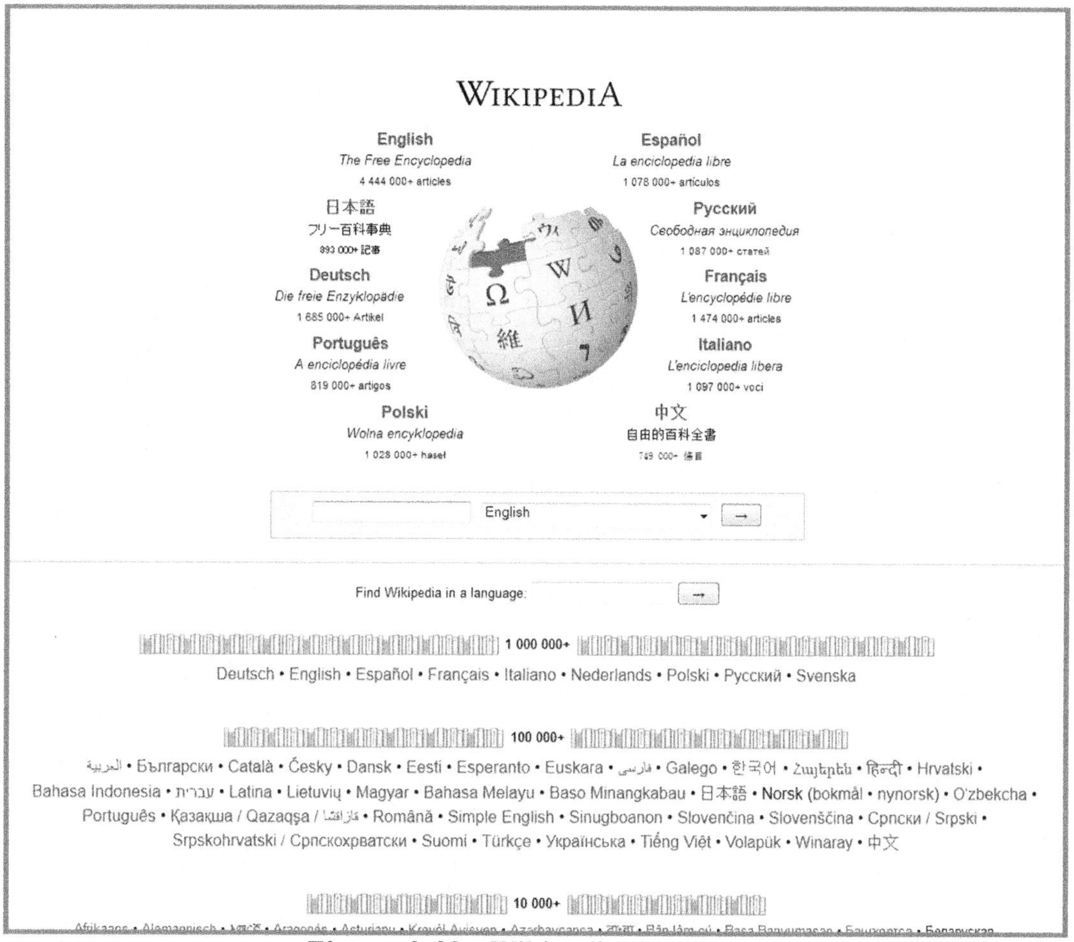

Figure 4.42: Wikipedia Home Page

The entry about Chicago has a great deal of information, including photographs. The contents include history, geography, cityscape, culture, economy, demographics, law and government, education, transportation, infrastructure, sister cities, and links to more about Chicago. At the end of this entry, as with all of the entries, there are references, a bibliography and links to items found on the internet. You can even learn that the name Chicago is a

Potawatomi word meaning wild onions!

Figure 4.43: The "Chicago" entry in Wikipedia

Suppose after reading about Chicago, you decide you want to visit the city. You could then use Wikimedia's Wikivoyage tool as your travel guide. If you click on the "Wikivoyage" icon in Figure 4.41, you come to a page shown in Figure 4.44. If you type in "Chicago" and click on the magnifying glass icon, you will see Figure 4.45, which tells you a lot about vacationing in Chicago. It outlines the areas of the city (and where you should and should not visit), the architecture for which Chicago is known, museums, navigation (including a map of the Chicago "L"), recommended areas to visit, Chicago's ethnic neighborhoods and festivals, and even recommended Chicago food, such as Chicago-style pizza (including recommended restaurants), the Chicago hot dog, and Chicago's Italian beef! It may not replace your Frommer's guide, but it certainly can tell you a lot about the place!

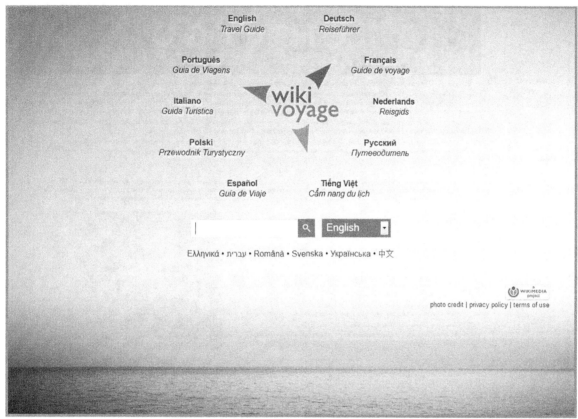

Figure 4.44: Wikivoyage Home Page

Figure 4.45: Chicago Page in Wikvoyage

eMail

A letter is a written message from one person to another. According to the online collection of the Bath Postal Museum (http://www.bathpostalmuseum.org/), the earliest letters were written on clay (about 2000 BC) and, later, on papyrus (in 1200 BC) in Ancient Egypt. The letters were transported through a sophisticated relay system in the Persian Empire (about 6 BC) which was later duplicated by Roman Emperors, for whom communication was critical. Later in Medieval times, Kings set up postal routes during wartime, or when they were traveling so they could continue to consult with their courts and ministers. By the 1800s, the broader population wrote some letters, but letter-writing truly became popular in the mid-1800s. In fact, the popularity of writing letters forced reductions in postage cost to make it more economical to keep in contact. It was at this time that the practice of sending valentines of embossed paper and lace became popular because the postage cost was reasonable. Throughout history letters have brought news of distant friends and relatives, messages of love, business records or bills, and even historical accounts of important lives to our doorstep.

The role of letters in communication has changed significantly since the 19th century. Historically, letters were the only reliable means of communication between two persons in different locations. As communication technology has diversified, letters have become less important as routine communication. Even when I was a child, the practice of writing letters was declining. Although families might be separated by large distances, telephone calls could be used to share special news, and the advent of the interstate highway system made traveling to see distant family more practical. Of course, we did still write letters to friends and family, and we had pen pals to learn of distant lands.

So, should we assume that this practice is lost and that future generations will never learn the practice of letter writing, and enjoy the benefits of keeping in touch with those far away? Of course not! People still want to hear news from their family and friends, and businesses will still want to send bills and advertise their products. All that is different is *how* we are doing it. Instead of the traditional approach to writing letters, we are moving to new media; one of these media is called email.

"eMail," short for electronic mail, is the most used tool on the Internet today. It can provide a wonderful connection to friends, family and long-lost acquaintances. The term email contrasts to the traditional approach that is now often referred to as "snail mail," reflecting the slowness with which paper-based mail travels. It reflects the lag-time between dispatch of a letter and its receipt, versus the virtually instantaneous dispatch and delivery of email.

eMail is not replacing all snail mail completely. Many traditional purposes for letters are still used, and probably for a long time will be used in society. For example, snail mail continues to be the mode of choice when the sender is not sure if the recipient has the technology to receive a message by other means. No telephone or computer is needed to read a letter. Similarly, local advertising which blankets a particular neighborhood or region is still done using snail mail because it is easier to find home or office addresses than the associated email addresses. Finally, important messages that need to be retained, such as receipts or legal documents, are still sent via snail mail because they can be kept more easily and securely.

But, for our typical communication, email has become a popular medium. Among the youth, it may be the only way to get a "letter!" It is quick, clean and convenient. Unfortunately, if not handled correctly, it can also overtake your life and/or give thieves access to your valuables. This chapter will talk about why you want to use email, and how it can be an asset. It will also talk about how to protect yourself from unwanted consequences and, of course, how to use email safely.

What about History?
Letters have been an important form of communication for centuries, especially in America. The country was founded by immigrants who left loved ones in the old country. Communicating about their new lives, and learning about their families' lives, required letters. As we expanded West, again people left their families for new land, and wrote home about their experiences. Some of these letters were saved. According to Lisa Grunewald and Stephen J. Adler in *Letters of the Century: America 1900-1999.*

> "Throughout the last hundred years . . . observers have lamented the fact that people don't write letters anymore. Yet letters have described most of the century's major events, have reflected or reflected upon most of its

social and cultural trends, have captured most of its political passions, and have been written by most of its principle figures. We may think we've heard the whole story, but that story resonates more deeply when we read the century's letters. Part of the reason for that resonance is the immediacy of letters. Letters are what history sounds like when it is still part of everyday life."

Archives of correspondence, whether for personal, diplomatic, or business reasons, serve as primary sources for historians. No one I knew as a child was involved in such weighty concerns that their letters would be saved by an historical museum. Yet, as I read through letters I collect from my ancestors, I do get insights into their worlds and dreams that I might not otherwise see.

Storing paper mail uses more physical space than storing email. However, paper is a very reliable storage medium. Documents printed on most common paper and left undisturbed for one hundred years will be easily readable. In contrast, items stored electronically and left for one hundred years may no longer be recorded. Further, and more disturbing, is that the way we store items electronically changes drastically from year to year; it may be difficult, or even impossible to read that same document even a decade or two after it was recorded.

However, the storage – and long term access – question should not stop you from using email for communication. If you want to save the letters, then do it! I have a special file on my email account for emails from my son while he was away at college. While they do not have his handwriting, they certainly carry his personality, daily thoughts and spirit. Clearly they provide me insight that I would not otherwise have into what is important to him right now. The same emails will help him remember part of his college experience and, one day, give my grandchildren insights into their father's development. So, I have printed them out to keep as part of his scrapbook of college. While I have relied upon email to get the information, I realize that a paper record will provide the long term storage of the information.

A Beginning

In the mid-1980s a friend decided that I should start using email (after all, I was a computer person). My response, which is probably similar to thoughts you have had is "why? I get all the correspondence I need now, why should I add email?" My friend just walked away. The next morning he came to my office and said "I sent you email." My response was to ask about the content. He declined to expose the content and said if I wanted to know I should check my email. Of course, I checked it. He went through the same routine for about two weeks, each time ending

The first email sent between two machines was sent by Ray Tomlinson to himself in 1971. The machines sat next to each other, but were connected through ARPANET, a military-based predecessor to the INTERNET. Tomlinson said the message was entirely forgettable... Most likely the first message was QWERTYUIOP or something similar. The program he developed was called SNDMSG, which was included as part of a time-sharing system, TENEX that was released in 1972.

with me checking my email. By then it became a habit and I started checking it before he asked just so I would know whatever new fact he shared with me. Over the years my reliance on email has grown significantly and I can no longer imagine life without it.

I share this story to point out that we *all* had a point in our lives when we thought email was irrelevant. Further, we only moved past the dislike of using the technology *if* we had a purpose to use email. People also move past poor typing skills *if* they have a reason to use email. It doesn't matter what your reasons are for not using email, once you have a reason for using email, you will use it.

Why email?

Most people start emailing because they want to communicate in a business or school setting or to keep in contact with loved ones. I have already mentioned how I got started using email. I also surveyed individuals over the age of 50 and asked them why they got started using email. Most of the people I asked started using email because of some need at work or while they were in college/graduate school. The second largest reason was to keep in touch with friends and family, especially children who were away at college or had moved out of town. The interesting group was the third most common, "unknown." These individuals could not remember a compelling reason they started, but knew they relied upon it now.

The reasons to *keep* emailing are limitless though. I rely upon email a great deal for work. Much of the communication with co-authors or editors about my research, students about my classes, or colleagues about any number of things is done using email. I also use email to inquire about product changes or orders for my household purchases. I also rely upon email for my family. Neither my husband nor I live near our families, and we use email as one method of keeping contact with them. A quick email about recent events or a funny story can help make you feel close to family.

eMail is a great way to get information to a large number of people quickly. The surveys I do for this book are all done by emailing to a list of non-randomly chosen people who were willing to answer my questions. When my husband had heart surgery, I used email to contact most of our families and friends when the doctors finished. I could not possibly have called all those people in a timely fashion, yet they all knew what each stage of recovery brought right away. Or, when we are planning our elementary school reunion, we use email to share ideas, schedules and plans.

eMail is also a great way to make new friends and acquaintances. As I mentioned in the previous chapter, there are bulletin boards on which one can post questions on the Internet. In order to get answers, you must have an email address to which a responder can send the answer. I used such a bulletin board for some genealogy work a number of years ago, and it turned out that the person who responded was my second-double cousin whom I did not even know existed!

We will next discuss listservs and discussion groups that bring together people from around the world to talk about a particular topic. I belong to some discussion groups for work, and others for fun. I have joined genealogy groups for specific surnames, regions of the country and even one group for descendants of a couple who lived in the 1700s. The focus of these groups is specific, but you can learn much, get questions answered and even make friends!

Electronic Mailing Lists, Listervs, and Newsgroups

People with common interests like to talk to one another. So, needlepoint enthusiasts might meet at a needlepoint store to discuss new stitches, fibers or canvas artists. Racing enthusiasts congregate at races not only to compete but also to discuss their sport. People join reading clubs to discuss the latest book. Widows often congregate to discuss how they handle their grief.

People with common interests also talk online. So, a reason to get an email address might be to be able to discuss a topic of interest. The world is a large place, and there are bound to be other people with similar interests with whom you can share your passion. You may be surprised to learn the number of interested people, and the world of information they have to share.

This type of widespread discussion uses an electronic mailing list. Just as some people refer to tissue as Kleenex, or photocopies as Xeroxes, you might also hear electronic mailing lists called "listservs," because an early electronic mailing list server was "Listserv."

Whatever the discussion list is called, it works the same. Someone sends an email to the server. That email is, in turn, broadcast to all of the people registered on the list. People can respond to the email, but that response is sent back to the server and then again broadcast to all of the people on the list. The lists can be managed in different ways. Some are "announcement lists" on which only a limited number of people can send email that is broadcast to the entire group. Most, however are "discussion lists" on which anyone in the group can send email.

Some lists are "moderated." That means that there is a "list manager" who reads each email before it is broadcast to be sure it is appropriate for the group. These moderators check the email to ensure they are high quality and on topic. Most lists are "unmoderated," however. This means that anyone who is a member of the mailing list can send messages to the group directly. In some cases, an individual can join the list only after being approved, while other lists allow anyone to join.

There are discussion groups on almost any topic you want. You can search for "listservs" (those that use the original technology) at http://lsoft.com/lists/listref.html.

Yahoo! Groups

Business & Finance
Computers & Internet
Cultures & Community
Entertainment & Arts
Family & Home
Games
Government & Politics
Health & Wellness
Hobbies & Crafts
Music
Recreation & Sports
Regional
Religion & Beliefs
Romance & Relationships
Schools & Education
Science

Yahoo! Groups is a popular source for electronic mail lists. If you already know what kind of group might interest you, just search for a discussion group by that name. Otherwise, Yahoo! lets you browse groups in 16 major categories. If you click on one of the general categories, such as "Hobbies and Crafts," Yahoo! provides specific categories within "Hobbies and Crafts," such as "Collecting," "Crafts," "Hobbies," "Models," and "Other." You can then click on one of those, such as "Crafts," to find groups for specific crafts, such as basketry, candle-

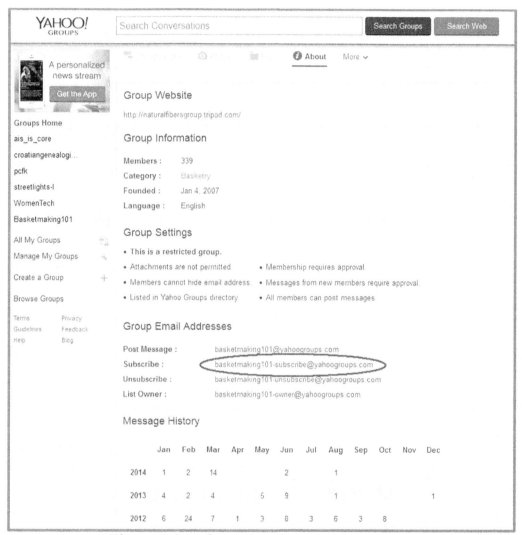

Figure 5.1: Information about a Yahoo! Group

making, crocheting, egg art, quilting, or woodworking. Clicking on one of those categories allows you to find the specific group that would interest you.

Suppose I followed the path described in the previous paragraph and found a group of interest in "Basketry," called "Basketmaking." When you click on "Basketmaking," you see a group information page like that in Figure 5.1. It shares information about the number of subscribers, the language of the group, the rules of the group and a history of how many emails have been sent in recent months. This group has few messages each month, but some have hundreds sent each month. If you decide the group is one that you wish to

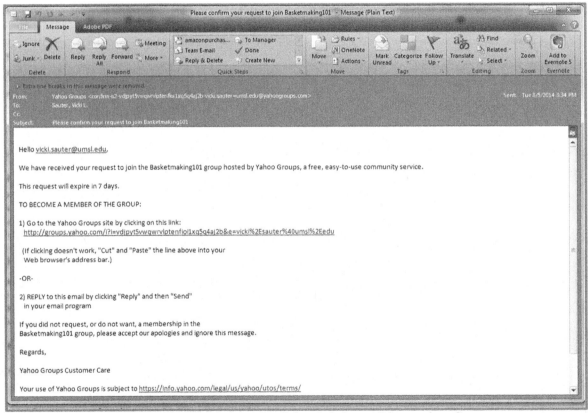

Figure 5.2: Confirmation eMail for Joining a Discussion Group

join, look for the link next to "Subscribe," circled in Figure 5.1. If you click the link, it will cause an email message to appear; send it. Most groups will then send you a confirmation such as the one in Figure 5.2. You must respond to that confirmation in order to be added to the list.

Google also has discussion groups. As with Yahoo!, you can search for a group with a particular key word, or follow clicking through categories to find a list of interest. In addition to sorting by topic, Google allows you to search for a group by region, by language, by volume of email, or by number of members.

These are just *some* of the discussions you can join. If you do not find what you want from these sources, try an internet search for "forum" and the topic of your interest. I will bet you can find something.

There is another kind of discussion group, however, called a "newsgroup." Newsgroups are posted to an electronic bulletin board rather than being sent to you via email. So, you must actually retrieve these messages; they are not sent in email. You can see a list of these groups at http://groups.google.com/groups?group=news.lists.misc.

Google Groups

Categories	Region
Arts and Entertainment	Africa
Business and Finance	Asia
Computers	Canada
Health	Caribbean
Home	Central America
News	Europe
People	Latin America
Recreation	Mediterranean
Schools and Universities	Middle East
Science and Technology	Oceania
Society	United States
Adult	
Other	

What is an email Address?

Once you have decided on an email provider, you must decide on an email address. Since the email address represents your online presence, a little thought about it is in order.

Consider a normal home address:

> 1234 Main Street
> Somewhere, MO 63155

This address has two parts. The second line identifies the town or city in which you live. Once you identify the city or town, you consider the second line which includes the specific location in that city or town. Knowing a street address without a city/town is useless because there may be many 1234 Main Streets in the world and the only way someone can know which you mean is to know the city/town first.

eMail addresses are similar in that they have two components, the "user name" and the "node." The user name is similar to the street address, representing the "who," and the node is similar to the city/town in the example above, representing the "where." The form of the email address is "user@node," which is read "user at node."

The node, which is everything after the @, represents the domain name (discussed in earlier chapters) from which and to which email is sent. If, for example, an email address is "email_user@yahoo.com," you can tell the person gets his or her email from the free service, Yahoo! On the other hand, someone using "email_user@whitehouse.gov" gets his/her email through the White House, and "email_user@monsanto.com" gets his/her email at the corporation, Monsanto. This node provides information about to what location to deliver the email. Once email has been delivered to a node, then the local server puts it in a specific mailbox on the node. The server identifies the appropriate mailbox through the user name, or all the information to the left of the @.

While the node or domain name (the material to the right of the @) is determined by the provider of the email, users generally have a great deal of flexibility in selecting the user name. Of course, that assumes that someone else does not already have that user name. So, what should you select? It depends on the reason for using the email. If you intend to use the email for something professional or serious, you probably want to select a professional or serious user name, such as a combination of your first and last name. In my case, for example, some possible "serious" user names might be "sauter" or "vicki.sauter" or vicki_sauter" or "vlsauter." On the other hand, I have one friend who first used email when she was to chair a national ballet competition for the National Society of Arts and Letters, and so chose a name that reflected the group for which she was volunteering, "dancediva4u."

If your intent is strictly personal, then something lighter or more playful might be used. One friend uses the nickname his sister gave him as children. Others have taken names that are spinoffs of television shows, such as "kingoswego" (from the television show King of Queens, except that he lives in Oswego), or the ever popular addition of "ster" to a name such as "walshster." I have been known to use my dog's name, Allie, such as "allie_mom" as a user name. Have fun, select something unique so that your friends and family will recognize it easily. However, as with naming children, be careful you do not inadvertently select something that could be seen as controversial or inappropriate. Controversial user names can cause people who might not know you well to ignore you, and even cause the filters at the email providers. Hence, I recommend you look at your user name carefully to be sure you didn't put together something that another person will read differently. "Lovemebaby" might simply reflect your affection for your grandchild, but someone else might read it as suggestive.

OK, How Do I Get an eMail Account?

Let us suppose you are now convinced that you want to try email. What do you do now? Get an email account! There are many places from which you can get email accounts, and most of them are free (although some of the free sites do show advertising). Some of the more frequently used free sites are Gmail (http://mail.google.com), Yahoo (http://mail.yahoo.com), and Microsoft (http://mail.live.com).

Suppose you decide to get your email address through Yahoo! First you direct your browser to http://www.yahoo.com, and select "Mail" (the top option on the left of the screen. That will take you to another screen that asks if you wish to signin to a known account or create a new account. Click on "Create New Account" and you will see a screen such as that in Figure 5.3. Complete the form and you will then have a new email account. Please read the next section first about selecting a name though.

What to Consider

As you consider various email providers there are a few things you need to consider. These include the following; they will generally be described on the email account's home page.

1. Spam Filtering – does the email provider try to eliminate unwanted junk email from your mailbox. This unwanted junk might just be cluttering up your mailbox, or it might be mail that is trying to fool you into sending money or

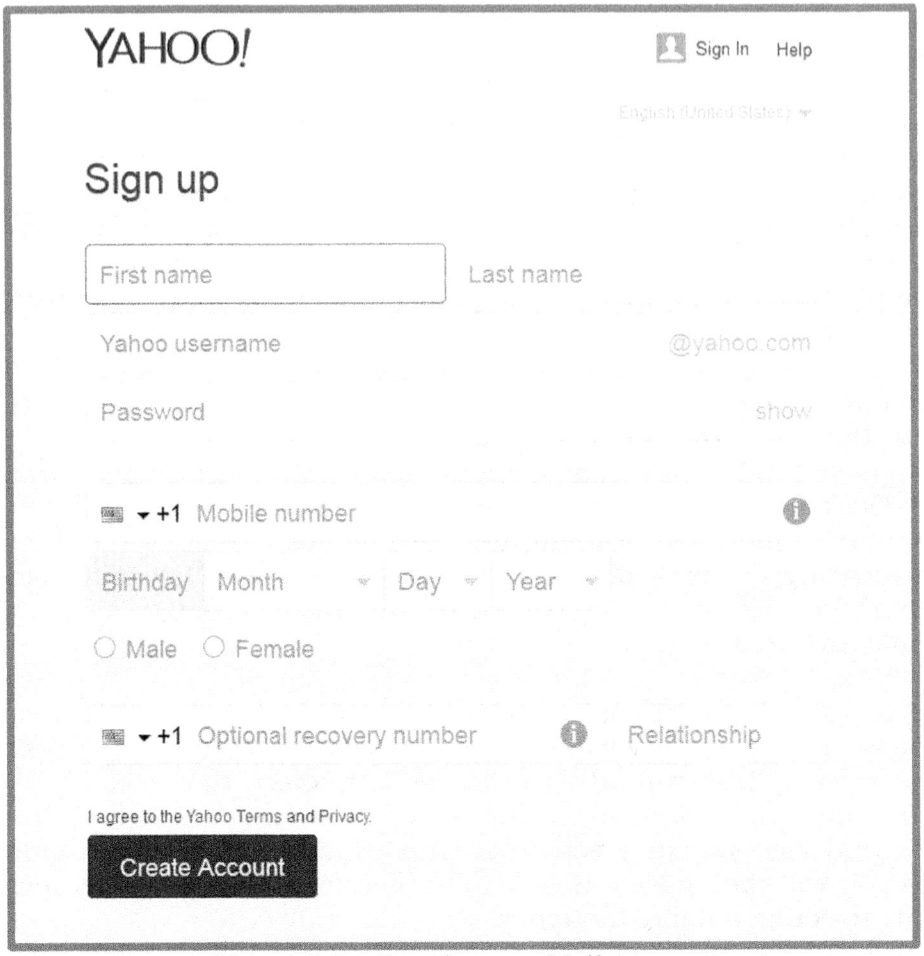

Figure 5.3: Creating an eMail Account

personal information to people trying to steal from you, or it might include messages that you find offensive.

2. Reliability - can you connect, and does the email work consistently? This includes not only connectivity, being able to even connect to your email provider, but deliverability as well. If your email provider is preventing you from receiving the email you requested, for example, due to over aggressive spam filtering, that could quickly also become unacceptable.

3. Support - if you have a problem, is there someone to help? Can you find a person to address the issue? Tied in with reliability, this means helping me with

connectivity issues that might come up, account recovery perhaps, and of course, dealing with issues related to missing email and spam.

4. Portability - can you take data to another provider if you so choose? This allows you to control how you back up mail and contacts, and even allows you to switch to another provider in the future should you desire.

There are many other features you might wish as well. You may find one interface easier to use than others. Some email providers will allow sub-accounts. Some email providers require you to login and use the account more frequently than others. For most new email users though, most of the standard email providers, such as Google, Yahoo! and Microsoft, will be a reasonably good choice.

How many email accounts do I need?

Most people begin with one email account. If their primary email account is associated with their place of business, they might get a second account for personal emails. If they do a lot of work for a particular organization, they might have a third account with that organization so as to keep those communications separate. Some people have several email accounts.

Most people have only one email account. However, you might consider having a second email account that handles just your e-commerce records. Most online vendors require an email address when you purchase an item so they can send you a receipt. Once they have that address, they also use it to send information about sales, special offers, and catalogs. Some are relatively infrequent, but others send materials several times per week. If you want to keep that traffic separate from your other communications, use a different email address. But, do not forget to check all of your accounts regularly.

The Mechanics of Sending an eMail

Before sharing how to use the email function, there are certain accepted practices on email of which you should be aware. Clearly all the rules of normal communication should be followed. eMail should be easy to read, should have well-formed sentences and correct spelling. You should read and re-read your email to ensure that it will not be misunderstood. The absence of non-verbal cues on which we depend heavily in face-to-face communication can make it easy for the recipient to misunderstand your message. You should also avoid cluttering your messages with excessive emphasis (such as stars, arrows and the like). It may make the message hard to follow.

If your messages are for business, for an organization, or for a specific purpose, keep messages to only one subject. Recipients who are not interested in the first subject may never get to a second or third subject, and it might be missed. It is also a good rule to include a descriptive subject line in your message. This may help the recipient to decide whether or not to read your email or how quickly to read the email. More important, a subject line will help focus the recipient on the subject of interest. Of course, if you are using email to send a personal letter, you are likely to have multiple subjects covered.

In addition, the convention in email is not to use all capitalized letters in your email. Online, capitalization is seen as shouting or yelling at the recipient, and is generally accepted as hostile. You should make sure your humor can be understood, especially among people who might not know you well; careful labeling and/or use of emoticons can help this issue (we will discuss emoticons later in this chapter).

All email systems will have their own way of accomplishing specific tasks, and the one you select may not be exactly what I show here. However, I am only showing common functionality that will most likely be available in your system once you look for it.

Once you login by providing your user name and password, most systems will show you a screen that lists the emails in your "inbox." We will return to a discussion of how to handle those emails sent to you shortly. You might come to a page that resembles the email system shown in Figure 5.4. To begin composing an email, look for a button or menu option that says either "new" or "compose" to indicate you would like to create a new email; this button is circled in Figure 5.4.

Once you select that button, you will have the new message template that is shown in Figure 5.5. Note that the system will have already filled in your email address on the "from" line. In this case, my address is example@provider.com, clearly a fictional email address.

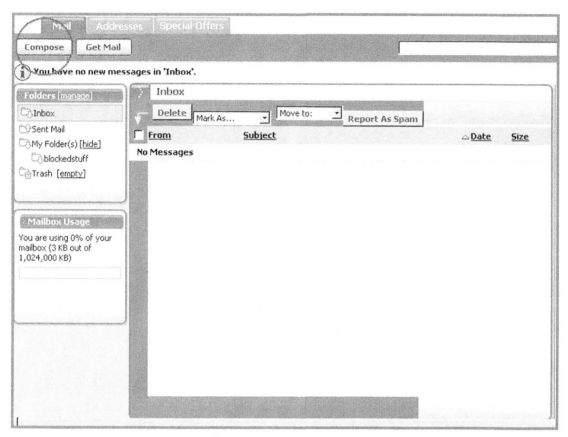

Figure 5.4: Basic eMail Screen

The first thing you need to do is to type in the email address to which you want to send the email. For example, suppose you want to send an email to someone at friend@hotmail.com. You would then type in that email address on the "to" line as shown in Figure 5.6. You can send it to multiple people by typing a semicolon[1] (;) and then listing the second email address, friend2@yahoo.com (also shown in Figure 5.3). As with any correspondence, you may address the email to one person and then send a copy to another person. When using email, you simply put the email address of the person being copied on the CC: line rather than the To: line. In Figure 5.6, you will see that friend3@gmail.com will get a copy of the email. Finally, if you want to send a copy of the email to another individual and not have any of the primary recipients be aware of that

---

[1]Most email systems use either a semicolon or a comma to separate email addresses.

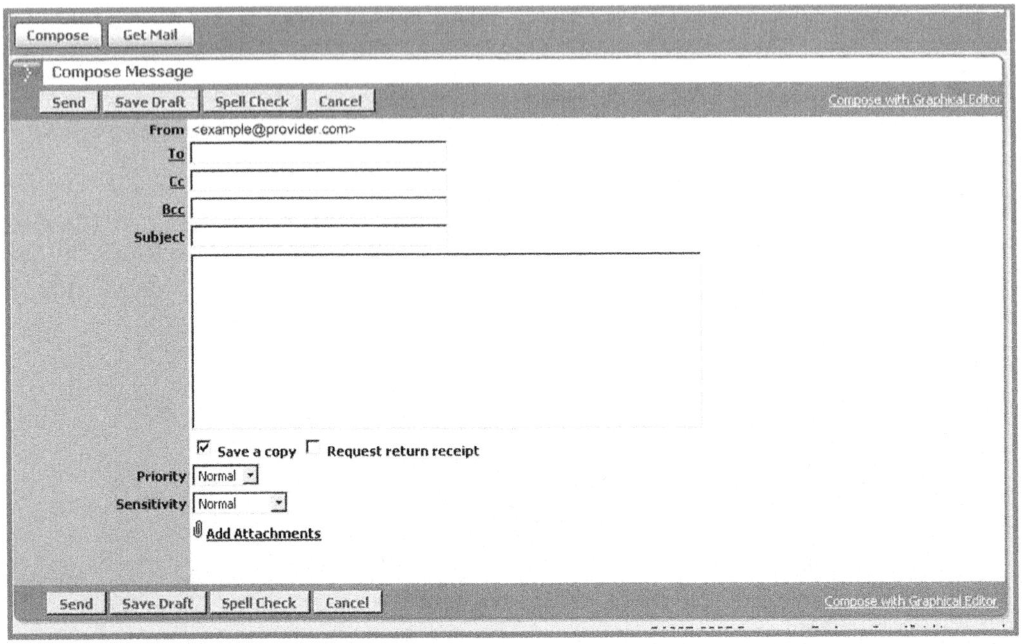

Figure 5.5: Blank eMail Template

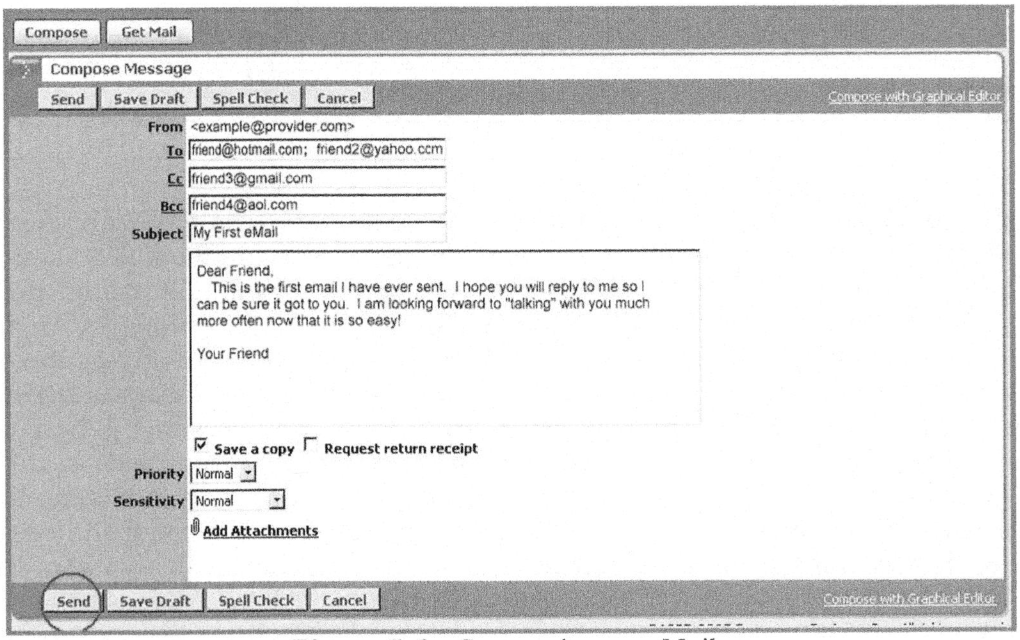

Figure 5.6: Composing an eMail

person receiving it, you want to "blind cc" the email to this person. To accomplish that task, you simply list that person's email address on the line labeled "bcc:" as is shown with friend4@aol.com.

The second thing you need to do is to specify the subject of the email, by typing it on the "Subject:" line. In Figure 5.6, the subject is listed as "My First eMail." You then type your message in the box as shown. When you are finished, you simply press the "send" key, which is circled.

When you receive your friend's email, the inbox will change from being empty (as in Figure 5.4), and will appear to them as Figure 5.7. To open the email, simply double click the mouse on the subject, "My First eMail" (that is underlined in Figure 5.7). You will view your email as it is shown in Figure 5.8. Note that it has provided the list of addresses to which the email was sent and copied, but *not* the address that received the bcc.

You will note that there are buttons across both the top and the bottom of the email message. These provide for the various functions now available to the reader. Suppose for example you wanted to reply to the email. You would simply pick the "reply button" (the left most button) and you would see a view such as that shown in Figure 5.8. In this mail program, you type your response after the original email as shown by the circled text. There are some options immediately below the message that you should notice. The first, which is already checked, tells your system to save a copy of the message. These messages are stored in your "sent mail" folder which generally is part of your list at the left side of the screen. This allows you to return to the message later and review what you wrote, resend the message or send it to someone else.

The second option (shown circled) is not selected. This option "request return receipt" asks the recipient's email system to send back a message automatically when the message is read. This is comparable to sending certified mail; the mail carrier obtains a signature from the person who took possession of the letter. In this case, the reader gets a popup message asking if it is acceptable to send confirmation that the message has been read. Not all systems will honor the request. Most systems ask the reader before sending the response, although some will go ahead and send the response without asking. In general, this is not an option you should select. Even if the recipient's system will allow the request, it can be very annoying to readers to need to answer the question before reading the email. Instead save this option for when you really need to know if someone has read your email.

Remember when you are constructing your reply to follow the conventions stated in the original email. In addition, before replying to an email, read it carefully to ensure you are not misunderstanding the intent of the email. As you construct your response, think about the person or people with whom you are communicating. Make
your content as clear as possible for that audience. It is also helpful if you include at least part of the original message in your reply message. You might label your response or the original message (or both) to ensure that it is clear

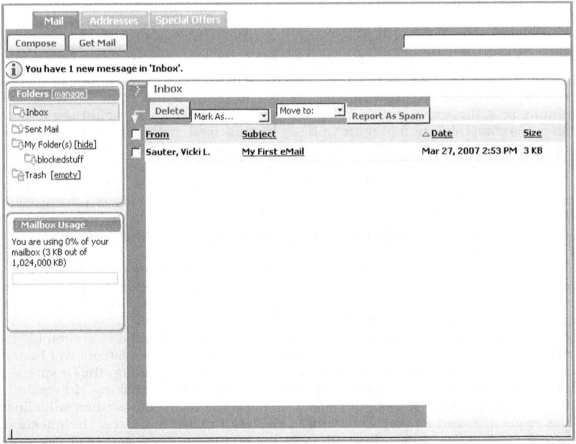

Figure 5.7: The Inbox with a Message

which is which. Many email systems have conventions such as preceding a response with initials or special characters. You should also keep your subject line intact from the original

email. Most email systems will add (automatically) "RE:" and the original subject to a reply. If your response is going off track of the original email, you might adjust the title to reflect that.

Once you are happy with your reply, you would move your mouse to the "send" button and click it as you did when you sent the original email.

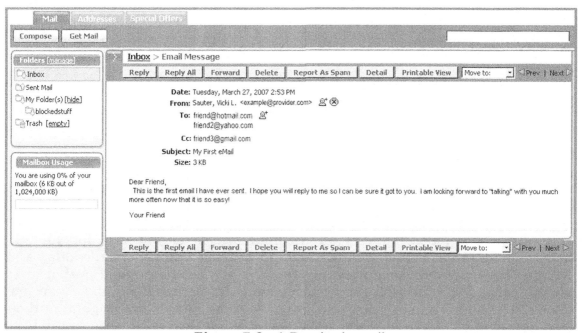

Figure 5.8: A Received email

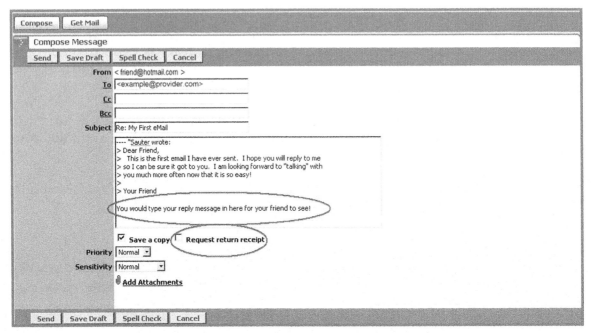

Figure 5.9: A Reply eMail Message

Reply vs. Reply All

If we return to the message in our inbox (Figure 5.8), we see that the second button from the left is slightly different from the one we just selected. That is, there is both a "Reply" button and a "Reply All" button. If the email is between you and one person, there is no difference between the two options. If, however, the original mail was to you and at least one other individual, you have a choice between sending your response just to the original author or to all the people who received his or her email. In our example above, we just chose the "Reply" button. So, our response went just to the original author. Had we selected "Reply All," the email would have been addressed not only to "friend@hotmail.com" (as was our example in Figure 5.9), but also to friend2@yahoo.com and friend3@gmail.com because they were a recipient and a copied recipient, respectively, on the original email. The reply would not go to friend4@aol.com because your system never "knew" of that recipient since it was "blind" copied.

While there is not a universally right or wrong use of these buttons, it is a good idea to remember the difference between them. If your response is meant just for the original author, then you should select "Reply." First, this keeps the others from receiving unnecessary mail. Second, your comment may be intended for *only* the one person. Many people have been embarrassed by sending a private statement to a list of people by hitting "Reply All" accidentally.

Forwarding

When you "forward" email, you are simply passing the email you receive onto some other person or group of people. It might be information that you forward or simply a good joke. You can forward it to one person or to a large number of people. The "Forward" button, the third from the left in Figure 5.8, works much the same way as the reply button, except that you will need to provide the email address of the recipient or list of recipients.

There are some things to keep in mind as you forward email. First of all, be sure that it is worth forwarding. There are many jokes and other humorous stories circulating around the Internet. Not all of them should be shared. Some should be share cautiously. Think about to whom you are sending the email and whether that person will appreciate it.

> ## Spoofing!
>
> Email that has been spoofed is one where the header information is designed to make the message appear to have come from someone it has not. Generally the goal is to make the recipient believe the email has come from a trusted source. The fact that the email might not be from whom you believe it to be makes it all the more important to validate information before forwarding email.

Second, if you are forwarding your email to a large number of people, consider using the bcc: option for the addresses. If all the addresses are "blind copied," recipients will only see their address not a big long list of addresses. This has two advantages. First, it will eliminate that large block of addresses that would otherwise appear at the top of email. As people continue to forward others' email, that block gets larger and larger and the recipient must scroll down substantially to find the eventual joke. That can be annoying. Second, and perhaps more important, it will protect the privacy of the people to whom you sent it. Other people will not know to whom you sent it, and will not have access to the email addresses of your friends and relatives. This means they will not get more unsolicited email.

Third, if it is a warning, make sure it is real. If it is a virus warning, take a minute to check it with McAfee (http://vil.mcafee.com/hoax.asp) or Norton (http://www.norton.com) to be sure it is a warning about a real virus. Many email messages warning people about viruses are just not true and simply upset the recipients. Do a search of a virus hoax site before you share the information. And, if you find the email to involve a hoax, share that information with the person who sent you the email originally.

Fourth, if the email says someone is going to pay you money for sending the email to everyone you know, do not bother with forwarding the email. eMail cannot be tracked in that way and, so far, no one has paid for forwarding anything!

Fifth, if the email involves a child is lost or kidnapped, go to The National Center for Missing and Exploited Children (www.missingkids.com/), or Snopes (www.snopes.com) and make sure it is real. I know the temptation is to forward the email as quickly as possible because your heart goes out to the child and parents. However, most of them are not real, or are out of date. Check the Snopes listing for urban legends or do an internet search for the child's name.

OK, I Have Read it, Now What?

You have read your email, and perhaps forwarded it or responded to it. Now what do you do? Generally there are two options: either you delete the email or you file the email.

If you no longer want the copy of the email, delete it. This keeps your inbox manageable *and* helps you keep under the maximum mailbox size[2]. The fourth button in Figure 5.8 deletes the email from your inbox. However, you should be aware that most email programs do not really delete the email from your box at that point. It has simply been moved to a temporary location, generally called "deleted mail," "trash," or something similar. You must then go to the "deleted mail" or "trash" and actually delete the mail. When you delete mail from this folder, most email systems will ask if you want to permanently delete your mail. After that deletion, it is not generally recoverable.

---

[2] Typically you are allocated a fixed amount of space in which to store your email. Once you have stored that amount of email, the system will quit sending and receiving email for you until you delete some of the older emails.

If, on the other hand, you want to save some of the emails you receive, you might want to organize how you save them. I have one friend who keeps everything in his inbox. So, he has more than 3000 items in his inbox and has trouble finding the specific email he wants at any given time. A better approach is to put those saved emails in folders and organize those folders. You might want to keep emails, organized by the person who sent them, or by the topic, or some other way to make it easy for you to find them again.

Consider again the received email shown in Figure 5.8. Towards the right side of the buttons (above and below the email) is a drop down box that shows "move to:." If you click on the right arrow, you get a list such as that shown in Figure 5.10. This is the list of possible folders in which you may save your email. When you just begin, as is shown in this figure, there are not folders in which you may save your email. But, at the bottom of the dropdown box, there is the "[new folder]" option. If you click on that option, your email system will ask you to specify the name of the new folder you would like to create. In my case, I labeled it "Friends." This action automatically moved the email message from the inbox to a new folder called Friends. In addition, it has added a folder labeled "Friends" to the list of possible options available the next time I want to file an email.

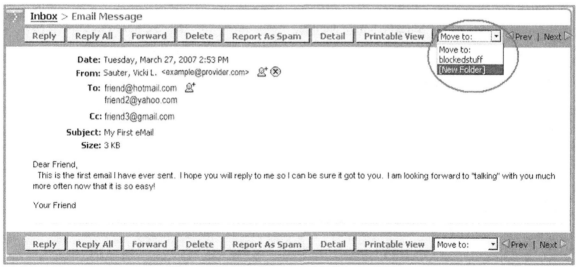

Figure 5.10: Saving eMail to a folder

If you look at the hierarchy of folders available to your account (which in most email systems generally appears to the left of the window in which you view your email), you should see folders that include "inbox," "sent items," "deleted items," and now, "friends." So, when you want to read the email in that folder, you simply double click on its name and you should see a listing of the email stored in that folder much like the listing in your inbox. All operations that you have on email stored in your inbox are also available in Friends folder.

Attachments

Sometimes when we send letters (also known as snail mail) to people, we enclose photos, newspaper or magazine clippings, or other enclosures. Of course there is a parallel in the email world; in cyberspace these are called s. Most email systems indicate there is an attachment with a paperclip. Consider your inbox shown in Figure 5.11. The first email has a paperclip notation toward the right end of the line whereas the second one does not. This tells you the new email[3] has an attachment.

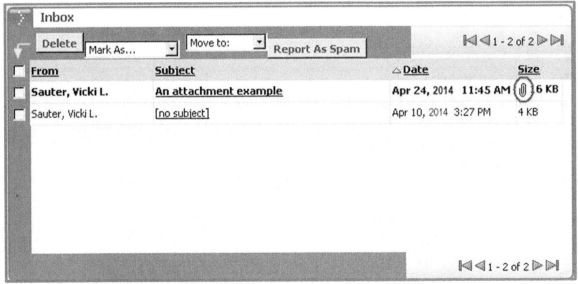

Figure 5.11: Inbox with an eMail with an Attachment

---

[3] You know it is a new email both because of the date and because it appears in bold characters. Many email systems denote a new item in bold. Once the email has been opened, the email appears in a regular-weighted font (such as the second email).

Once you open your email, you may see your attachment, such as the picture in Figure 5.12.

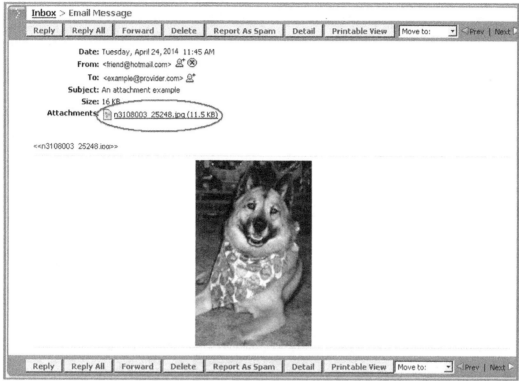

Figure 5.12: eMail with an Attachment

Or, you may need to open the attachment by double clicking on the attachment name (circled in the figure above). This may open another program, such as a graphics program, a word processing program, or spreadsheet program, depending on the type of attachment you have received.

Suppose you want to

A Warning

NEVER open an attachment from someone you do not know. Such attachments may be malicious programs that do harm to your computer. Sometimes by the time you realize the attachment is bad, your computer is already infected and the damage is done. We will discuss more about this later in this chapter and again in the last chapter.

Remember also that email addresses can be "spoofed" so that even though it *looks* like it is from someone you know, it might not be from that person. If you are not expecting an attachment, always verify the source.

send an attachment with your email. In order to accomplish this, the photo or document must be saved on your computer first. If it is saved, then you can attach it through the settings on your email system. Begin by composing an email such as shown in Figure 5.13. Click on the paperclip which may be a button or may, as it is shown below, appear on your email form. This may open another screen that prompts you to "browse" your computer to find the file you wish to attach as shown in Figure 5.14.

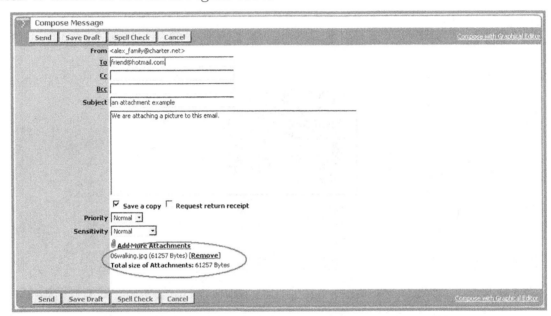

Figure 5.13: Sending an Attachment – Step 1

Once you select "browse" it will take you to your document files as shown in Figure 5.15. Or, your email system may skip the step shown in Figure 5.14, and take you directly to your documents files so you may select the file you wish to attach. You simply highlight the file and click the "open" button (or some systems may have a button that says "attach").

Once selected, you may have an intermediary step that brings you back to a screen similar to that in Figure 5.14, but with the name of the file included. Or, it may simply bring you back to your email form such as shown in Figure 5.16. You should see a notice that you have an attachment and the name of the file that is attached. This is circled in Figure 5.16. Once you finish writing your email, you can now press the "send" button and message, along with the attachment, is on its way!

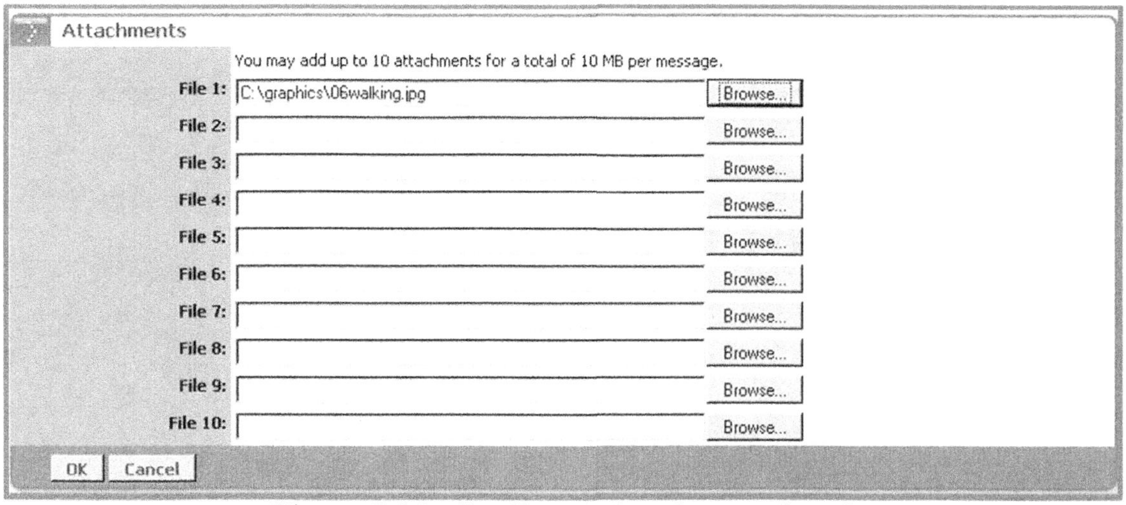

Figure 5.14: Sending an Attachment, Step 2

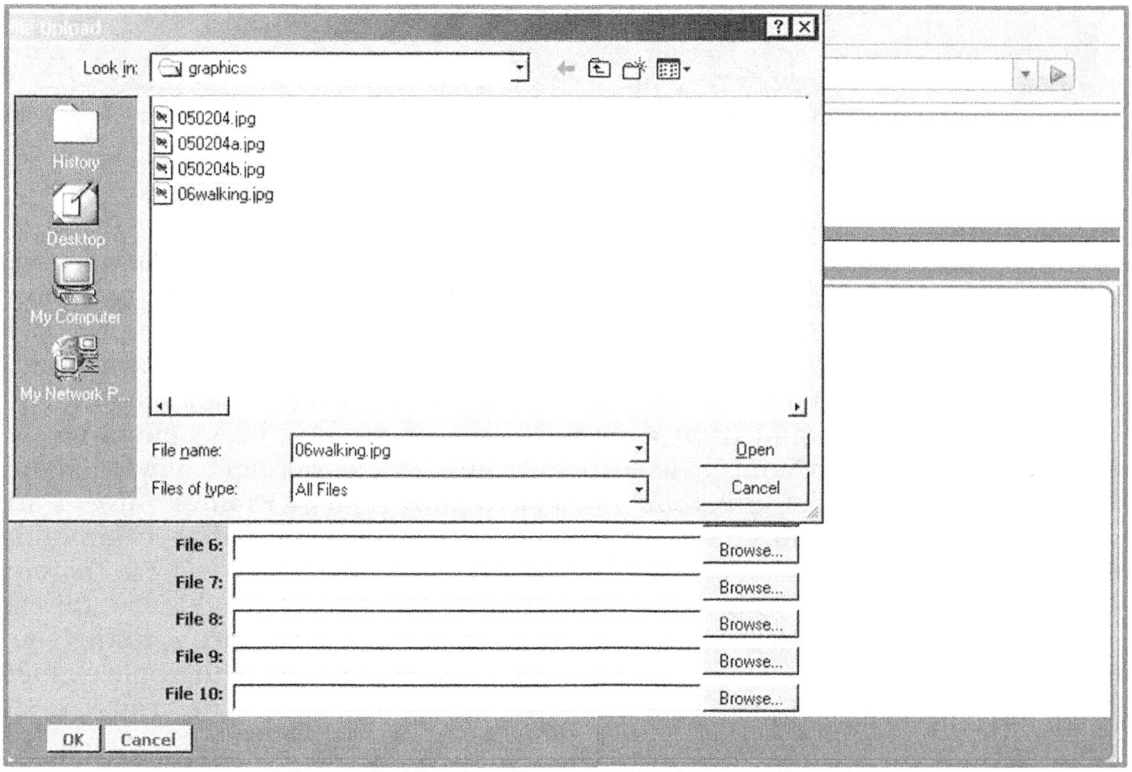

Figure 5.15: Sending an Attachment, Step 3

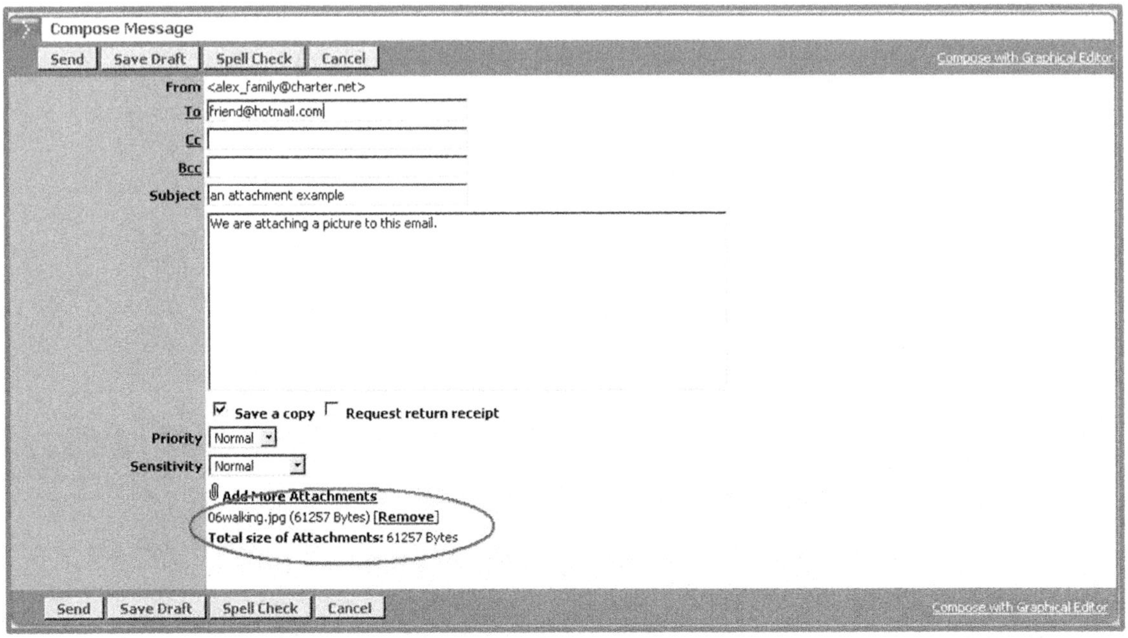

Figure 5.16: Sending an Attachment, Step 4

Signatures

Although you have identified a user name that somehow reflects who you are, you should also think about inserting a "signature" that identifies you more precisely to put at the end of your email. An email signature is simply a few lines of text that are *always* appended to your email. As with the user name, what appears in a signature depends on why you use your email account. At the very least, you should have your full name at the end of an email so the reader will know with whom he is corresponding. Professional or official emails should always have that affiliation associated with it. For example, if you are treasurer of the condominium association, you should include that information on all emails sent to the condominium owners. In those cases, where there is an official purpose for your email, you might want to also add an address and/or telephone number to your signature. Similarly, if you are sending your email to someone who is acting in an official capacity, such as the police chief, you should include your address and telephone number in case he or she needs to contact you. I would, however, not include a home address and home or cell telephone number if you send emails to people you do not know. There is no reason to share contact information that might be used for nefarious purposes.

You can also let your personality shine some with your signature. One friend of mine always has a small picture of a rose next to her name.

Many people have quotes or sayings that are meaningful to them. For example, my University email account signature includes the quote in Figure 5.17.

Figure 5.17: A Clever Quote Often is Part of an eMail Signature

> No trees were killed in the sending of this message.
> However, a large number of electrons were terribly inconvenienced.

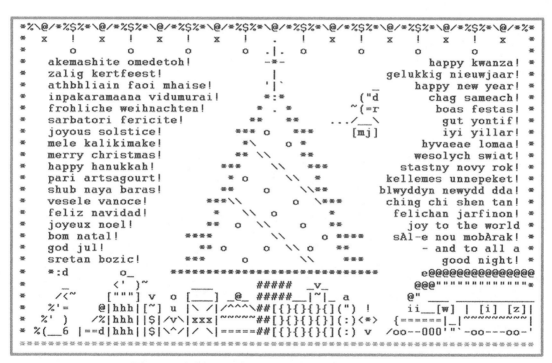

Figure 5.18: A Text-based Holiday Signature

Figure 5.19: A text-only signature that shows
a map of the state of Missouri

The amount of flexibility you have with your signature depends upon your email system. If your system does not allow graphics as part of an email, then you must limit your signature to a combination of characters available on the keyboard. That doesn't mean it must be boring, however. One signature used during the Christmas season looks like a holiday scene in Figure 5.18. Others have figured out how to make the characters into a map such as that shown in Figure 5.19.

Of course, if your email does allow graphics, you are unlimited in how you might express yourself. You might use one of the signature creator programs or scan your actual signature and use that as part of your email signature.   Or, you might find a small graphic to use. One friend always uses a picture of his workplace in Figure 5.20 with her name as his email signature.

Figure 5.20: eMail Signature with Graphics

Not all email systems allow users to embed graphics in their signature files. Some free email account providers will only allow the use of graphics if you upgrade to their premier system. Some of these systems will, however, allow you to embed emoticons (that will be discussed shortly). So, you could have a signature such as the one in Figure 5.21.

Figure 5.21: Signature with Emoticon

Even if your provider does allow graphics in your signature, you should be cautious about using them in email. First, some of your recipients of email may not be able to see the graphics. Further, the use of graphics does increase the size of your email which may cause problems for the recipient, depending on the amount of email storage space he or she has available.

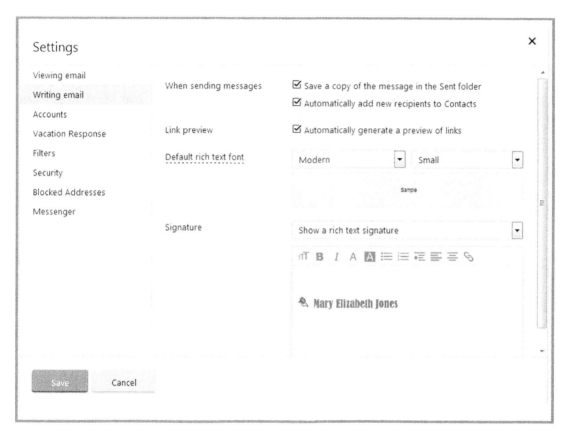

Figure 5.22: Creating a Signature for eMail

As said earlier, the advantage of using a "signature" is that it will always be appended to your email automatically. How one sets a signature depends on what email service you are using. For example, if you use Yahoo, you check your settings (by clicking the small gear in the upper right hand corner of your screen) and you will see a screen such as the one shown in Figure 5.22. To create your signature, you paste images and type text in the signature box and press the "save" button.   As you can see from the dropdown box, this signature uses the "rich text" option. That gives you more flexibility in terms of how your signature is displayed. If you use another option, such as "plain text," you will not have control over the font, layout, or color, and will not be able to use graphics.

Stationery

Another way to personalize your email is to use stationery. As in the paper world, stationery is simply a decorative background that is attached to an email message. If the receiver's email system allows it, he or she will view your email on the decorative background rather than on a plain white background. For example, Figure 5.23 shows an example of email stationery sent to me by one friend.

Figure 5.23: Example Stationery used with eMail

Most email systems will allow you to customize your standard email with stationery. This might involve setting the background color, the font color or using some background or foreground image, or even sounds with each and every email. Thus each time you send the email, you can either always have it sent with the same color, images and font, or select those things each time.

Where do you get the images? Any image can be incorporated, so if you have a small image, such as a picture of a flower or flag, you may add it to your stationery.   Some email systems have some pre-defined stationery types available through their systems. Or, you can import stationery available on the internet. Some of these are available for free, and some require a payment for downloading the stationery. As with the concern about the signature, you need to realize that not everyone will be able to view the stationery with their email systems. Further, each additional image, especially if it is large, makes the email size larger which can affect both your storage and that of the recipient.

Abbreviations/Acronyms

eMail is often much more informal than snail mail letters. This, combined with bad typing skills on the part of many users, has resulted in the use of some standard acronyms or abbreviations that are commonly used in email. If you have never seen them before, they can be quite confusing. Once you get accustomed to them, they do not seem so foreign.

Common Acronyms

AFAIK: As far as I know
BTW: By the way
IMHO: In my humble opinion
LOL: Laughing out loud
TTFN: Ta ta for now
FWIW: For what it's worth
ROTFL: Rolling on the floor laughing

Of course, there are some acronyms that are particular to a profession or field or interest area, and some that are more common among different age groups.

Trivia

According to the *Guinness Book of World Records*, the longest acronym is 56 letters: NIIOMTPLABOPARMBETZHELBETRABSBOMONIMONKON OTDTEKHSTROMONT. It means "The laboratory for shuttering, reinforcement, concrete and ferroconcrete operations for composite-monolithic and monolithic constructions of the Department of the Technology of Building-assembly operations of the Scientific Research Institute of the Organization for building mechanization and technical aid of the Academy of Building and Architecture of the USSR." The length of this acronym does seem to defeat the purpose of making it easy to remember.

Should you encounter another acronym, not included in this list, you can check it by searching for it with your favorite search engine. Some of the places that I like to look for explanations of acronyms are shown below.

www.acronymfinder.com/ — The Acronym Finder
acronyms.thefreedictionary.com/ — The Free Dictionary
www.muller-godschalk.com/acronyms.html — Muller-Godschalk.com

Emoticons

One of the problems of email communication is its inability to convey non-verbal cues, and unlike snail mail, email is immediate. Your mood when constructing the email might not be obvious to the person or people to whom the communication was sent. If you were being silly or sarcastic in an email, the recipient might interpret the response as serious. This can lead to some miscommunications. So, when email was still totally character-based, people created a short-hand to convey facial expressions. These were called Smileys or Emoticons. Smileys are small (usually less than 5 characters) combinations of characters that all appear on one line intended to convey emotions or attitudes that, in face-to-face communication, would be conveyed by facial expressions or other nonverbal communication. Early on, they were intended to be simple to type and recognize as long as one turned one's head to the side.

Common Emoticons

:-)	A smiling face
:-D	A large smile or laugh
:-))	Really happy
:->	Sarcasm
;-)	Winking, indicating you do not mean what was said
:-*	Kissing
:~x	Tongue tied
=:-O	Scared
:-p or :-)~	Tongue sticking out

As time progressed, of course, people got more creative with their emoticons. In addition to emotions, they might represent objects such as (:::::[]:::::) to indicate a bandaid or <;;;;;;;;;;;|===0 to indicate a sword. Others designed emoticons to represent famous people. With a little imagination, you can see Abraham Lincoln in ==):-)= or a snowman in (:>]}( )( ) or even Marge Simpson in ######:o) Some later individuals created emoticons for which one did not need to turn one's head. For example, °¿° might represent a normal face while ._/. or `_´ might

Graphical Emoticons

☺	Smiling Face
☻	Large Smile or Laugh
☺	Sticking out one's Tongue
☺	Rolling one's Eyes
☺	Thinking
☺	Angry

represent an angry face, ;_; might represent crying, and ^_~ might represent a wink. These "no turning" emoticons are not frequently used, however.

The advent of instant messaging (which will be discussed in the next chapter) and online chatting brought graphical representations of the smileys. These are sometimes referred to simply as "graphical emoticons," or "graphical smileys," but sometimes are referred to as "emoji" or "emojicons." Most systems will allow you to use these graphical emoticons in your email. Further, if you enter a sideways emoticon, the system will convert it to the graphical version automatically. The goal of the emoticons is to provide an image that is easy to discern. However, should you find that you have an emoticon that you do not understand, you can look it up on http://Muller-Godschalk.com, which has a fairly complete collection of emoticons.

Etiquette

You might at this point ask if there are any rules of etiquette for email. As with any other social group, there are certain accepted practices of which you should be aware, and we shall discuss them shortly. It is important to remember, however, that there are social conventions among people that go beyond the realm of email. Clearly, polite society recognizes polite communication whatever the medium, and email users expect the same. Generally, it is useful to have a well written document as well to make it easier for the recipient to understand your point. If your email is for a particular club, organization or place of work, remember the code of conduct in that group and follow it as you would in face-to-face settings.

First, think about your email and whether it is appropriate to put your message in that medium. eMails can easily be forwarded, printed and saved. If what you want to say is confidential or hurtful, you might not want to use email. Remember, although *you* delete the email, not everyone does. Do not put anything in email that you do not want the world to see.

The second accepted practice among email users is DO NOT USE ALL CAPITALS IN YOUR EMAIL. Capitalization always adds emphasis to your point. However, in the world of email, capitalization is considered shouting. Do not shout in your email any more than you would shout in face-to-face communications. Some email users I know avoid all use of capital letters in an e.e. cummings approach to prose. Clearly it avoids the image of shouting, but it can also be difficult for the recipient to read.

Third, respond to email as you would respond to a telephone call. Some people find it very annoying to send a message and never receive a response. While this takes time, it is generally accepted practice to send some reply to an inquiry. However, if you do not know the sender of the email and it is not a wanted email (see next section on Spam), then *never* reply to it.

If you reply to an email, be aware of how you are replying. In all email systems, there are two reply options, one labeled "reply" and one labeled "reply all." The first (reply) sends your email only to the person who sent the email to you. The second, however, sends your email to both the person who sent the email and anyone who was copied on the original email. If you intend your message just for the original sender, you might be terribly embarrassed if the entire group reads your response. Alternatively, if your goal was to inform the entire group about your answer, you will have missed your opportunity if you simply chose the reply option.

Most email systems have a way of marking an email as urgent. When that email appears in a recipient's inbox, it is marked with a red exclamation point to get the recipient's attention. This is a good system to help people identify really important messages. But, if all of your messages appear this way, the identifier loses any significance. So, use the urgent marker sparingly.

Many systems also have a way of asking for a return receipt that the email was read. These popups are annoying to users because it adds an extra step in reading email. It also clutters the sender's inbox with those acknowledgments. When the message is urgent and you need to be sure the recipient has read the message, then use this option. Otherwise, ignore it.

Many people believe society should be more cautious as to what email we forward to others. One way to keep in touch with others is to forward meaningful stories, photos and jokes to one's friends. But, not everyone has the same sense of humor and not everyone wants to receive these items. Be cautious and think about your recipient before automatically forwarding something. In particular, think hard and long before sending chain letters that promise either good or bad luck.

If you do forward email, remove the heading material before you do. The headings often include a list of people to whom (and from whom) the email has been passed previously. It may include several peoples' signatures as well. Hence, the recipient needs to scroll down (sometimes a long way) before seeing the content you intend. By removing this material, you shorten the email *and* protect the privacy of those people who received it previously because their email addresses are not constantly rebroadcast (as discussed below).

Similarly, think about whom you include in a carbon copy (cc:) of your email. There are two reasons to be concerned about this. First, you are sharing the email addresses of all of the recipients with all other recipients. If they know each other, this is fine. However, many people do not like sharing their email address with unknown individuals. Respect their privacy and be cautious about how you do this (you can always use bcc: if you need to copy them). In addition, you may be sending a statement that you do not intend by copying another individual. If it is a confidential conversation and you copy someone else, a recipient may be hurt or offended. Follow your common sense and the practices of the group you are emailing to make this decision.

Finally, always make sure it is obvious from whom the email was sent. This includes signing the email and/or using a signature (as discussed earlier in this chapter).

Spam

We all have tons of junk mail that fills the mailbox outside of our homes. There are applications for new credit cards, advertisements, lots of catalogs, and other items that most people simply pitch when going through the mail. Unfortunately, there is a similar phenomenon in the email world, and it is called spam.

Spam is any unwanted and unsolicited email that is delivered to your mailbox. Usually the email is a result of bulk mailings by an advertiser, a prankster or a "phisher" (which we will discuss in the next section). However, today the term is also used to reflect any unsolicited message that people do not want to receive. The term "spam" for unwanted email originates with a 1970 Monty Python sketch in which two customers are ordering from a breakfast menu on which almost every item includes spam.

Spam, a processed meat made by Hormel, was one of the few meats available (and not rationed) in Britain during WWII. Many Brits, and Americans as well, grew to dislike this product, thereby leading to the skit. Computer technologists, who have a propensity to like Monty Python, coined the term, given overabundance of unwanted email and most users dislike of it. How you handle the spam depends on the source of the spam.

Catalogs

When you purchase something online, most catalog companies will send you a confirmation, a receipt and often updates about your order online. It is very convenient to receive and store these messages in an email folder, and track your purchases online. What they do not tell you is that they also add you to their promotions and advertising lists, which can generate several emails per week. Further, they do not tell you that they sell these lists to other catalogs (just as paper catalog companies sell their mailing lists to other companies).

To me, these are among the most frustrating spam messages. Yes, I want to purchase from these people, and sometimes I even want to see their advertisements, but I want to do it on *my* terms. I do not want to have them disturbing me every time I read my email.

On the other hand, this form of spam is the easiest to manage. My solution is simply to have one account that you use *only* for purchases for which you provide your email account. Many providers, such as yahoo or gmail will provide you with an email account (or as many email accounts as you wish) for free. Suppose I have an email account called VSauter@yahoo.com that I use for my regular correspondence. I might create a second email account, VSauter_purchase@yahoo.com, SauterPurchases@yahoo.com or even Vsauter1@yahoo.com Then *every time* I make a purchase online, I would use the VSauter_purchase@yahoo.com as my email account, and keep VSauter@yahoo.com for my correspondence. This means, of course, that you will need to check two email accounts, but it will also be easier for you to manage your mail.

Scams

One of the first mass-emailed spam messages was the famous Nigerian scam shown in Figure 5.23. This version of the email was taken from the Snopes site (http://www.snopes.com/crime/fraud/nigeria.asp) on May 28, 2007. It has also been circulated from other countries including other African nations such as the Ivory Coast or Sierra Leone, and even some Asian countries. The names may change and the text may change some, but the idea is always that you will obtain a significant amount of money if you only set up an account and help these people.

Snopes, which provides a wonderful resource to check on emails such as this, reports that sometimes the email varies by mentioning that the person would like to leave all his money to the church, or that the reader has won some foreign lottery. According to Snopes, which cites an unmentioned 1997 newspaper article, in the United States, in the first six months of 1997, known losses (because many people do not report their loss) were over $100 million!

Scams such as this are not just in emails. Apparently this same scam has been around for many decades in the form of letters and letter faxes. In the 1920s, the scam mentioned Spanish prisoners, but it was much the same idea.

Other scams include companies promising to sell popular pharmaceuticals by mail at a fraction of the cost of a drug retailer, and often with no prescription needed.

Sometimes these companies do send the purchaser *something*, but it is always from an offshore pharmacy, and is never the brand name. Other times, they send nothing and the purchaser has nothing to show for the money.

Often there is nothing you can do to eliminate these messages. You should *never* respond to the message, that simply tells the sender that the email address is active, and will result in your getting *more* email messages. Many email providers, including those that provide free email accounts, now provide some spam filtering. If your provider does filter, you may never see these kind of email messages. If not, or in addition, you might want to filter your own email messages. Later in this chapter, we will discuss how to filter your own messages. If you have no idea where they got your email, by all means *do not answer* the email, even if the message suggests they will take you off if you request it. Usually all that does is to tell the sender that the email address is actually an active address.

Chain Letters and Hoaxes

When I was a child, I remember many chain letters sent to me by friends and acquaintances. They all included a message about what you had to do to get good luck, lots of money, recipes, photos or postcards. You were instructed to add your name to the bottom, remove the top name, and forward it to ten friends. You were also required to send something to the person whose name you had removed. Of course, the chain letter also came with a warning about the bad things that would happen to you if you broke the chain. The modern version of these chain letters is available via email. The email version, like the snail mail version of my youth, is nothing more than a pyramid or Ponzi scheme that is illegal in most states.

A variation on the normal chain letter concept is the hoax. The hoax is an email that sounds plausible enough to be true. It comes from someone you know, almost always says it was verified by someone, and pleads with you to forward it to everyone you know. One popular form of a hoax is the one that promises you will get money if only you forward an email to everyone you know. Consider the email shown in Figure 5.24.

REQUEST FOR URGENT BUSINESS RELATIONSHIP

FIRST, I MUST SOLICIT YOUR STRICTEST CONFIDENCE IN THIS TRANSACTION. THIS IS BY VIRTUE OF ITS NATURE AS BEING UTTERLY CONFIDENTIAL AND 'TOP SECRET'. I AM SURE AND HAVE CONFIDENCE OF YOUR ABILITY AND RELIABILITY TO PROSECUTE A TRANSACTION OF THIS GREAT MAGNITUDE INVOLVING A PENDING TRANSACTION REQUIRING MAXIIMUM CONFIDENCE.

WE ARE TOP OFFICIAL OF THE FEDERAL GOVERNMENT CONTRACT REVIEW PANEL WHO ARE INTERESTED IN IMPORATION OF GOODS INTO OUR COUNTRY WITH FUNDS WHICH ARE PRESENTLY TRAPPED IN NIGERIA. IN ORDER TO COMMENCE THIS BUSINESS WE SOLICIT YOUR ASSISTANCE TO ENABLE US TRANSFER INTO YOUR ACCOUNT THE SAID TRAPPED FUNDS.

THE SOURCE OF THIS FUND IS AS FOLLOWS; DURING THE LAST MILITARY REGIME HERE IN NIGERIA, THE GOVERNMENT OFFICIALS SET UP COMPANIES AND AWARDED THEMSELVES CONTRACTS WHICH WERE GROSSLY OVER-INVOICED IN VARIOUS MINISTRIES. THE PRESENT CIVILIAN GOVERNMENT SET UP A CONTRACT REVIEW PANEL AND WE HAVE IDENTIFIED A LOT OF INFLATED CONTRACT FUNDS WHICH ARE PRESENTLY FLOATING IN THE CENTRAL BANK OF NIGERIA READY FOR PAYMENT.

HOWEVER, BY VIRTUE OF OUR POSITION AS CIVIL SERVANTS AND MEMBERS OF THIS PANEL, WE CANNOT ACQUIRE THIS MONEY IN OUR NAMES. I HAVE THEREFORE, BEEN DELEGATED AS A MATTER OF TRUST BY MY COLLEAGUES OF THE PANEL TO LOOK FOR AN OVERSEAS PARTNER INTO WHOSE ACCOUNT WE WOULD TRANSFER THE SUM OF US$21,320,000.00(TWENTY ONE MILLION, THREE HUNDRED AND TWENTY THOUSAND U.S DOLLARS). HENCE WE ARE WRITING YOU THIS LETTER. WE HAVE AGREED TO SHARE THE MONEY THUS; 1. 20% FOR THE ACCOUNT OWNER 2. 70% FOR US (THE OFFICIALS) 3. 10% TO BE USED IN SETTLING TAXATION AND ALL LOCAL AND FOREIGN EXPENSES. IT IS FROM THE 70% THAT WE WISH TO COMMENCE THE IMPORTATION BUSINESS.

PLEASE,NOTE THAT THIS TRANSACTION IS 100% SAFE AND WE HOPE TO COMMENCE THE TRANSFER LATEST SEVEN (7) BANKING DAYS FROM THE DATE OF THE RECEIPT OF THE FOLLOWING INFORMATIOM BY TEL/FAX; 234-1-7740449, YOUR COMPANY'S SIGNED, AND STAMPED LETTERHEAD PAPER THE ABOVE INFORMATION WILL ENABLE US WRITE LETTERS OF CLAIM AND JOB DESCRIPTION RESPECTIVELY. THIS WAY WE WILL USE YOUR COMPANY'S NAME TO APPLY FOR PAYMENT AND RE-AWARD THE CONTRACT IN YOUR COMPANY'S NAME.

WE ARE LOOKING FORWARD TO DOING THIS BUSINESS WITH YOU AND SOLICIT YOUR CONFIDENTIALITY IN THIS TRANSACTION. PLEASE ACKNOWLEDGE THE RECEIPT OF THIS LETTER USING THE ABOVE TEL/FAX NUMBERS. I WILL SEND YOU DETAILED

Figure 5.24: Text of the Nigerian Scam Spam

THIS TOOK TWO PAGES OF THE TUESDAY USA TODAY - IT IS FOR REAL

Subject: PLEEEEEASE READ!!!! it was on GOOD MORNING AMERICA

!!!! It was on the news!

To all of my friends, I do not usually forward messages, But this is from my good friend Pearlas Sandborn and she really is an attorney.

If she says that this will work - It will work. After all, What have you got to lose? SORRY EVERYBODY.. JUST HAD TO TAKE THE CHANCE!!! I'm an attorney, And I know the law. This thing is for real. Rest assured AOL and Intel will follow through with their promises for fear of facing a multimillion-dollar class action suit similar to the one filed by PepsiCo against General Electric not too long ago.

Dear Friends; Please do not take this for a junk letter. Bill Gates sharing his fortune. If you ignore this, You will repent later. Microsoft and AOL are now the largest Internet companies and in an effort to make sure that Internet Explorer remains the most widely used program, Microsoft and AOL are running an e-mail beta test.

When you forward this e-mail to friends, Microsoft can and will track it (If you are a Microsoft Windows user) For a two weeks time period.

For every person that you forward this e-mail to, Microsoft will pay you $245.00 For every person that you sent it to that forwards it on, Microsoft will pay you $243.00 and for every third person that receives it, You will be paid $241.00. Within two weeks, Microsoft will contact you for your address and then send you a check.

Regards. Charles S Bailey General Manager Field Operations
1-800-842-2332 Ext. 1085 or 904-1085 or RNX
292-1085 Charles_Bailey@csx.com Charles_bailey@csx.com

I thought this was a scam myself, But two weeks after receiving this e-mail and
forwarding it on Microsoft contacted me for my address and withindays I receive a

Figure 5.25: Text a Chain Letter Spam

The one I hate most are the amber alert messages because they are so hard not to forward. For example, see the message shown in Figure 5.26. They provide details of a disappearance and/or abduction and always include a photo.   You want to forward it because you want the child to be found. There is no harm in forwarding it because nothing bad will happen except that you will unnecessarily take the time of everyone to whom you forward the message, and all those who receive it after that point.

I know. You look at the message and think, "but this one *might* be real... I should forward it just in case." You are right, it might be real. But, before you forward it you should check to see if it is a known hoax. One easy way is to conduct a search using your favorite search engine. If it is a hoax, you are likely to find many sites that link to it. Another way is to check known hoaxes. Earlier, we discussed snopes.com, which has information about many urban

PLEASE LOOK AT PICTURE THEN FORWARD

I am asking you all, begging you to please, forward this email on to anyone and everyone you know, PLEASE. My 9 year old girl, Penny Brown, is missing. She has been missing for now two weeks. It is still not too late, Please help us.

If anyone anywhere knows anything, sees anything, please contact me at zicozicozico@hotmail.com

I am including a picture of her. All prayers are appreciated!!

It only takes 2 seconds to forward this on, if it was your child, you would want all the help you could get. Please.

thank you for your kindness, hopefully you can help us.

Monzine Jang
Office Administrator   [Photo deleted]
G208, Health Sciences Centre   [Phone number deleted]
Faculty of Medicine   [Phone number deleted]
University of Calgary   [Fax number deleted]

Figure 5.26: Fake Amber Alert eMail

email hoaxes at http://vil.nai.com/vil/hoaxes.aspx, including information legends, including email hoaxes. McAfee provides an up to date listing of known about the hoax and what damage, if any it can do to your computer.

Malware and Viruses

We will discuss security in the last chapter of this book. However, it is important right now to note that email is a major source of security problems for your computer. The primary source of this security problem is the attachments to the email. An attachment is anything sent along with the email that is not viewable in the main message window. For example, photographs that are sent via email are sent as attachments. Similarly, documents, such as newsletters, spreadsheets, or other emails being forwarded. Sending such items as attachments makes it easy and convenient to share.

However, some attachments are programs intended to infect your computer. Depending on the kind of program in the attachment, it can do anything from being a little annoying to totally destroying your computer. Such programs are computer viruses and malware (short for malicious software). Attachments might include either viruses or malware (or both). The program runs the minute you open the attachment. Once you realize that something bad is happening to the computer, it is too late to stop the program.

There are other programs you can run that protect your computer from viruses and malware or fix the damage if the computer has contracted a virus or malware. These will be covered later. In the meanwhile, the most important thing you can do to protect yourself is to follow these two rules.

First, *never* open an attachment if it is from a person you do not know. The subject line might be intriguing, and it might be something valuable. However, it is more likely spam, and when opened, the attachment will infect your computer. Simply delete the email.

Second, even if you know the person who seems to be sending the email, *never* open an attachment unless you are expecting it, and believe that it is uninfected. If your friend has malware running on his or her machine, the malware might attach a malicious code without your friend's knowledge. In addition, email addresses may be faked so that a given email *appears* to be from a known person, but in fact it is not. If you are not expecting the attachment then, do not open it until you are sure it is ok.

Phishing

If you read the word phonetically, it appears to be "fishing." Rather than using a worm to entice fish to get caught on a hook, phishing uses an email lure to entice unsuspecting users to provide passwords, financial information, and other sensitive information. Phishers send messages that appear to be official and trustworthy to unsuspecting users. Generally they bait the user by stating there has been a breach of security, such as someone else using their account, that requires them to change a password or enter other critical information. For example, below are example texts from such email.

> "We suspect an unauthorized transaction on your account. To ensure that your account is not compromised, please click the link below and confirm your identity."
>
> "During our regular verification of accounts, we couldn't verify your information. Please click here to update and verify your information."

Phishing almost always uses phrases such as:

> Verify your account.
> If you don't respond within 48 hours, your account will be closed.
> Dear Valued Customer.
> Click the link below to gain access to your account.

Always be suspicious if the email uses these or similar phrases.

Security Update   ⑦ Need Help?

Official Notice for all eBay users

Dear eBay User,

During our regular udpate and verification of the accounts, we couldn't verify your current information. Either your information has changed or it is incomplete.

As a result, your access to bid or buy on Ebay has been restricted. To start using your eBay account fully, **please update and verify your information by clicking below :**

http://www.ebay.com.us:eBayISAPIdllVerifyInformation

Regards,

eBay

Please Do Not Reply To This E-Mail As You Will Not Receive A Responce

Copyright 1995-2003 eBay Inc. All Rights Reserved. Designated trademarks and brands are the property of their respective owners. Use of this Web site constitutes acceptance of the eBay User Agreement and Privacy Policy.

Figure 5.27: Example of Phishing

These emails always use official looking logos. Finally, there is always a link in the email and instruction to click on the link. If you look at the link carefully, it is *close* to a legitimate link for that company, but not quite. Or, it may be masked (that is the words say the right thing, but when you click on it, your browser goes to a different site).

For example, consider the phishing example in Figure 5.27.

What should you do if you get this email? **Delete it immediately.** But, what if it *is real* you ask. The first question you should ask yourself is whether you provided your
email address to the bank or other company noted in the email. If not, then delete the email and move on. If you are still not convinced, then log onto your account and find out. But, ***never*** get to your account by clicking on the link. Remember, the links, while they look legitimate, are re-directions to fake sites (that look just like the real one) that exist for the sole purpose of collecting the account and password information
you enter. The site may appear to have problems logging you in. Or, the site may tell you that nothing is wrong. Meanwhile, someone is using your account and password to log into your account and steal your money or identity information.

If you really want to check your account, open a new page in your browser and log onto your account. If there is a problem, you will always receive some kind of message. By typing the url directly, you are making sure that you are logging into the actual company.

Sometimes phishers request that you call a phone number instead of going to a website. As with the email, you cannot be sure of that location. Instead of calling the number they conveniently provide to you, check your last statement or other records and call the phone number listed there. This too protects your information.

If you believe you have received a phishing email, you may report it to the FTC (in the United States) by reporting it to reportphishing@antiphishing.org. You may also forward the phishing email to spam@uce.gov. If you believe you have been a victim of phishing, you can report this to the FTC. More information about how to make a complaint can be found on the FTC website at http://www.ftc.gov/bcp/edu/microsites/idtheft/.

Handling Spam
Most email providers do some spam filtering before your email ever gets to your mailbox. In some systems, you never see the email. In other systems, they may put the messages suspected to be spam in a bulk mail folder automatically. If you are confident in your mail system, you can simply empty

that folder without considering any of the email. If you are not sure whether desirable email might have been inappropriately classified, you may open the folder, scroll through the senders and even open the mail if you wish.

Clearly this is good because it means *you* do not need to sift through all of those emails. However, this can also be bad because *you* might *want* email from that domain. For example, one email system with which I am familiar blocks email from travelocity.com. So, when the daughter of a friend who uses that email system sent her travel plans, her father never received them. Clearly, he did not want to block travelocity.com. On the other hand, most email systems do not block the domain yahoo.com. However, you might find that all you get is spam from that domain, and you *do* want to block it. In the first case, you want to "allow" a blocked address; in the second case, you want to "block" an address. Most systems allow you to do these functions through the preferences or settings option.

Most email providers will allow you to select a message and report it as spam, thereby increasing the effectiveness of the spam filters at the provider level. This is done by selecting a message and clicking the "spam" button shown below. Please note that your email system will have a way to do this, but it might be slightly different than the one shown in the figure.

Thereafter, all email from that source will either put in a directory for spam suspects or automatically deleted depending on your system. Some email systems are more sophisticated in how they allow you to filter your email.

Consider the screen in Figure 5.28. In one system, this is how you specify what specific email addresses or domains you would like to allow or block. This example shows how the user allowed two domains, travelocity.com and umsl.edu in the top box. However, the user blocked yahoo as discussed earlier in the bottom box. In addition, although the domain umsl.edu is allowed, the user has blocked a specific email address, student123@umsl.edu; this is also indicated in the lower box. So, while all other email addresses from umsl.edu are allowed, student123 will have his or her email blocked.

Notice that this system allows two options for blocked email. You may have it automatically deleted by selecting the first option. In that case, you will never have the opportunity to review the messages to see if you really wanted some of them. Alternatively, if you select option two, all of these messages will be placed in a special folder called "blockedstuff" until you review them and delete them if desired.

Please note that many systems allow you to "organize" all of your incoming email using such rules. For example, suppose I want all emails from a particular individual or mailing list put into a folder automatically either so that I can save them, but not need to deal with them with my normal reading of email. I might construct a rule such as the one shown in Figure 5.29. When new messages are received, the system will check the sender of each. Any that are from Andrew Peara will be put in a folder labeled "correspondence" for action at a later time.

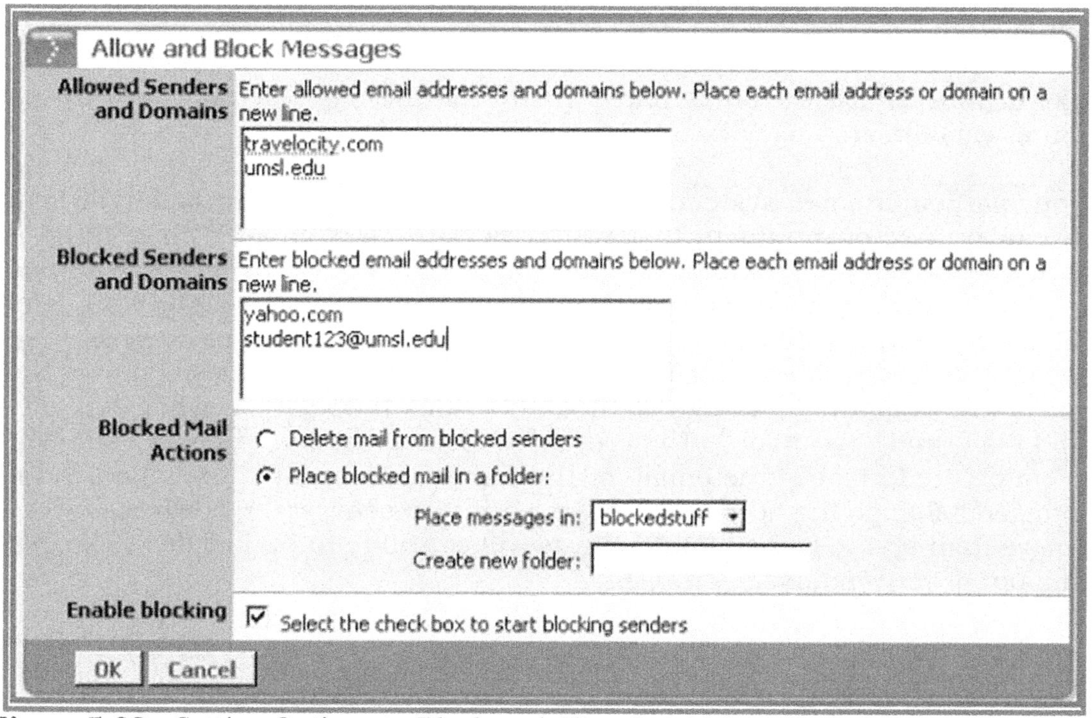

Figure 5.28: Setting Options to Block and Allow Particular eMail Sites and Addresses

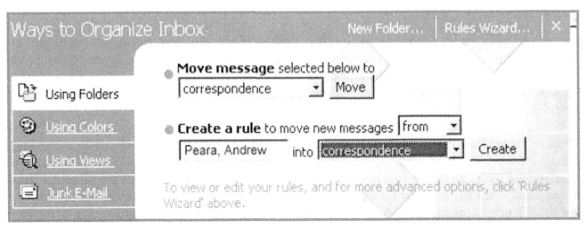

Figure 5.29: Creating a Rule using Microsoft Outlook

You may also create a series of rules and control the order in which they are considered by your email system. Consider the rules shown in Figure 5.30. In each case these show the sender of the email. If you click on one, then you view the rule. They might move a message, they might ensure the message stays in your inbox, the rules might delete the message, or even forward it to another email user.

If your particular email system does not allow you to filter your email for spam, you can try add-on products that will work with your email system to do the filtering. One popular package is SpamBayes. This is a free package available at http://spambayes.sourceforge.net/ that can be used with your email package to control your spam. What is different about this package is that it "learns" your preferences for email as you identify messages as spam over time. That is, the computer package creates new rules based upon what you say is "good mail" and "bad mail." The created rules may be based on the subject of the email, the format of the email, or the sender. Thus, as those who send the spam send change the account from which it was sent or the spelling of words, or move from text to images, SpamBayes will continue to build rules to keep the spam out of your mailbox.

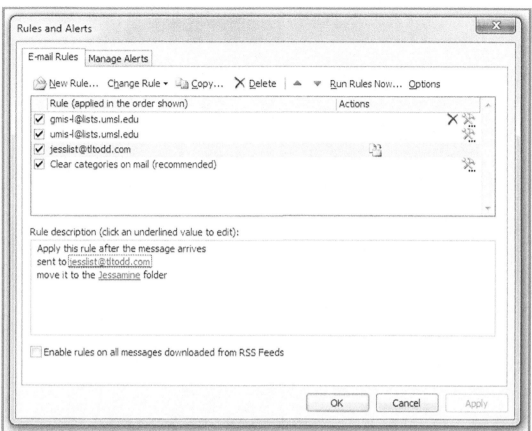

Figure 5.30: Automating Rules for Handling eMails

Blogging and Social Networking

Perhaps you have finally become more confident in your use of the Internet; you are using email and surfing websites. Then you start hearing about "blogs" or seeing references to RSS Feeds. Your child or grandchild might refer to his or her "Facebook page" and you feel like you are still confused. These too are part of the Internet, but you might not have ever run across them. So we will talk about these terms, and a few others briefly so you know what they are and how they might be used.

What are Blogs?

A blog is simply a special web page. The term "blog" is short for web log, and refers to a web page that provides comments on a topic, such as news, politics, travel or food. They generally are presented in reverse chronological order, with the latest entry at the top. Sometimes blogs are nothing more than an online daily chronicling of what is happening in one's life, and other times the blogs many chronicle a civil war.

There are blogs for everything. You can search for cooking blogs, travel blogs, hunting blogs, sports blogs, crafts blogs, news blogs, celebrity blogs, or political blogs. Almost anything you can imagine. There are those people who ask questions hoping for advice from anyone who reads their blogs, those who provide advice. Then there are also those folks who try to make a point. For example, some waiters are blogging about stingy tippers on sites such as WaiterRant.Net.

Whether a blog is of interest to you depends, of course, on whether you are interested in the topic and whether the person is a good, engaging writer. I have a friend who has several blogs on topics of professional interests. They are always useful and clever, but they probably would not be of interest to you at all. However, even though you do not know him, you might be interested in his personal blog that chronicled the year he, his He has wonderful observations and an

> The term "weblog" was coined by Jorn Barger on December 17, 1997 to describe the process of "logging the web" as he surfed. The shortened term "blog" was coined by Peter Merholz, " who jokingly broke the word weblog into the phrase we blog in the sidebar of his blog Peterme.com in 1999.

Figure 6.1: An Example of a Personal Blog

adorable child whom he regularly photographs. An excerpt of his blog is shown in Figure 6.1. In earlier years, this person might have kept a journal of his parenting and of his travels. It would not be as rich because he would not have been able to integrate the photos with the text as easily. It certainly would not have been as easy to share because he would have to duplicate his pages and mail them; many of the wife and young son spent in New Zealand. people who enjoy his blogs probably would not have had access to them.

Another example of a blog can be found with the electronic military paper, *Stars and Stripes*. Consider, for example, Figure 6.2 which shows the ombudsman blog for the paper. You can see that the blog includes entries by the blogger and its readers. This is a common feature of a blog; it provides people the ability to share comments and develop a sense of community around the

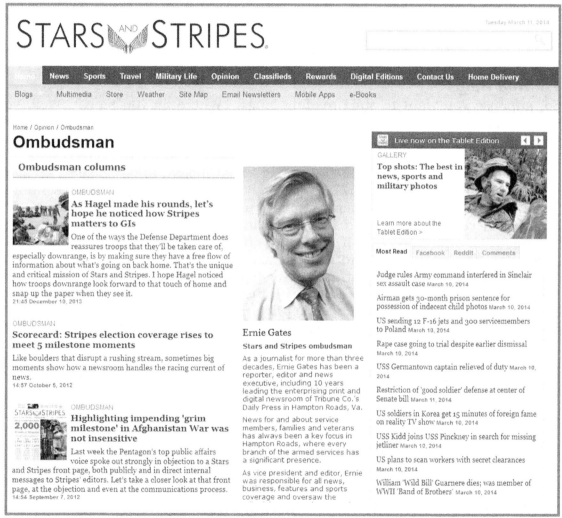

Figure 6.2: Stars and Stripe's Blog

entries. The blog page also provides links to other blogs of interest, and other news of interest; these kinds of links are also common.

Sometimes blogs contain only photographs. After publishing my book, *Street Lights of the World*, I found that I still collected photos of streetlamps, and still wanted to share the photos. So I started the blog at http://streetlightsoftheworld.wordpress.com as shown in Figure 6.3. Unlike my friend's blog discussed earlier, this one simply has photos. Blogging photos is a fun way of sharing photographs without the hassles associated with setting up your own website because blogging sites have already done most of the work for you.

Finding Blogs

So, suppose you want to start reading blogs. Where do you start? Well, you would find blogs the same way you do any web page – either you already know the address (someone has recommended it, or you saw it referenced in an article) or you search for the blogs using your favorite search. Two places that claim to provide the best searches for blogs are Google - blogs (http://blogsearch.google.com/?tab=wb) and Technorati (http://technorati.com/). When searching use specific terms to find blogs. For example, if you are interested in politics in Michigan, use *both* "politics" and "Michigan" as search terms. If, instead, you want to find blogs for politics in a particular city, such as Grand Rapids, use "Grand Rapids" as a search term; don't just scroll through all of the Michigan blogs. In addition, remember safe computing! These blogs are posted by individuals without any screening or editing. You will need to practice skeptical reading of the blogs until you have evidence that the writer is accurate, informative, and/or entertaining.

Navigating Blogs

There are a variety of ways one can navigate a blog. After the image, there are two buttons, "home," which always takes you to the most recent post, and "about." The "about" button takes you to the author's description of the reason for the blog. This generally gives an overview of why the author is blogging and what you should expect to see there. On my blog, I explain how I got started taking photos of streetlights, where people can find my book, and how I see the blog as the continuation of the book.

If you click "home," you will always see the most recent entry in the blog. Scroll down to see other posts. When you get to the bottom, you will see a link to "older posts." In this way you can see everything from last to first.

You can also get to recent posts with the navigation on the right side of the blog. These entries link to the five most recent entries available in the blog. So, maybe you are interested in Pennsylvania. You might click on the third entry, "Danville, Pennsylvania" to see a photo of a streetlight in Danville near the Susquehanna River.

Those are not the only navigation options available. Below the "recent posts" shown above is a list of Archives that is sorted by month (these are not shown in the figure, you must go online to the page to see). So, you can scroll down and click on "August 2013," for example, and see photographs of a streetlight in Ballwin, MO and some from a Hindu Temple in a southwestern suburb of St. Louis. You can always select the "home" button at the top of the page to return

Figure 6.3: A Photography Blog

to the most recent entry.

Below the Archives list is a word cloud of locations as shown in Figure 6.4. A "word cloud" or "tag cloud" is a visual key representing how frequently words are used to describe the content on the blog; the larger the word, the more frequently that tag is used. So, you can see that I have many photos from Missouri, Illinois and Ohio, but not nearly as many from Turkey. When I post my photos, I tag each one with a location that includes the city, the state (if in the United States) and the country in which the streetlight was photographed. In this way, viewers can select to see only photos from Havana, or Milano, or St. Louis as a way of navigating the site.

Figure 6.4: Word Cloud of Locations

Locations

Ballwin Besançon Brentwood Burlington Canada Chicago Cleveland Cuba Europe France Havana Illinois Italy Japan Kentucky Maine Milano Missouri New Hampshire Oak Park Ohio Osaka Port Elizabeth Portsmouth Sapanca St. Louis Turkey U.S.A. Uncategorized Vermont

If you scroll to the bottom of the page, there is another word cloud, shown in Figure 6.5. This cloud provides a visualization of tags of the names of the photographer, and descriptive key terms, such as the type of building or the type of architecture. I am lucky that I have many friends who take photographs of streetlights when they travel and share them with me; it is only right to give them credit for the photo. So, if you only want to see streetlights in the Prairie School of Architecture, or of those near a church, or those taken by Ray Creely, you only need to click on that term. As with the location description above, the larger the word, the more photos you will see.

Allan Friedman architecture art deco arts bank Board of Education Board of Public Works Book bridge Bruch Creek Canada church columbus park convent court house Dave Gellman David Bird design Dick and Virginia Navarro Ekin Pellegrini estate sale Fireworks franklin building Frank Lloyd Wright gas lamps Halifax Harbor Hindu Temple Iron Heritage Festival Jennifer Gosnell Joe Martinich John Cunningham Keith Womer Lake Erie law macaroni grill medieval Melanie Whapham Metzenbaum Mike Martinich-Sauter newport kentucky ohio river park Prairie School Printers Row Randy Kiefer Raphael Hotel Ray and Susanna Creely religion religious building restaurants Rokas Varanavicius seagulls sheridan road St. Gregory the Great St. Louis street lamps Susquehanna River train station Vicki Sauter Voinovich Ward Parkway Welcome

Figure 6.5: Word Cloud of Photographers and Key Terms

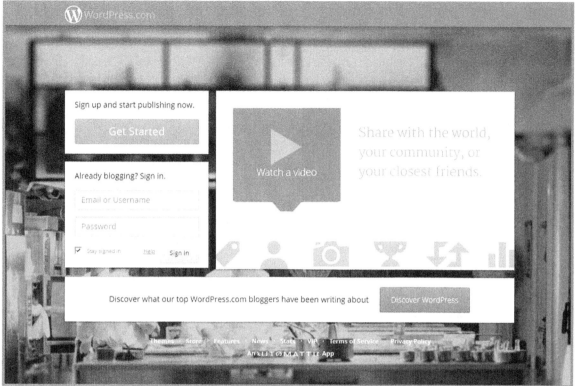

Figure 6.6: WordPress.com Home Page

The nice thing about blogging software is that these navigational tools as well as the layout and background are provided to you. Your only task as a blogger is to provide the content! Consider the blogging site, WordPress.com. If you go to their home page, you will see an option to login or to watch a video that provides an overview of blogging, as shown in Figure 6.6.

When you first log on, you will be at a page helping you to find blogs of interest, either by the name of the author (if you know friends who are blogging) or by topic. These options are shown on the right panel of Figure 6.7. Along the top you will see a menu of "reader," "stats," "my blogs," and "freshly pressed." As you can see the "reader" option helps you to find blogs of interest searching either by subject, tag or author. When you follow specific blogs, they appear on this page so that you can find them easily. The "statistics" option gives you information about how many people have read your blog or clicked on links that you have provided. When you select the "Freshly Pressed" option, you see recently edited posts. For example, when I selected that option, I found the most recent blogs included "Nostalgia in the Land of Boiled 7Up," "The Exxon Spill: 25 Years of Tears," "Rojava, Syria: Fabio Bucciarelli in the Land of the Kurds," "On Animal Play and Game Creation," and "The Irish Chef." Browsing these options is a fun way to find things in which you never thought you had interest, but now see as interesting!

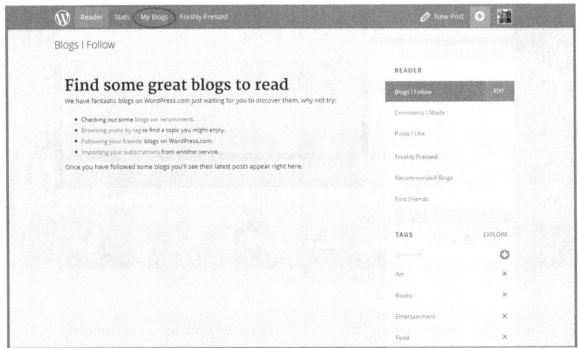

Figure 6.7: Navigation of WordPress

Creating Your Own Blog

But instead of finding interesting blogs, let's return to the circled option, "My Blogs." This gives you access to your own blogs. Figure 6.8 shows my page with both of my blogs. We will look at those shortly, but first let's consider the option of creating a blog. Select "Create Another Blog" as shown in Figure 6.8, and you will see Figure 6.9.

Before your start the blog, you should think about why you are blogging and make your choices accordingly. There are probably as many reasons a person

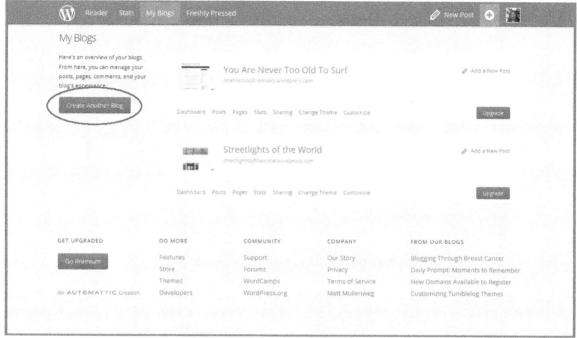

Figure 6.8: Creating a New Blog

blogs as there are bloggers. Most people simply want to express themselves and record their thoughts in a way that is similar to using a diary as a young adult. Others use the blog to document special experiences and share them with others. Even if the events are not unique, some people use blogs simply to keep in touch with friends and family. Alternatively, people blog to share their knowledge or skills with others. This might include providing a repository for information that you think is important, influencing how people think about something, motivating others to action, or perhaps just to entertain people. Of course, one might blog to network with other professionals, meet new people or to make money.

While you can have any title and any address, it is best if these have something to do with the topic on which you are blogging. So, for example, suppose you were interested in blogging about your vacation to the Dalmatian coast of Croatia. You might name the blog "My Time in Dalmatia" (the second box in the figure above) and select a blog address of mytriptodalmatia.wordpress.com (the first box in the figure above). You should not worry too much about it because you can always change your choices later.

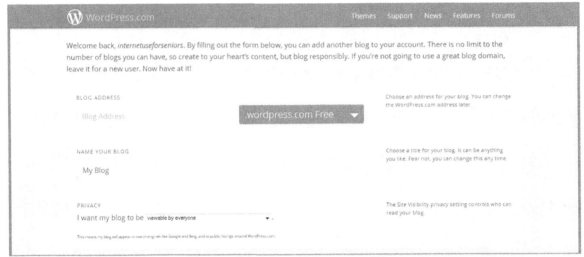

Figure 6.9: Specifying your Blog

As a general rule, blogs are viewable by everyone. But, you can change that so the blog can be viewable by everyone, but not added to search engines (making it harder for people to find your blog if you do not tell them about it), or keeping it private (which allows you to decide who can view the blog).

The next thing to select is the theme for your blog. WordPress has over 250 free or low cost themes you can use for your blog. They all have easily controlled functions and professional looking graphics. You simply need to add your text. You might want a minimalist look like "Spun," a more colorful look like "Matala," a more traditional look such as "Blogum," or a bolder news-focused theme such as "Bold News." These themes can be seen in Figure 6.10; other themes can be seen on the WordPress site.

Before going on, it is important to talk about safe blogging. First of all, if you are blogging about something personal, keep it private, unless you want the world to know about it. For example, you might be using your blog to talk about your wonderful grandchild, and share photos of him or her. That is wonderful, and I am sure you will want your family and friends to know about it. However, you do not want the pedophile in the next neighborhood to know about her, or the kidnapper who is hanging around school to be able to get details that will help him lure your grandchild into a waiting car. Yes, I know that sounds harsh, but you need to remember that letting everyone read your blog, means *everyone*, even unsavory types. My advice is that if you are blogging about a child to mark your blog "private" and only tell people you trust about the site.

Sometimes, however, you want everyone to know about the information in your blog, but you do not want that information associated with your identity. Many people have learned that their independent blog, maintained away from their workplace, can have negative ramifications if they are not careful. Employers

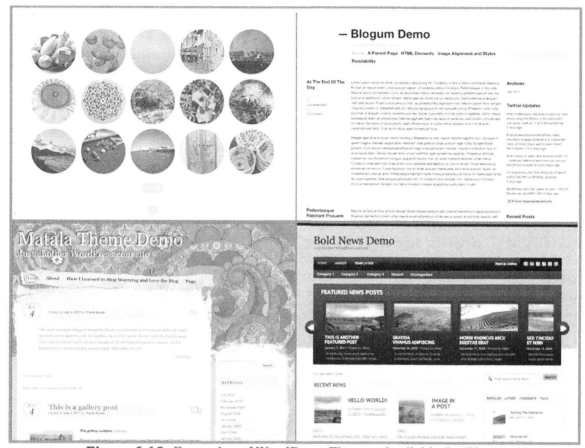

Figure 6.10: Examples of WordPress Themes Available for Blogs

have been known to take action against people who blog negatively about them, and individuals have been known to sue about inappropriate stories on blogs. If you think your blog falls in that category, you can keep it private *and/or* blog anonymously.

Blogging Anonymously

Blogging anonymously is more than just using a nom de plume (although that is critical). When you adopt a new name, you should not adopt anything too close to your real name, your nickname, or anything that might be associated with you. For example, Vic Saut is too close to Vicki Sauter to believe that using that name will keep your identity secret. Second, you must be careful not to share any details of your life. Do not suggest where you work in a way that can give it away. For example, do not say that you work for one of the two private coeducational academies in Ladue (when there are only two such institutions), or make up a name for one of the two. You can instead say you work in a private coeducational academy in the Midwest and maintain your privacy. Further, do not provide any details of the institution that will identify it or some of your coworkers. Keeping these ideas in mind, keeping the blog private or at least not searchable, and perhaps keeping it password protected will help to keep your identity secret.

Updating Your Blog

Once your blog is created, updating it is quite easy. When I get a new streetlight, I need to update my blog. So, I return to WordPress' "MyBlogs" page. As we saw, I can "add a new post" simply by clicking the pencil icon on the far right of the page under "Street Lights of the World." This brings us to the dashboard as shown in Figure 6.11. Notice the template in the middle of the screen; this is where you enter your information about the posting. You enter the name of the blog, which in my case is the city with the new streetlight. My new street

Most states do not have laws protecting bloggers, and so companies can fire you for what you blog. Unfortunately, the First Amendment only protects your freedom of speech from the government, not from your company. However, many states have laws that protect your freedom of speech when you discuss politics, unionization or whistleblowing topics. Unfortunately, today blogs are sufficiently popular that you cannot assume what you say on your blog will not affect your real life.

light comes from Covington, Kentucky, so I enter "Covington, Kentucky U.S.A." where the template says "Enter title here."

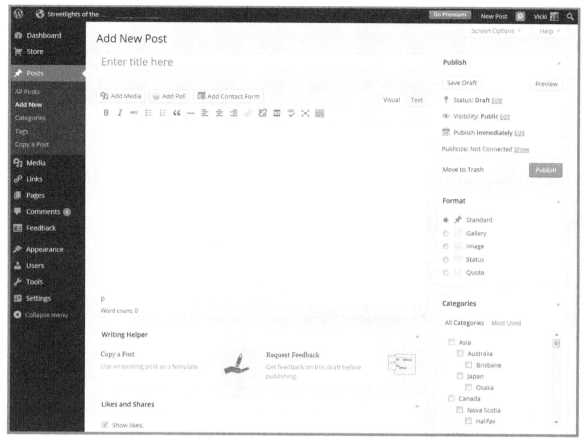

Figure 6.11: Blog Template

The next step is to add the photograph to the page. You can press on the "add media" button to add the photographs from your computer. Selecting this option will bring you to a page that will allow you to select an image already in the library for the blog (probably something you have used before, or to upload an image. If you press the "select files" button, it will allow you to search your computer for the desired photo and add it to the library. Figure 6.12 shows the screen that will appear after you upload a photo (the newly uploaded file has the check in the upper right hand corner). Notice the area circled on the right encourages you to provide documentation for the photograph, including a caption, alternative text and a description. You can also specify the requirements for the photo here. Once the documentation is finished, select "insert into post" on the lower right side and you will now have a post.

This post is not finished, however, because we need to provide categories for the photo so viewers can select it by location or photographer. Notice on the right, bottom of the blog template in Figure 6.11 there are categories which correspond to the location in which the photo was taken. As it turns out, I do not have any photos from Covington Kentucky, so I will need to add that town. I press "add a new category" and type in the box, "Covington." The second box provides the parent category which is the state of Kentucky, so I change

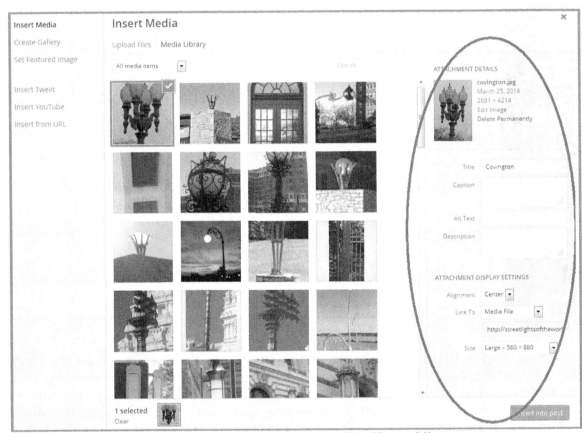

Figure 6.12: Adding Photos to a WordPress Library

the parent to Kentucky. Since Kentucky was originally created under the U.S.A., Covington is automatically related to that parent as well.

The next step is to add the tag for the photo. In this blog, I use tags for two purposes, to demark something about the photo and to identify the photographer. Since I know nothing about the location, I will add the photographer (who has not previously been featured on this page) in the box and press the "add" button.

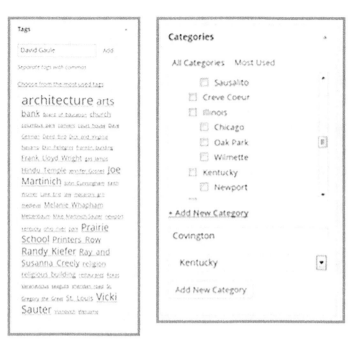

Figure 6.13: Identifying Tags for Blog Entry

Since there are no other functions that I wish to set, I am ready to examine the draft of the page. Notice at the top of Figure 6.11 there is a button labeled "preview". If I press that, I will see how the page will appear, even though it will not be published yet. My preview is shown in Figure 6.14.

Note that the picture appears, and that it is categorized as being from Covington and taken by David Gaule. If all looks acceptable, you return to dashboard and select the blue "publish" button on the right side of the screen. Now the blog is available for everyone to see and you are now a blogger!

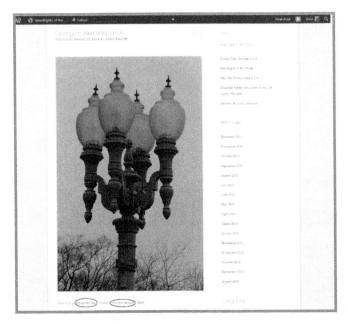

Figure 6.14: The Preview of a Blog

I talked with about a hundred friends to ask what blogs they read regularly. They identified many specific people, communities, teams, etc., and many work-related blogs, but they did identify some general ones that you might enjoy as well they are listed below.

Educated Nation	http://www.educatednation.com/
Extreme Presentation	http://extremepresentation.typepad.com/
Eye of the Tiger	http://grnvlteach.typepad.com/eye_of_the_tyger/
FiveThirtyEight	http://fivethirtyeight.com/contributors/nate-
Scientopia	http://scientopia.org/blogs/
LifeHacker	http://lifehacker.com/
Major League Baseball	http://mlbnewsblog.com/
NY Times Crossword Puzzle	http://rexwordpuzzle.blogspot.com/
Travel	http://www.bbc.com/travel
Uncertain Principles	http://scienceblogs.com/principles/
Wall Street Journal – Law	http://blogs.wsj.com/law/
The White House Blog	http://www.whitehouse.gov/blog/

You can search on blog sites, such as WordPress, and, of course on your general sites such as Google (http://www.google.com/blogsearch). As discussed in previous chapters, you may need to

Remember there is a blog associated with this book, called "You are Never Too Old to Surf." You can read it at http://internetuseforseniors.wordpress.com

experiment with the search terms until you find the specific kind of blog that you want.

Instant Messaging

When I was a child, people wrote letters to others who lived far distances. But, if the people lived next door, you might talk over the fence; or if they lived a few blocks away, you might use the telephone to call them. The formality of written correspondence, and the time lag of letters were not conducive to the kinds of communication you had. Instead, you wanted informality and immediacy in

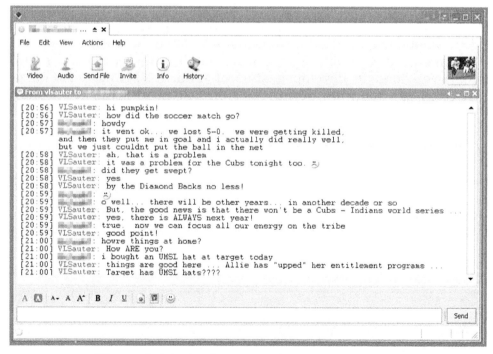

Figure 6.15: An Example of Instant Messaging

your communication. Both the topic of, and the frequency of, communication demanded a different form of communication.

Although email can be *almost* instantaneous if the other person is also at his or her computer, there often are slight lags due to the mechanics of sending the emails. Many people today, want faster, less formal communications over the computer. They use something called "instant messaging" or IM for short. As the name suggests, the IM sends a short message to another person immediately. If the person responds when the message is received, then the communication resembles a conversation.

So, what *is* Instant Messaging? Figure 6.15 shows an IM session between me and my son. As you can see, this IM session is totally text and fairly informal. Each party (in this case there were only two of us) can type in the bottom section and send messages to the other. However, if one party types faster than the other, thoughts get interwoven and there may be multiple "discussions" happening at the same time. It is literally a real-time conversation that people type.

With IM, conversations tend to be informal. Spelling and grammar often are not observed. Emoticons and abbreviations are often substituted in the text, making it somewhat confusing for the uninitiated. Since the conversations are so informal, you tend to develop a style of talking. People who IM together frequently often can tell from deviations from a typical style when one's mood changes.[1]

Most IM programs allow graphics, video and audio sessions in addition to the text, if you have a web camera, microphone and speaker attached to your computer. When those are used, the user sees pictures and hears sounds from the other user. An example of this is shown in Figure 6.16. Some friends were determined not to let their young granddaughter, Kailyn, forget them when she moved. So, they use IM to read a story to Kailyn and share stories of the day.

---

[1] This observation was made by my cousin, Wayne Sauter, when we were conversing using IM when I was working on this chapter. He noted that I did not sound like myself. I replied that I was writing and that I was focused. After that exchange we discussed how moods were shared by how one replied on IM.

Figure 6.16: Instant Messaging Using a Web Camera

The image shows four shots. In the first pane, you see Grandma and Grandpa reading a book. Kailyn not only hears them reading, she can see them reading when she looks at her monitor. When Grandma and Grandpa look at their monitor, they see Kailyn, including her activity and facial expressions, as shown in the second pane. Later, their son, Mark, and Kailyn talk about the day's events, and Grandma and Grandpa can both see and hear the discussion (as shown in the third pane). Of course, when their granddaughter looks at the monitor, she sees her grandparents smiling. While it may not be as good as hugging, everyone keeps engaged.

Some programs allow people to play games, such as chess or backgammon over the internet. Further, they allow multiple people to join in the same conversation, if they are all approved by the originators.

According to the Pew Internet and American Life Project, 40% of all adult users of the Internet, or 53 million adults, use instant messaging regularly. In fact, almost a quarter of these users of IM use it more frequently than email, and about 20% of them use it regularly at work. As you might expect, though, IM is primarily a tool of younger generations. The Pew report stated that only 15% of those 50-59, 10% of those 60-68 and 9% of those over 68 used IM.

As I have described earlier in this book, I surveyed a group of 100 people about their instant messaging behavior. Of them only twelve were IM users. The first person never initiated the conversation, but used it to "talk" with people in different time zones. The second person, who is not generally a leading edge technologist, used IM to be able to send text messages to her daughter's Blackberry; this use was particularly convenient because her daughter is hearing-impaired. Some of the others used IM to communicate with people at work. Many people began to use IM tools to speak with their children who were away at college. If this is your goal, it is important to know that IM use is decreasing among college age students. Technologies are changing and if we want to be able to communicate with younger generations, we will need to change the technology we are willing to use.

Since, I use IM to keep in contact with a variety of people, I like to have a tool that is flexible and will handle multiple accounts. So, I use a tool called Trillian which manages IM accounts from a variety of providers. As with many such tools, Trillian is available in a basic version, which is available for free download (from http://www.trillian.com), and an enhanced version for which the company charges. This will allow you to manage communications if you have multiple children or grandchildren and they select different providers!

RSS Feeds

RSS stands for "Really Simple Syndication" and is simply an online system that sends notifications to your computer that the content on a web page has changed. Obviously, these notifications only need to be sent out if a web page changes frequently, and so they tend to be associated with news sites or blogs. So, rather than you needing to check a page frequently to determine if something has changed, you can subscribe to the RSS and you will receive notification when it has changed.

The notification from these sites is sent to an "aggregator" that is associated with your web browser. In this way, the notice is fairly passive and does not interrupt your normal activities, but you can track changes easily.

In order to begin receiving these notifications, you must subscribe to the RSS news feeds. If a page supports RSS feeds, there will be an RSS symbol on the page, such as that shown circled in Figure 6.17 which appears on the website of "Morning Edition" (an NPR broadcasted show).

Figure 6.17: Notice that an RSS Feed is Available

If you click on that link, it will take you to a page offering the option of subscription through only one service, such as in Figure 6.18.

Figure 6.18: Sign up to RSS Feeds

Generally, you will want to subscribe using Live Bookmarks (as shown above) since this sends it to your browser anytime, and not just when you are logged using the browser. However, some people would like to receive their feeds through other services such as their Yahoo! or Outlook pages.

Once you have subscribed, you will have a new item at the top of your tool bar as shown circled in Figure 6.19. Your web browser is your "aggregator" for that site. If you click on orange symbol next the name of the site, you will get a list of articles that have been saved to it. Whenever you are ready to do so, you can read one or more of the articles.

If you move your mouse over any of those stories and click on it, your browser will be redirected to the story. In this way, you can keep track of what has changed on the original page without needing to check it frequently, and read only those stories that are of interest to you.

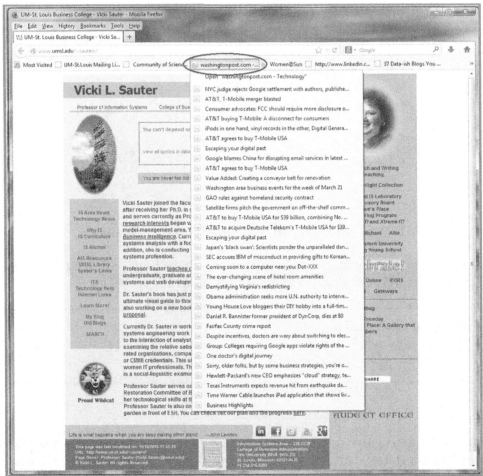

Figure 6.19: Using the Aggregator in your Browser

Social Networking Sites and Microblogging

You might have heard the terms Facebook, LinkedIn, Twitter, InstaGram, Tumblr, or several others and wondered what they meant. They are all part of the Internet, and are really "just webpages." However, they serve a specific purpose – they are "social networking sites." A social networking site is one that allows you to describe – or perhaps invent – yourself and to make connections with other people. The tool is a way to connect with your real-life friends and associates *and* to make other friends and associates and connect with them as well. It is, from a web perspective, what we all do in real life. The basic program allows you to describe yourself and to "declare" as friends or colleagues (depending on the application) other people who have also created pages. Obviously this means that you can search for people you know already have created pages, and you can invite those you know who have not created pages to join the network.

These sites can also be described as microblogging sites because they allow you to share your thoughts, concerns and more, just like the blogging sites. However, they allow you much less room than the blogging sites. In fact, Twitter allows you only 140 characters to share your thoughts!

Each social networking site allows you to describe yourself, express views, write notes to others, share capabilities, state your qualifications, You have some control over what you put on the site and how it is arranged to reflect your interests and personality (within certain constraints). You can create and join organizations in all of the social networking sites, and you have unlimited access to people within your "network." Depending upon the kind of site, you can express views; share photos, videos and favorites; describe your qualifications; pose questions; and play games. You can advertise events, and check whether people are signed onto their computers. You can also create new organizations, and meet people with similar interests. Or, you can search your network and find people you think might be interesting to know and invite them to be your virtual friend. Finally, you can ask people you know to "introduce" you to others whom you would like to meet.

The social networking sites are different and work differently, though, and so we will review each of them.

Facebook

Facebook is the most popular of the social networking sites, with (as of January, 2014) over 1.23 billion *active* users across the world who used the site at least

Facebook began as an application only for college students. The concept was created by a Harvard alumnus who wanted to replicate the paper "facebooks" used by some universities with incoming classes to help students get acquainted with one another. Originally only available to college students, it allowed new students to virtually learn about their new university and meet people also going to their university (and therefore available in their "network"). In 2005, the site was opened to high schools, again with each high school being defined as a network; students could automatically see anyone in his or her high school, but needed to be invited to see anyone else on Facebook. In 2007, Facebook opened membership to anyone with an email address.

once per month. While the greatest number of users is in the United States, they represent less than 20% of the total users; other large groups of Facebook users can be found in Brazil, India, Indonesia and Mexico.

Although Facebook was introduced as a tool for college students to learn about fellow students, once it became available for anyone with an email address, it quickly grew as a communications forum for adults. In fact, many high school and college students have curtailed their usage because parents and grandparents are too likely to see their posts, and so the forum is no longer as "cool" as it once was.

Facebook is much like a party. Its goal is to provide a forum for sharing things of interest in your life with your friends. If at the party, all of your friends discuss politics, especially if they do not agree, you will not have a successful party. The same is true of Facebook. You need to have a variety of people with interests similar to yours posting messages. You may be patient with friends who share photos of food and wine they order at restaurants, or quizzes they have taken, if they also post items that peak your interest. So, when you are deciding whom to have as friends on Facebook, you need to plan it much as you would a cocktail party: who has what interests and how do those interests complement your interests. Facebook can be a total waste of time or it can be an informative and fun experience. The difference is the friends you select. Only you can decide what group of friends you want and how you spend that time.

I began to use Facebook when I first thought about this book (about 2005), and my son was in college. I thought to include it then because it might be a way for parents and grandparents to interact with the younger generations. I thought it would be fun to watch my son's development through college. My son is now through college and law school, and we are still Facebook friends.

However, if asked, I would tell parents of college age or older students to be cautious about how you proceed. First, you cannot just look at the page unobtrusively; your child or grandchild must grant you permission. Although my son has granted me "friend" status, in college he strongly objected to my "friending" (or attaching to) his friends and associates. Further, most of his friends are amazed that he would give me access. This suggests most children and grandchildren would not grant such access. Second, and more important, much of what happens on a Facebook page does not make sense out of context. While I can read what he has been doing and the interactions he has with others, the posts are subject to *much* misinterpretation. They make comments based on what is happening in their lives. So posts may have something to do with music, television or a class they shared. Since you don't have that experience, often you will misinterpret their comments, especially if it is a sarcastic comment about the event. If you do read their comments, you undoubtedly will be tempted to guide them about what is, or is not, appropriate to put on their page. I recommend that you do because kids tend to forget how they can be tarnished by something they post. However, the cardinal rule is **never guide them about their behavior on their Facebook page**. Talk with them on the phone, drop them an email or use the "message" option in Facebook. Otherwise you run the risk they will drop you from their friends list and you won't see anything.

Some people spend a significant amount of time sharing their thoughts and activities on Facebook. Today there are many applications that can help someone share anything from their photos to their writings to mapping where they have been and want to visit in the world. Some people, of course, can take this to an extreme and use this as a way of building monuments to themselves: "The Pharaohs built statues. Caesar put his visage on coins. We use Facebook and MySpace."[2] So, what is the problem with that? In her article, Ms. Rosen cites a researcher, Rob Nyland, who found that heavy users of these sites actually are less involved with their communities and *actual* social networking. These heavy users, who are primarily high school and college students, become more withdrawn from human interaction, and that rarely is a good result.

In addition, the users get so involved with documenting their lives, they forget that once they post something on the Internet, it is *permanent*. Even when someone "removes" information from a site does not mean it is gone from the Internet. Sites get backed up, copied and downloaded, and people lose their control over the information. Now at a distance, most of us are glad that our late teens and early twenties are not highly documented for the world to see; these young users have not yet come to that realization. College personnel monitor these sites and can learn when students break college rules, scholarship obligations or team requirements. Job recruiters check the sites to obtain more information about prospective employees. Students suffer the consequences. Worse yet, there are a number of predators of various kinds who survey the pages looking for victims, and the students suffer the

---

[2] Rosen, Christine, "What are Facebook friends for? The Pharaohs built statues. Caesar put his visage on coins. We use Facebook and MySpace," *Christian Science Monitor*, October 10, 2007.

consequences there as well.

Why Use Facebook?

The first step in using Facebook is to decide why you are using it. I try to keep contact with students and alumni to keep them engaged, involved, and connected to each other. I also use Facebook to keep in contact with some of my colleagues. I get great insights into what they are reading and some of their research via their Facebook posts. But, I also use Facebook to connect with family and friends who are scattered across the globe. In fact, I use Facebook as a way of searching for old friends with whom I have lost touch. As my elementary class planned for its reunion, we created an organization for our class and searched for our classmates in hopes we could attract more people. Informal associations of professionals have also created groups so people can interact better. These kinds of applications might be more useful for the average reader of this book.

Using Facebook

You start Facebook by, of course, creating a Facebook account at http://www.facebook.com. Once you press the green button that says signup, you will be faced with a page such as that shown in Figure 6.20.

Figure 6.20: Signing up for Facebook http://facebook.com

Once you have signed up, Facebook begins to try to help you find friends by asking you to share your contacts from other sources as shown in Figure 6.21. I recommend you do not do this, but rather find your friends on your own. As we will discuss later, it is not good to have accounts tied together, and you may not want to be friends with everyone who is on your contacts list. So, simply click on "skip this step," which is circled in the figure.

Step 2, shown in Figure 6.22, asks you to begin to share information about yourself. There are several ways you can address this request for information. First, you can simply ignore the request and press "skip" as circled in the figure. Or, you can put in some or all of the information requested. If you do provide the information, you can select who can see the information. For example, I entered my hometown of Chicago, Illinois. Next to that box (and also the other three) is a drop down box as highlighted with an arrow in that

Figure 6.21: Step 1 of Facebook Signup

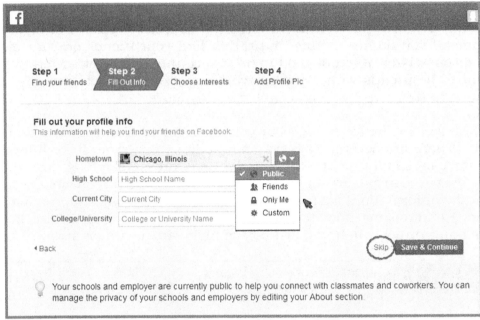

Figure 6.22: Step 2 of Facebook Signup

figure. You can select that anyone can see the information (public), that only your friends (people whom you have friended on Facebook) can see it, that only you (and Facebook, of course) can see it, or that you have custom settings. These settings allow you to share it with "friends of friends," meaning there must be some connection between you, but not necessarily someone you know, or only with specific friends whom you list. Alternatively, you can specify that you don't want to share it with specific people. These options are shown to the right.

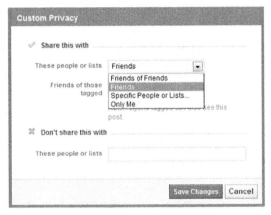

In Step 3, you can select interests, such as movie stars, musicians and bands and more. If you select these interests, Facebook will attach your page to the page associated with that interest, and you will get information from it. I recommend you skip this stage at this time. You can always search for pages associated with interests later. Finally, in Step 4, it asks you to upload a photo or take one with a webcam (if you have one attached to your computer. Whatever photo you put up there is public, so everyone who can see your page sees the photo. However, there is a wide range of items that show up as Facebook photos. Some people use a photo of their pet, a child or grandchild, or a recent vacation venue. Others select photos of books they enjoy, a still from a recent movie or even a bouquet of flowers. So, you can put your photo there so people can be sure you are you, or provide a photo of something else.

Figure 6.23 shows how you upload a photo. First select the option of uploading by pressing the button that is circled. The system will automatically bring up access to your files and you can navigate to the one you wish to select. The system will then substitute the photo you have selected for the outline of a person that was there previously. If you are happy with the photo and with the settings you have selected, then press "Save and Continue." This will take you to the introductory Facebook page that allows you to search for friends, learn about your privacy settings, and of course, update your profile (if you did not already do so in the previous step).

Let us begin talking about Facebook by looking at my "home page" shown in Figure 6.24. This is the page that I see when I start Facebook. The page is broken into three parts. The middle section is referred to as the "feed" or the

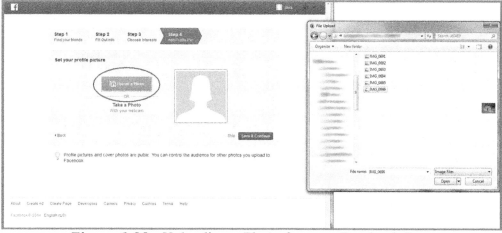

Figure 6.23: Uploading a Photo for your Facebook Page

Figure 6.24: Basic Facebook Page

"wall." So if someone says they are posting something to your Facebook Wall, this is where it will appear. In fact, when people whom you have friended post something on your page, it will appear in this section. At the top of the page, circled, is where you post. Simply begin typing where it says "What's on your mind" and hit "post" when you are finished. So, if you type "Hello World" as shown to the right, it will appear on your feed and the feeds of all of your friends as the second image. In fact, whatever you said there, or whatever photos you included will be posted on all of your friend's pages.

Notice that my feed shows a post from my cousin who is active in her local historical society showing an activity from the previous evening's events. Some posts contain photos (like this one) or videos. But they always include a short post where the individual states whatever is on his or her mind. It is because of this short "blog" section that Facebook and other social networking sites are often called microblogging sites. In addition to the message, you see the message includes how long ago it was posted (40 minutes), so you know how current the message is. As you scroll down the message, you have less timely messages posted.

At the end of the message, there are three options, labeled "like," "comment," and "share;" they are noted in Figure 6.23 with the arrow. You are not obliged to respond in any way to a posting. If you want to provide positive feedback about the posting, but have nothing to add to it, you can just click "like." You can see the note that 96 people have looked at Cindy's post and clicked that they liked it. If you want to post a message about the post, you click "comment," and you can place a short comment about the post under the post. You can see that five other people have posted comments and yours would be the sixth. When you post it, the original poster and each of the five people who commented on it will get a notice that something has changed. Further, everyone who goes to Cindy's page will be able to see your comment.

The third option is that you can share the post on your Facebook page, and thus all of your friends can see what has been posted. To do this you click "share" and you will have the ability to repost the original message with your comment (but not with the comments that were made on the original post) for your friends to see.

The left section of the page is for navigation. At the top are the photo you uploaded earlier and your name. You can select your news feed (which is the default position when you begin Facebook), to view your messages, or to see what events are happening that week. We will come back to this.

Figure 6.25: A "Page" in Facebook

Under that section there are two options, "pages" and "groups." Facebook pages are sometimes called "fan pages," because they were created for an artist, band, or form of entertainment. Later pages were created for causes or community efforts, brands, products, local businesses and even companies or institutions. One of the pages I follow is shown in Figure 6.25.

This page was created by and is managed by an organization in St. Louis called Craft Alliance Center of Art and Design (formerly Craft Alliance). The organization provides classes for people to learn, studios where people can practice, galleries where people can exhibit their work, and a store where they can sell their art and design. So, the page lists current classes and outreach, information about exhibits, and of course, what is featured in the store. You can go and see what is featured at the site whenever you are interested. Or, you can "like" the page by pressing the circled button and then when they post information it will automatically appear on your wall to view. You can "like" as many pages as you wish and follow all of your favorites.

Groups work much the same as do pages, except they are created to allow collaboration among people who share some common interest, such as clubs, or just people with a certain interest. They can be created by individual users, and then members can post content, such as links, media, questions, events, documents and comments. Groups can be "open" and all of their information is available for reading by anyone; however, one must be a member to post items to the group. Or, groups can be "closed" which means others can see the group and its list of members, but the content of the group is closed. Finally, groups can be "secret" so that the public cannot even see the existence of the group, much less the content. As mentioned earlier, we created a group to find former classmates of my elementary school. I also belong to a group concerned about the ecology of a nearby river. Another group is for a particular programming product, and still another is for a summer camp I run.

Under "pages" and "groups" you have access to applications that run through Facebook. The most popular kind of application is Games. There are hundreds of free games including action, adventure, arcade, card and casino, puzzle, racing, shooting, and trivia games. Some of them you play alone, but many allow you to play with others. If you find one you like, you can issue requests to play to others. The request will appear in the person's feed and can be accessed under games.

All of these applications are written by third-parties and, according to Facebook, "enhance your experience on Facebook." That means that the information you provide to the application or game is stored on the servers of the group who created the game. Facebook does not have access to those data. Before you begin a game, you should learn as much about the application as you can. If you click on the game, you should see a description of the application, the kinds of information you will be asked to share, ratings of the application and which of your friends play the game.

On the right hand side of the screen there are four categories of information available. At the top (or over to the side, depending on the size of your screen) is what Facebook calls "The Ticker;" it is a list of your friends and their activity

---

An Example of Facebook Use

Andrea will spend next semester studying at a university in Budapest, and—so she can make the most of her time in Hungary —she wants to learn as much as possible before she leaves. For a couple of semesters, Andrea has had a profile on Facebook but hasn't posted much information about herself and doesn't use the site frequently. Because she attends a relatively small college without extensive resources for study-abroad students, she decides to find out what she can learn from other Facebook users.

Andrea starts by updating her profile to include information about her upcoming semester in Budapest and her major. She joins several Facebook groups related to studies abroad and international student exchange programs. Through these groups, Andrea finds students at her own college who have studied abroad—even some she knows but who never told her they had studied overseas—and many more from around the country. Contacting members of these groups gives Andrea insights into aspects of studying abroad that she otherwise would not have gained until she got there. She searches for users with "Budapest" or "Hungary" in their profiles and finds dozens of students from that part of the world or who have traveled there. From their perspectives, Andrea learns about the current and past political climate of former Soviet Bloc nations. This, in turn, leads Andrea to other Facebook searches focused on European politics and culture generally.

As the weeks progress, Andrea's Facebook profile becomes increasingly detailed. She creates several new online groups, one of which quickly has more than 200 members. Other Facebook users regularly contact Andrea, sometimes with questions, sometimes with answers to questions. By the time she leaves for Budapest, she has a good understanding of what to expect in terms of the study-abroad program and of local culture, restaurants, and weather. She has also met online several students from other universities who will be studying in Hungary next semester and whom she will meet for lunch in Budapest her first week there.

---

in real time. You will see a small icon with a photo of your contact and his or her name. You will typically see that the person "likes" someone else's comment, or commented on someone else's link. But it can list status and friendship updates, photos and videos, application activity and comments. In this way, you are privy to the discussions that your friends have with other friends. By hovering over the story, you can join in the conversation or listen to people's music. In Figure 6.24, you can see that one friend commented on hunter-jumper horses, and that another commented on his own photo.

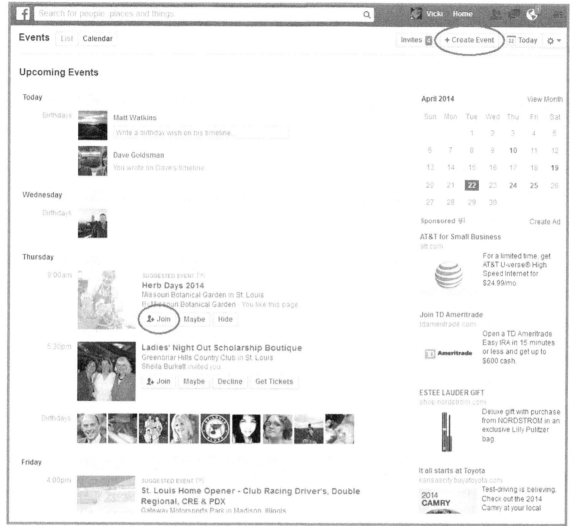

Figure 6.26: Facebook's Events Page

The second kind of information is "trending" information. Trending shows popular topics that are being discussed on Facebook around the world. Referring back to Figure 6.24, you can see on the day I took the image that there was much discussion about (a) Ford recalling vehicles because of steering and seat back issues, (b) the new Battlestar Galactica movie, and (c) Ben &

Jerry's free cone day. If you click on something that is trending, you can go to a page where discussions about that topic are aggregated . In that way you can join in the popular discussion.

Another thing you can do on this page is to create your own event. Start by pressing the "Create Event" button at the top, right corner of the page (it is circled). You will get a popup such as the one to the right that allows you to create invitations to the party. You can give it a name, provide details, and of course, provide the location and time. There are two parts of the form I need to highlight. First, as you look at the bottom, the default option is to allow guests to invite other guests. This is a great option when your event is to sponsor an event at which you want to create a huge crowd. Alternatively, you can select

specific individuals to invite. You can select from the general public, friends of guests, and finally just those people whom you would like to invite. If you are trying for a small, manageable party, you need to control your invitations by inviting only specific people.

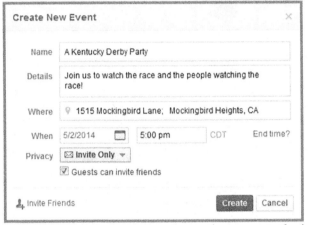

The final kind of information you can expect to see in the third column of your Facebook page is advertisements. Facebook allows advertisers to target specific ages, locations and interests when they post their advertisements.

Now notice the top of the page, defined by the blue stripe. From the left, the first thing you see is a text box with the instructions "search for people, places, and things." This is the "Search Box." You can use this box to find friends and organizations to which you want to affiliate. As you type the name, Facebook will begin to look for people with that name (or whose name begins with the letters you have selected. When you find the name of the person in whom you are interested, simply hit Enter and you will go to that person's page. If you would like to become friends with that person, you simply click the "friend" button.

Becoming someone's friend takes both of you to agree about it. So, when you clicked the "friend" button, you indicated your interest. The person then receives a message of your request. To work through this, suppose instead that someone has requested to friend you. Return to Figure 6.24 and notice the three highlighted icons (shown in white) toward the right. These highlighted icons tell you that Facebook has something to share with you. The first icon of the two people with the number 1 indicates that someone has asked to friend you. If you click on the icon, you will see the person who made the request, and two buttons which allow you to accept the friend or ignore the request.

The last icon, of a globe, indicates that someone has commented on your post. In Figure 6.23, you will see the number 2 adjacent to the icon. This means that two people have either "liked" your post or commented on it. When you click on the globe, it will tell you who has done this and on what post. You can click on the entry and Facebook will take you to the original post.

The middle icon is of a "word bubble," and the fact that it is highlighted means that one of your friends wants to "message" you. A "message" is a private, text-based discussion between you and a friend. These messages do not appear on your feed, and others cannot join them. You may have your chat feature turned off (I do most of the time), but Facebook still saves an attempt to chat. Click on the icon and you will see all the recent messages sent through chat. You can click on the most recent one, see the full message, and reply to it if you wish.

If you wish to start a chat with someone else, or at least send that person a private message, click on the words in the top right "Send a New Message." You can then type the person's name, hit return and begin typing your message. It will be available to the person, and only that person, the next time he or she logs in. You can send a message with just text, or you can incorporate photos and video, or add attachments.

The most important thing to know about Facebook, however, is about security and privacy settings. Return to Figure 6.24 and notice the icon of a "lock" to the far right that is not highlighted. When you click on it, it becomes highlighted in white and a drop down box appears. Click on the bottom of this drop down box, "See More Settings." The default is to go to your privacy settings and tools, as shown in Figure 6.27 below.

Facebook also allows you to create "events" and invite your friends to them. Generally you will find announcements of some kind on right side of your screen below the ticker. If you click on the "birthdays" or "events" logos and select "see all," Facebook will take you to an announcements page. Here you get announcements about friend's birthdays, activities that are happening that week and events to which you have been invited. Birthdays are part of the registration for Facebook which people can elect to share or not; if they share them, you will get a notice on their birthday. Anyone can create an event. On the right size of the screen (under "edit profile"), you can click on "Events" and you will see a screen such as Figure 6.26.

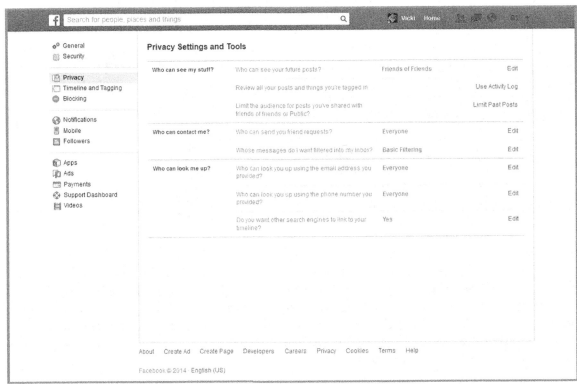

Figure 6.27: Facebook's Privacy Settings

Notice my events page already has things on it. Under "Today" it notes two people have birthdays. I could write a greeting in the box under the first person's name and it will post that greeting on my friend's wall. When I do, it will look like the second person under "Birthdays."

Under "Thursday" of that week, I see that the Missouri Botanical Gardens (a Page which I have "liked") has invited me to an event called "Herb Days," their annual sale of herbs of all kinds. If I want to accept this invitation, I would simply click on the join button that has been circled in the image. Once I do, this announcement will appear on my home page.

As a general rule, it is important to lock down your privacy settings tightly so you control what happens to the content that you post. You will see that mine are more open than I will recommend because I want my posts to be reposted. But if you are posting photos of your wonderful grandchild, talking about an upcoming trip, or are describing your spouse's recent rehab experiences, you might want to keep that just among people whom *you* know. The first, and most important option is "Who can see my stuff?" You will see that my privacy setting says "friends of friends." That means people can easily share posts that I provide with their friends, most of whom I probably do not know. If you click on "Edit" at the right, you will see that your options are public, friends of friends, friends, only me, and custom. If you select Public, that means *anyone* can see your post, whether they are your friend or not. I strongly recommend against using that option, especially for sensitive posts. You do not know who that will be or why he or she is interested in your post. You can limit the option by selecting "Friends." Under this condition, only people whom you have accepted as a friend can see what you posted. If someone attempts to share your postings on his or her wall, they will not be allowed to. The last option is "Custom." This allows the post to be shared with only a select group of people whom you specify. You can develop a list, such as "family" to which you send photos of children, or "close friends" with whom you share personal details.

You can also rewrite history when you "review all of your posts and things you're tagged in." If you click "Use Activity Log," you will view all things that you have posted, commented upon, liked or shared. To the right of each comment is a pencil, which if clicked, allows you to drop that item from your timeline. People will not be able to see that you ever selected that. If you do nothing, the comment, share, post or photo will continue to be viewed on your page. The final setting in this group is to limit the audience of your old posts. If you originally shared something as "public" or "friends of friends," selecting this option will change who can see the old posts; if selected, then only friends will be able to see the option.

A second kind of privacy option is who can contact you in what ways. The first option is who can send friend requests. Some people want to control this because they do not want to respond to peoples' requests. My recommendation is to leave it open to everyone; you can always ignore the request. You can also control the filtering of messages. The "Basic Filtering," which Facebook recommends, allows messages primarily from friends, but also some "people you may know." These people you "may know" might be friends of one or more of your Facebook friends or they may be organizations or companies that advertise to you. If selected, Facebook posts advertising in your feed if they believe it is something in which you might have interest. The other option is "Strict Filtering," which Facebook describes as "mostly see messages from friends ... messages from people you want to hear from may go to your Other folder." Since it has never been clear to me what the "other" folder is, I keep using the basic filtering. You will notice after using Facebook for a while that they have a strange algorithm for deciding what to show you anyway; you do not seem to have control over it, and the algorithm seems to change over time.

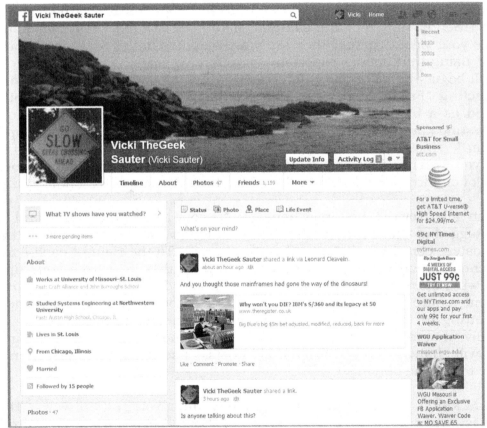

Figure 6.28: Facebook Timeline

The third kind of privacy addresses who can even see that you have a profile. The first two options, include whether people can search for you with the email address you provided and/or the telephone number you provided. Your options are everyone, friends, or friends of friends. Since I encourage people to link to my Facebook page, I have left that option as open as possible. If you would rather the world not know you have a Facebook page, you might want to limit your accessibility through only friends or friends of friends. While I keep my email address available to anyone, I do hide my telephone number and address information; I recommend you keep these things hidden as well. You can also turn off search engines' access to your page. This option really gives you the option of being found by the search engines quickly or slowly (not at all is not an option). Again, you should select the option according to how comfortable you are in being found by people who may have been out of your life for some time.

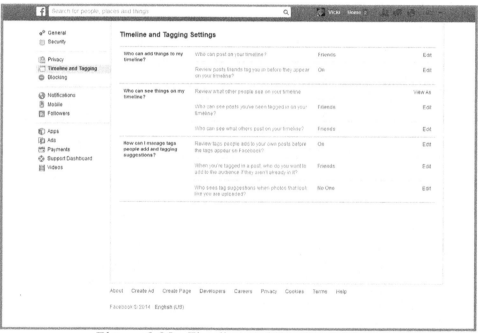

Figure 6.29: Timeline and Tagging Settings

Another way of thinking about privacy has to do with who can share what with you. To begin this discussion, we need to talk about your "timeline." The timeline is what others see when they view your information on Facebook. My timeline is shown in Figure 6.27. You can get to your timeline by clicking on your name at the top of the page (right next to "home").

The timeline shows information about you, provides access to your photos and friends list and all the items that you post or that others share with you. So, a friend could make a comment or post an article on your timeline that he or she thought you would be interested in reading. Not only can you see what your friend wrote, but everyone who comes to your page can see what he or she wrote. However you can control whether people have the right to do that by controlling your "Timeline and Tagging" settings as shown in Figure 6.28. Go to the top of the page again, and select the final icon, the downward faced arrow. Then select the "timeline and tagging" option from the menu at the left of the page and you will see a page such as the one in Figure 6.29.

The first option in Figure 6.29 allows you to give the right to your friends to post on your timeline. The alternative is to allow no one but yourself to post on your timeline; there is no option for opening that further.

Figure 6.30: A Tagged Image in Facebook

Another way people can share information with you is to "tag" you in a photo associated with a posting. Tagging is a way of identifying a person in a photograph. When you look at a photograph in Facebook, you can move the mouse around the photo. If a photo is tagged, then the person's name will appear on the photo, as shown in Figure 6.30.

If you are tagged in a photo, then the photo and anything posted along with it will appear on your timeline. The second privacy option shown in Figure 6.30 allows you to review those posts before they appear on your timeline if the option is enabled. Since everyone who can see your page sees those posts, it is recommended that you enable that option.

As an aside, let us talk about how to tag someone in a photo. If you go to your photos, open one and it will appear like the image on the left side of Figure 6.31. At the bottom of the photo, in the black region, there are some options. The first is to tag the photo (it is circled). Once you select that option, a small square will appear on your photo, as shown in the right photo. If you move it over the person you want to identify and then click, you get a list of people with whom you are (Facebook) friends. Scroll down to select the person in the photo. When you are finished, select "Done Tagging" with your mouse (this is circled in the photo to the right. Thereafter, anyone who can see the photo will see who is included in the photograph.

Figure 6.31: Tagging a photograph

Returning to the timeline and tagging settings, and Figure 6.29, the next option is who can see things that are posted on your timeline. You can control who can see posts in which you have been tagged as well as what others have posted about you. For each of these, you can allow everyone (whether or not they are your friend), friends of friends, just friends, only you or a list of people to see what is available there. So, to protect your privacy, you can either control who can write on your timeline and tag photos, or you can control who can see them, or, of course, both.

The third category of settings in Figure 6.29 address how you want to manage tags. The first category of settings controls what happens to your friends' posts when they tag you. Specifically, it controls whether or not you must approve tagging done by other people in *your own posts*. Suppose you post a photo such as the one in Figure 6.30, but you do not tag the individuals. A friend could tag them. If the friend tags photos, and if you enable this first option, then *you* must approve that tag before others can see it. This is recommended.

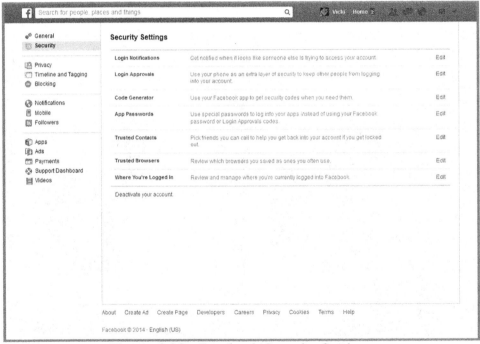

Figure 6.32: Facebook Security Settings

The next setting controls who can see posts in which you are tagged by someone else. Remember, if someone else posts a photo of you, it is *his or her privacy settings* that control who may see it. If you want to share, you can do so by allowing all friends or a custom list of people to view it automatically. Alternatively, you can set it to only you so that your friends cannot see these other posts.

The last setting on the page controls automatic tagging of photos. Facebook has a photo recognition system that scans all photos that are uploaded and attempts to identify people in photos before they have been tagged. According to Facebook, this "saves time... especially when labeling many photos from one event." Further, Facebook argues that "suggestions can be ignored and no one will be tagged automatically." Personally, I set my option to "no one" because I do not want people misidentified, especially not myself.

Those are the privacy settings, but there are also security settings. Return to the last icon at the top of the page (the downward arrow), and select "settings." Then, select the second option, "security," as shown in Figure 6.32. These are settings to help ensure others do not use your account.

The first option provides you an alert if Facebook perceives that someone else is trying to break into your account. This might be because you are logged into a machine you do not regularly use and/or there have been a large number of attempts to login with the wrong password. If Facebook perceives there is a problem, you can opt to receive an email with the information, such as the one above. It is a painless system, and one that could help you protect your account, and perhaps your identity.

facebook

Hi Vicki,

We detected a login into your account from an unrecognized device on Monday, April 28, 2014 at 5:52pm.

Operating System: Windows 7
Browser: Firefox
Location: St Louis, MO, US (IP=134.124.127.7)

Note: Location is based on internet service provider information.

If this was you, please disregard this email.
If this wasn't you, please secure your account, as someone else may be accessing it.

Thanks,
The Facebook Security Team

Please note: Facebook will never request your login information through email.

This message was sent to vicki.sauter@umsl.edu at your request.
Facebook, Inc., Attention: Department 415, PO Box 10005, Palo Alto, CA 94303

A second way of protecting your Facebook page from use by unauthorized users is to add a second level of approval when Facebook is being used by browsers or computers other than where you usually view it. On these other machines, Facebook will require a security code to get access. If you select this option, you must provide the number of a cell phone. When Facebook detects unusual access, it texts a code to your cellphone, which must be entered for access. The security settings allow you to put passwords on your applications, to specify what kinds of browsers are available, and to check on what machines you are logged in.

Another setting that I would like to highlight, however, is the "Trusted Contacts." These are people who know you and whom you can trust, who can vouch for you and help you regain access to an account if you are locked out. I would keep it a small number of people who really know you; personally I have my husband, my son, and my best friend.

The various settings help to protect you, but in fact you still must rely on common sense to keep yourself safe. There are a large number of scams that affect Facebook, either to get your password or money or money. For example, messages like the one below are aimed at getting you to disclose your password.

> WARNING : Your account is reported to have violated the policies that are considered annoying or insulting Facebook users. Until we (http://www.facebook.com/security) system will disable your account within 24 hours if you do not do the reconfirmation.

> If you still want to use Facebook, Please confirm your account below:

> [URL deleted]

> Thanks.

> The Facebook Team

Facebook's response is:

> Spammers and scammers sometimes send phony emails that have been made to look like they're from Facebook or another reputable website. These emails can be very convincing, and the "From:" field can even be spoofed to include "Facebook" or "The Facebook Team."

> If an email looks strange, don't click on any of the links in it, and delete it from your inbox immediately. Be especially wary of emails that ask you to update your account, tell you to open an attachment, or warn you to take some other urgent action.

There are also a series of scams that claim companies are giving away items such as:

> Gift cards to the Cheesecake Factory, Starbucks, Tim Hortons, Wallmart
> Apples, iPods, iPhones on MacBooks
> Southwest Airline tickets.

Often when you click on these, you get directed to questionnaires asking for lots of personal information. Remember, there is no free lunch! Not only will you be disappointed, you run the risk the scam is trying to download viruses to your computer, reveal confidential information or even take control of your computer.

Another scam comes in this form:

> Just so everyone on my friends list knows that I completed this and I am done! Facebook has changed their privacy settings once more!! Due to the new "graph app" anyone on facebook (including other countries) can see your pictures, likes & comments. The next 2 weeks I will be posting this, and please once you have done it please post DONE!!! Those of you who do not keep my information from going... out to the public, I will have to DELETE YOU! I want to stay PRIVATELY connected with you. I post shots of family that I don't want strangers to have access to! This happens when friends click "like" or "comment"... automatically, their friends would see our posts, too. Unfortunately, we cannot change this setting by ourselves because Faceboook configured it that way. PLEASE place your mouse over my name above (DO NOT CLICK), a window will appear, now move the mouse on "FRIENDS" (also without clicking), then down to "settings", click here and a list will appear. REMOVE the CHECK on "LIFE EVENTS and "COMMENTS & LIKES". By doing this, my activity among my friends and family will no longer become public. Now, copy & paste this on your wall. Once i see

Following these instructions simply blocks your friends' updates from appearing on your timeline. According to Facebook, only your settings affect who sees your materials.

Many scammers prey upon us with stories of sick people, and missing children. Messages such as

> "this child's got a cancer. facebook is ready to pay 3
> cent for every share. we don't know is it true or not,
> but let's everybody share. maybe it's true and then..."

are often spread simply because it *might* be true. Facebook, Microsoft and others are *not* sending money when you post these messages. You should never send money in response to one of these messages without substantial checking on its veracity. Likewise, you need to be suspicious of any postings that promise to show unlikely photos, especially lewd, crude or gory ones.

A heartbreaking message that has appeared in Facebook, via emails and even via telephone, goes something like this:

> I'm writing this with tears in my eyes, my family and I came down here to London, England for a short vacation unfortunately we were mugged at the park of the hotel where we stayed, all cash, credit card and cell were stolen off us but luckily for us we still have our passports with us.
>
> We've been to the embassy and the Police here but they're not helping issues at all and our flight leaves in less than 3hrs from now but we're having problems settling the hotel bills and the hotel manager won't let us leave until we settle the bills.
>
> Am freaked out at the moment. I Need Your Help Urgently...

These people obviously are trying to steal your money. Be careful before you send any!

There are two sites on Facebook that I recommend you "like" and follow. The first is "Facebook Security," a group that provides updates about how to protect your security on Facebook (and generally in cyberspace). The second is called "Facebook and Privacy," with updates on protecting your privacy, and discussions on the threats to your privacy. You can find both of these groups by typing in their names on the search bar.

The last, and perhaps most important message about Facebook is to take care not to post things that you do not want available to a potentially very large audience. Once something is on the Internet, it is there *forever*. Files get saved by friends *and Facebook* and can reappear when you least expect them. So, think first, so you don't spoil a surprise party, announce a pregnancy before the mother is ready to announce it, or even be the person responsible for identifying Clark Kent as Superman!

Twitter

Twitter is the most challenging social networking site because they really take the "micro" part of microblogging seriously: messages sent through Twitter can be no more than 140 characters each. Generally these messages, which are called "Tweets," are like headlines, and they direct you to a website with more information. Early tweeting was associated with celebrities and their fans. Many of the tweets were inconsequential and so people dismissed the tool as frivolous. But, there are many good reasons to use it. The most important use of Twitter is to drive people to your website or blog by providing context for it. For example, every time I post something in my blog, I send out a tweet so people know to look at it. This saves people from needing to check the blog page regularly. Many not for profits use Twitter to announce and encourage fundraising campaigns. Many corporations and professionals use Twitter to announce new results or papers available on a given topic. One CEO even resigned via Twitter with his 47 character haku:

> Financial crisis
> Stalled too many customers
> CEO no more.

Twitter can have a big impact when it is used for the right reasons. In 2007, Twitter kept the followers of the California fires informed of the locations of fires, minute to minute. In 2008 during the Mumbai attacks, officials were able to get eyewitness accounts, information about the dead and wounded, emergency numbers, and even locations of hospitals needing blood donations using Twitter. People in Caribbean countries have used Twitter during natural disasters to find people and check on conditions. In 2009 during Iranian elections, Twitter was used as rallying tool and a way of communicating with the outside world. In 2010, demonstrators in the Arab Spring used Twitter and other social networking tools to organize, communicate, and raise awareness of their problems. Of course, not all uses are positive. It is hard to forget the problems of Anthony Weiner and the images he tweeted that seemingly ended his political career.

As with all social media, Twitter is only as useful as the people you "follow" (similar to friending in Facebook). If you only follow movie stars, you will only get social gossip, and if you only follow people who tweet about their food, you will not get much interesting reading. However, you can learn first-hand about your politicians' attitudes on topics by following their tweets. You can get truly balanced reporting by following news sources from a range of political viewpoints. I follow people and organizations in my field, and I am directed to research reports, journals, and even popular reports on topics of professional importance to me. But, you can follow whomever you wish and get as engaging and stimulating information as you want.

First, we should cover some vocabulary. The product is called "Twitter," but the activity is "Tweeting." For example during the "HiddenCash for ...." Campaign where individuals were giving away money and sending people hints as to where it is hidden, the benefactor "tweeted messages about the location on the money."

So, the message itself is called a "tweet," as in, I saw several tweets with hints about how to find the hidden cash. If you see a tweet from someone else, you, "retweet" the message, while giving credit to the original tweeter. If you want to ensure that you see all tweets by an individual, you "follow" that individual (or company).

As I said earlier, sometimes tweets are part of a movement, such as the Arab Spring. Or, they may be part of a smaller movement, such as people who saw a concert, or people interested in a particular organization or topic. People generally do not want to search all possible tweets to see what someone says about a concert, or the organization, or the hobby, but they still want to know what people say about these topics. For this, Twitter uses a "Hashtag." Hashtags are part of messages that begin with "#" and use a word/phrase so that interested individuals can know the tweet has a message of interest. So, for example, people interested in events in Chicago might use "#ChicagoEvents" at the end of their message to indicate they have a suggestion, a question or an answer about what is happening there. Or, if people want to know about anything happening in Chicago, including mayoral appointments, highway slowdowns, new store openings, business news, political news, sports and more, they might just, use "#Chicago."

Using the hashtag helps you find people of similar interests even if you do not know them. Twitter also keeps track of the use of the hashtags. When many people are using the same hashtag in their message, the topic is said to be "trending." Right now, the items that are trending right now (but they will be different when you read this section) are Rihanna, Chicago, Starbucks, Stay Classy, MusicAwards2014, Doctor Strange, iOS8, and Tupac Said It. Those are the topics most discussed today in St. Louis. Or, of course, you can search for a particular hashtag that is of interest to you.

Unless you "direct" a message, all tweets are open and *anyone* can follow them and read them. So as with Facebook, be careful that you are not divulging information that you would rather strangers not have.

As with other social media, you begin by creating an account. When you first go to Twitter.com, you will see the screen shown in Figure 6.33. You should take some time to browse the site and see what opportunities are available to you. When you are ready, you can set up an account. Select "sign in" in the upper right hand corner of the page. You will be sent to a page that is labeled "Sign in to Twitter." Ignore that section and go to the bottom where it asks "New to Twitter? Sign up now." Select that option. That will direct your browser to a short signup page that asks for your name, email address and a password. Follow the instructions and press the button labeled "Create my account."

Figure 6.33: Twitter's Home Page
http://twitter.com

Once you have completed your form and confirmed your email address, you will be faced with a page such as that shown in Figure 6.34. Notice on the left are items that are "trending" and on the right are people recommended for you to follow. But you have no tweets posted both because you have not made any and you are not following anyone who might have made some. Before we explore the page, we will make our first tweet. In the box to the left that is labeled "Compose new Tweet," type your first tweet. For example, you can tweet "Hello Twitter World #Intrnet4Seniors" and then press the "Tweet button that will have appeared under your entry window.

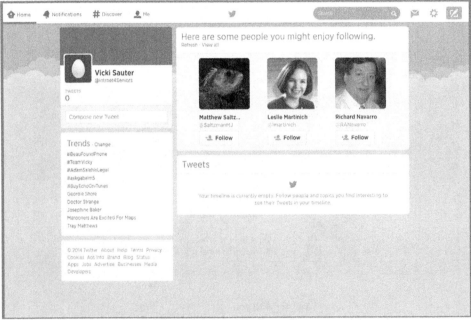

Figure 6.34: Twitter Page

Now instead of that blank screen on the bottom right, you will now see a "1" under Tweets on the left (indicating you have sent 1 tweet), and see a record of your posting such.

So, you have created your first tweet. You have also used a hashtag so that you can find other people who also have used that hashtag. To find out who else has used it, go to the gray oval at the top right corner of your screen and type in "#Intrnet4Seniors." The result of my search will look like Figure 6.34. Your search may have more names and will include others who are reading this book, who use the same hashtag. These people are likely to be readers of this book. However, at this point, I am the only one who has used the hashtag. My image is an egg until I change it.

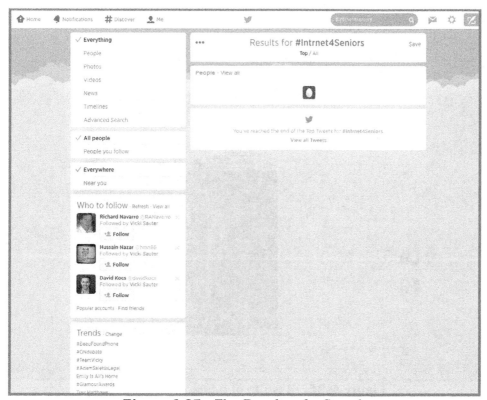

Figure 6.35: The Results of a Search

Now you need to find things of interest. You can search for hashtags (as described before), people, or just interesting topics. Let us start with trying to find a specific person. Type a name in the gray oval at the top of the page (marked with an arrow in Figure 6.36); as you can see, I typed in my colleague's name, "Perry Drake." Twitter will pick up everything having anything to do with Perry or Drake.

Everything is selected because that is the default search in Twitter. Look at the menu on the left of the page (marked by an arrow). As you see, "Everything" is checked. If you click instead on "People," you only get people who have Drake or Perry in their name as shown in Figure 6.37. The first one happens to be the Perry Drake I wanted. If I want to see his recent posts, I can click on his name. Or, I can "follow" Perry and ensure that his tweets are always summarized for me when I log into Twitter. To follow him, simply press the "follow" button to the right of his name (indicated by an arrow in the screenshot). By pressing the

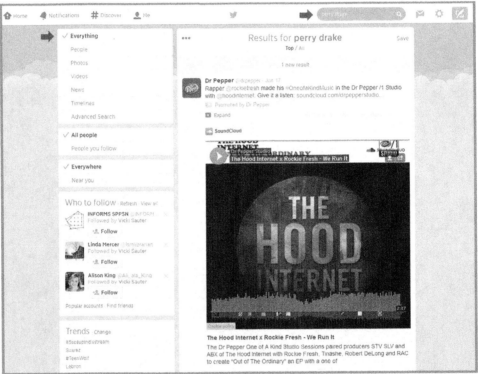

Figure 6.36: Results of a Search in Twitter

gear image to the left of that button, you have other options such as tweeting to him, adding or deleting him from a list, or blocking or reporting his tweets (if they are offensive).

If the search did not show the person I wanted early in the list, I could also search for him by his handle, @pddrake. These always start out with the "@" and generally have some of the person's name on them. If you select photos, videos, or news you get ones that have been tagged with that name. Similarly, "Timelines" allows you to look at anyone's timeline that happens to mention perry or drake. Finally, the last option is an advanced search. This allows you to search on a specific phrase, list of words or hashtags, only in specific languages, or even date specific.

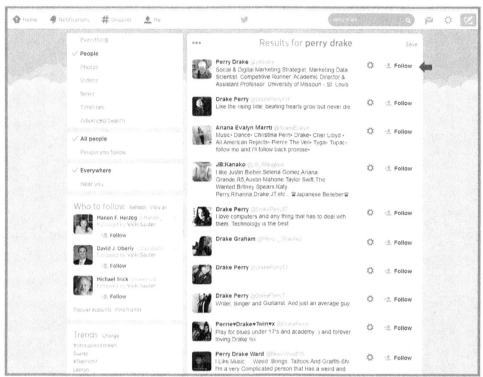

Figure 6.37: Searching only on People in Twitter

Now that you know how to tweet, how to use hashtags, and how to search for hashtags, let us return to the home page and personalize your page. In the upper right corner of the page is a gear icon. Click on it to bring down the menu. The second to the bottom is "settings;" select that one. The default page will have information about your account and contact which you probably do not want to change. However, the menu on the left of that page shows that you can adjust your security and privacy, your password, your notifications, profile, design and more. For example, if you would like to change the design of your page, you would select the item labeled "Design" and you would see a page like that shown in Figure 6.38. You may select a premade theme or provide one of your own, change the background color and theme color. If you provide your own background image, you will need to decide if you want to use a large image that is centered in the background or a small image that is repeated to cover your background. This set up is completely for your comfort; it is not used except on your desktop.

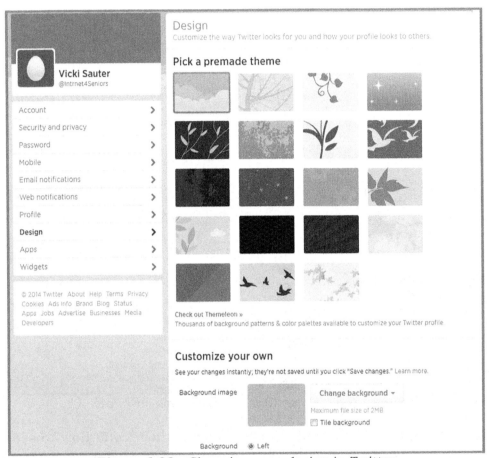

Figure 6.38: Changing your design in Twitter

You can also change your profile by selecting "profile" from the list of options. If you do, you will see the screen in Figure 6.38 and will be able to add a photograph of yourself, and provide additional information about you including where you live, your website and even a photo. All of these changes will appear anytime someone sees your page, or profile, or finds you from a search.

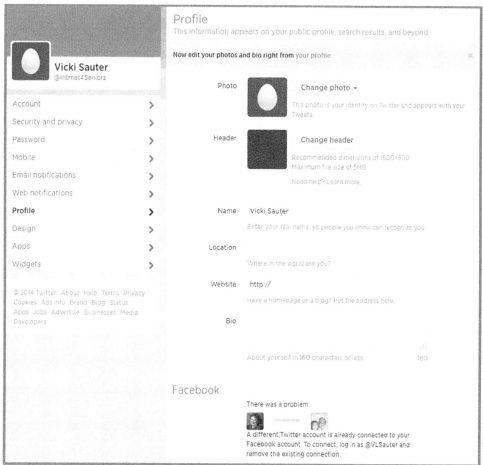

Figure 6.39: Changing Twitter Profile

LinkedIn

LinkedIn differs from other social networking sites in that it is used primarily for professional networking. The site allows users to create a profile of their education and professional background similar to a resume (although you cannot upload an actual resume). You can summarize your background, list specific jobs (with years and explanations), provide your education, list organizations with which you have some affiliation or for which you volunteer, list honors/awards, languages spoken, publications, and more.

Figure 6.40 shows the top of my LinkedIn page.

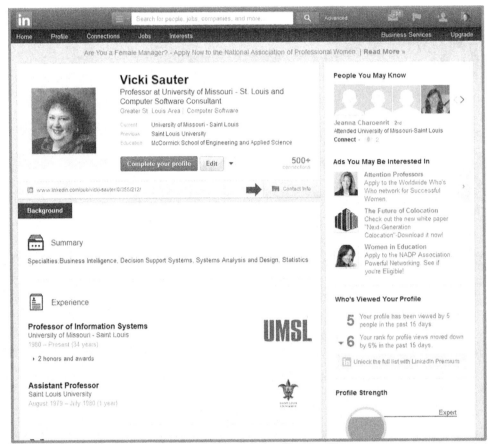

Figure 6.40: LinkedIn Profile

As you can see, there is summary information about me; more specific information comes later. However, one thing you should note is the "contact information" marked by the arrow. People list their email address, their Twitter handles, webpages, blogs and sometimes even telephone numbers here. It is a great way to find contact information you may have lost.

You do not have "friends," but rather have "connections" in LinkedIn. You can invite whomever you wish to be a connection. However, people who receive those requests have the option to be your connection or not. If they believe you do not know them, or are simply trying to build your connection list randomly, they can respond with "I don't know" and LinkedIn interprets your request as spam. If the site sees too many notifications of you spamming other people, you can lose your ability to invite people to be your connection. You build your network by finding connections. In addition to your direct connections, you have access to the connections of all of your direct connections, and the connections of their connections. So, if you see that someone you know actually knows someone you want to meet, you ask the person to "introduce" you to his or her other connection.

Much like the other social networks, when you login, your "home" consists primarily of a page of updates such as that shown in Figure 6.40. On the left of that image are updates that my connections have posted. It may be something that happens automatically, such as an update about promotions or work anniversaries. Or, it may be a statement about something you have recently read or experienced. This is where the "news" per se is shown. On the right side, you first see suggestions for connections. These will be people who are connected with others you know or who work at the same organization and you do or who are involved in the same not for profit organizations. Remember, LinkedIn discourages you from adding people whom you do not know, and will suspend your ability to add connections if too many people report that you tried to connect to them and they do not know you. Beyond that are data regarding pages you have recently visited and other statistics of your network. Finally, at the bottom are jobs, groups, and companies that might be of interest to you.

As with other social networking sites, groups allow people to associate more easily. People with similar interests, in similar jobs, in the same industry, who graduated from the same university can affiliate as a group and thus have easier access to one another. These individuals can post content, questions or jobs that they will be sure others in the group will see. In that way, people can get advice or reactions to ideas, find jobs and even increase their stature among fellow professionals.

Personally, I belong to a variety of groups on LinkedIn. First, of course, as professional societies, some associated with groups from my alma mater, Northwestern University, and those associated with where I work, University of Missouri – St. Louis. But, I also belong to organizations that connect me with people who have similar specialties, such as Decision Support Systems or Systems Thinkers. There are others to which I belong that link people in the St. Louis community, and other women in technology.

Figure 6.41: LinkedIn "Home" Page

These groups probably will not be of interest to you. However, you can search for a group that might be of interest to you. Go to the top and middle of the LinkedIn page for the search box and type in a topic of interest. For example, if you are interested in craft in some fashion, search for that and you will find over 1000 groups to join! Of course, there are a lot of crafts available. If you search for fiber craft, there are three groups of interest to them. There are over 200 groups pertaining to power tools, and over 300 with something to do about gardening. So, no matter what your interest, you are bound to find a group of interest because there are over a million interest groups on LinkedIn.

LinkedIn also provides information about others who attended the same college or university as you did. All of my degrees are from Northwestern University, so I only get that one page. If I click on "connections" (in the dark band at the top of the page) and select "find alumni," I see a page similar to that in Figure

6.42.

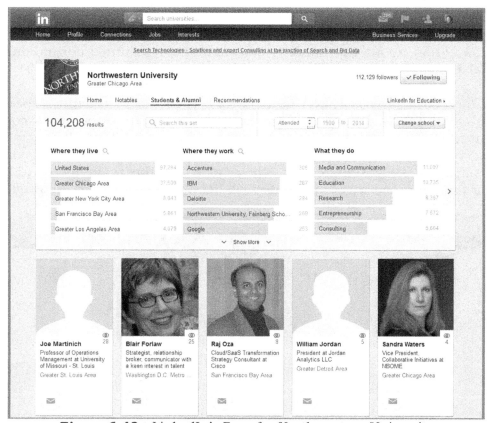

Figure 6.42: LinkedIn's Page for Northwestern University

From this page, you see you can go to Northwestern's profile page, find notable people who attended the institution, find students and alumni, and comment on the institution. The lower section of the page profiles people from Northwestern to whom you are connected. In between are some summary statistics about Northwestern alumni. From here you can investigate where they live, where they work, what they do, what they studied, in what are they skilled and to how many you are connected. Please note that these statistics are collected by LinkedIn by summarizing profile pages of those who are registered. So, they are not the official statistics, nor are they even necessarily inclusive of all groups of alumni. But they are an interesting way to view the University.

As mentioned earlier, there is also a profile page for the University. If you select

"Home" from the university menu above (in the pale gray area), you can see more information about the University. While it does provide some similar statistics, such as where people work and what they do, it does give some descriptive information such as a summary and contact information. There is also information about the student body and faculty, and information about financial aid.

One of the best sources of information you can find on LinkedIn, especially if you are looking for a job or a volunteer opportunity, however, is its company information. There are two types of information available. If you are just starting, you might look at the jobs that are advertised through LinkedIn. To have companies suggested to you, click "jobs" on the main menu (the dark menu at the top of the page). LinkedIn will list options based on the profile you

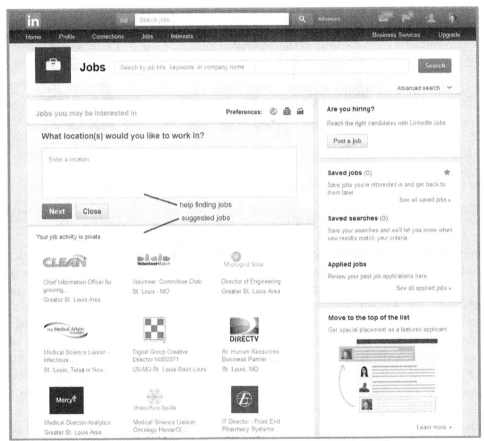

Figure 6.43: Searching for Jobs in LinkedIN

have created, as shown at the bottom of the page in Figure 6.43. These will be jobs in your local area requiring the kinds of skills that you have.

Or, you can have LinkedIn help you find a job with specific characteristics. You will see in Figure 6.42 the box at the top asking where you would like to work. You can specify the location, such as Chicago or Paris, by typing then in the box. When you are finished, click the "Next" key at the bottom of the box. Then LinkedIn will ask you how large of a company you seek. Move the slider to an option that is comfortable for you and hit "Next." Finally it asks the industry in which you are interested. Once you have answered those questions, LinkedIn will give you suggestions that meet your criteria. Of course, you can adjust those criteria and see what other options appear.

Figure 6.44: Researching Companies in LinkedIn

The second way you can research companies is to select the "interests" tab on the main menu and select "companies" from the drop down box. Then type the name of a company in which you are interested in the search box at the top of the page. I entered "Nestlé." LinkedIn responded with Figure 6.44. If you click the "see more" at the end of the first paragraph, you get a greater description and statistics about the company as shown in Figure 6.45. There is much to learn about their products, the groups within the organization and even possible jobs there. Did you know, for example, that one of Nestlé's specalty is in pet foods? Not exactly the chocolate bar that you probably first associated with it! Such information can be quite helpful during an interview for a job. It is not that you cannot get the information without LinkedIn. Rather that it is so easy to get the information using this tool.

Figure 6.45: Corporate Information on LinkedIn

Below the corporate information are recent updates about the organization In the case of Nestlé, they seem to be running a sweepstakes for new employees and they are hiring an HR Manager in Kansas City. Both are good if you are interested in joining that company.

On the right side, you see, at the top, people to whom you are connected on LinkedIn who work for Nestlé. In addition, you see that your connections have 483 second degree connections (to whom you can be introduced by one or more of your connections). This is an easy and direct way to network. Below that is a link to jobs and more information about different pages associated with Nestlé.

If you use LinkedIn completely, you can learn about jobs early, learn more about the company so you can ask better questions and understand if you will fit there, and know more about the people with whom you will be interviewing. Likewise, if you work for the company, you can learn more about potential employees sand understand if they will meet your needs.

As you can see, all of the social networking sites behave in similar ways: you build a profile, you find connections, and you share information. What differs among them is what kind of information is being shared and who belongs to them. Most of them allow you to affiliate with others of similar interests. Most of them allow you to select who can see what information. They can be fun, informative and useful. But, they can also be a significant time drain and they can be used for fraud and other negative activities.

Surfing Safely

A few months ago there was an article in my local newspaper about a woman who found photos of herself at questionable sites on the Internet. She was confused because she had never put them anywhere on the Internet – she only had them stored on her home computer. In another publication, there was an article about a man who had credit card and other personal information stored on the computer and suddenly he was a victim of identity theft. He did not know how the thief got the information because he never shopped or banked online. Recently, a friend complained that her computer had gotten slower and slower over time, and then she could not access some of her programs and files. What do these stories have in common? They all began with someone who used the internet, but did not do so safely. In each case, the user did not know what could happen, and so they did not know how to protect themselves.

In today's world, we need to be vigilant about our computer security even if we do not fully understand what could happen or how it could happen. This should not be surprising. Many of us provide security in our homes even though we do not know how to pick a lock, forge a key, or cut out a window. We provide security devices for our homes because we do not want someone in our homes, taking our possessions, and harming those we love. Some people have simple locks while others have dead bolt locks and locks on their windows. Still others have security systems, bars on their windows and perhaps guards. We provide "enough" security to fit our level of comfort with the risk we take. That is, we consider the amount of crime in the neighborhood, the acceptable level of risk, and the amount of inconvenience we are willing to tolerate for that security. Depending on where we live, what possessions we have, and who lives with us, we select different security options.

Similarly, we provide security devices for our computers because we do not want someone using the computing resources (without our knowledge), and we do not want someone taking our photos or personal information, especially if they use it to steal identities, harm loved ones or cause us embarrassment. In addition, not providing security on your computer may mean that even though no one steals anything off of your computer, you may be providing your computer to host a child pornography site, send spam and phishing messages to unsuspecting users or facilitating attack messages to corporations to disrupt their e-business – all without your knowledge!

Computer safety is similar to home safety in that we all make choices about what is enough, and how much inconvenience we are willing to tolerate. Unfortunately, crime has moved its way out into small towns and the country, so people there need to be more aware of their attention to security. Likewise, online crime (and mischief) has moved beyond the early questionable sites to be important for all of us to consider.

It is not a question of making our home or our computers theft-proof. Although we might have locks on the doors and windows, that is only a deterrent; a determined thief can *always* get in some way no matter how much security we provide. There is no such thing as complete home security. Similarly, it has been said, "[T]he only truly secure system is one that is powered off, cast in a block of concrete and sealed in a lead-lined room with armed guards - and even then I have my doubts."1

We know to lock our doors because we have seen other people do it since we were children. Providing security for a computer is more confusing because it is not obvious what needs to be done, how it should be done and how to stay one step ahead of a problem.

Of course, if you never connect to the internet, you may not need to worry about these issues of security. But if your life will include surfing, there are some basic things you must do to keep the computer safe. This chapter will describe a number of steps that will address many of the problems people face on the computer. Some are software related. Some are habits. They are all needed to make your experience good.

Do You Need Patches?

If you ever knitted, or observed someone knitting, you probably know about the problem of dropped stitches and the holes they can cause in the finished product. The process of knitting involves looping the yarn and pulling loops through each other to produce sweaters, socks and many other things. A graphic representation of this process is shown in Figure 7.1[2].

---

1 Dewdney, A. K., "Computer Recreations: Of Worms, Viruses and Core War" *Scientific American,* March 1989, pp 110.

2 **Error! Main Document Only.** This schematic is adapted from the one available at "Knitting," *Wikipedia Free Encyclopedia,* last modified 13:48, 16 August 2007, page viewed August 21, 2007, http://en.wikipedia.org/wiki/Knitting.

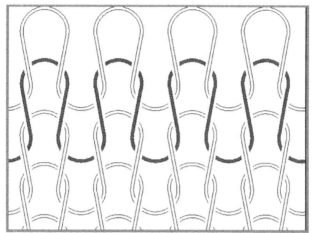

Figure 7.1: Knitting Schematic

When one "drops a stitch" the loop is pulled without having another loop pulled through it. Hence, instead of looking like Figure 1, your item will look like Figure 7.2. It has a hole in the spot where the stitch is dropped (this is noted with an arrow). Often these dropped stitches are not noticeable to the knitter. The hole may not even be noticeable to the person using the knitted item. However, this hole leaves the item vulnerable. Not only could a small item slip through the hole, if one pulls at that dropped stitch, one could make much of the garment become unwoven. This makes the hole larger and makes your knitted good unable to complete its mission of being warm, decorative and/or of covering some other item.

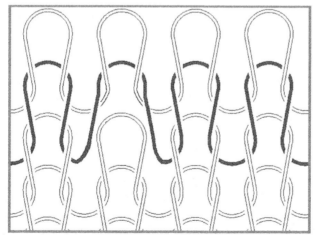

Figure 7.2: Knitting Schematic with Dropped Stich

Unfortunately, when people write software, they can commit errors that are similar to dropping a stitch during knitting. The error often is not noticeable to the person committing it, and may not even be noticeable when the software is completed. But, the hole can leave the software vulnerable. Pins and buttons will not slip through the holes in the software, but other small pieces of code can get through the hole unobserved and then cause your programs not to work properly. As with knitted goods, the larger and more complex the program, the more likely you will be to find holes in the code.

In today's world, many programs have holes. So, what do you do? Unfortunately, the analogy needs a change here from knitted goods to woven goods, such as shirts, pants and gloves. When a child's pants get holes in the knees from play or when a favorite shirt gets a hole, often we place a patch over the hole to keep the hole from getting larger *and* to provide the same protection, warmth and coverage of the original fabric. Some patches are made from the same material and are woven into the torn material to make them basically indistinguishable. Others are made from quite different fabric and are sewn or ironed into place with no effort to blend with the original covering. Some patches hold quite securely while other patches are put on with less care and can come open often.

When holes or other flaws are located in software, the manufacturer creates patches to cover them and to correct the problem. These might be called "patches" or they might be called "service packs" or some other name that suggests a similar mission. Don't worry, you do not need to fetch the needle and thread, or even the iron. Software patches are programs that are installed to work with your existing programs. They patch the hole in the fabric of the program, correct errors in the program, and sometimes even introduce new features to the software.

Companies introduce patches at various rates depending on the severity of the problem, the likelihood that the problem will be encountered by its users and other factors. However, when those patches are available, you should apply them to your system.

Perhaps the most important set of patches to consider are those to your operating system. The operating system is the main software controlling your computer. It represents the set of programs that allows information to be displayed on the monitor, sent to the printer, and input from devices such as keyboards and mice. It also controls how the other programs work and how they interact together. In simple terms, the operating system is "the boss." Most people have one of the Microsoft Windows operating systems. If you use an iPad, or a computer from Apple, generally referred to as a Mac, then you run a Macintosh operating system. Other tablets generally run a version of the Android operating system. There are other options too, but we will not address those here.

For those of you using Windows products, you can set the system to update automatically, or you can do it yourself. To update the system, click the "Start" button in the lower left of your computer as you would to run any program. This brings up your normal menu as shown on the left side of Figure 7.3. Select "All Programs" (highlighted with the arrow), and you will see the menu on the right side of Figure 7.3. Of course, your list of programs may differ from mine, but you should find the Windows Update toward the bottom of the list; this option is noted with an arrow.

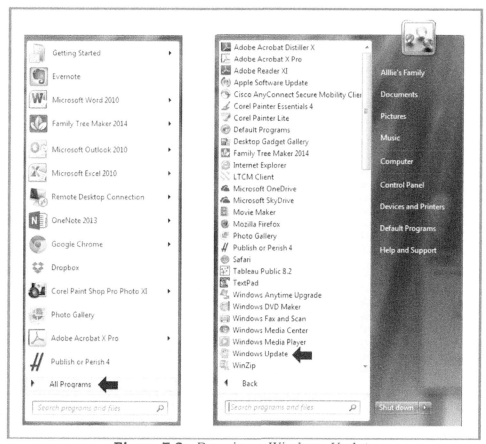

Figure 7.3: Running a Windows Update

Your computer will then display a screen such as the one in Figure 7.4. In this example, the operating system is fully patched with the required, and more critical, patches. You can see, however that there is one optional update available (note is highlighted with an arrow).

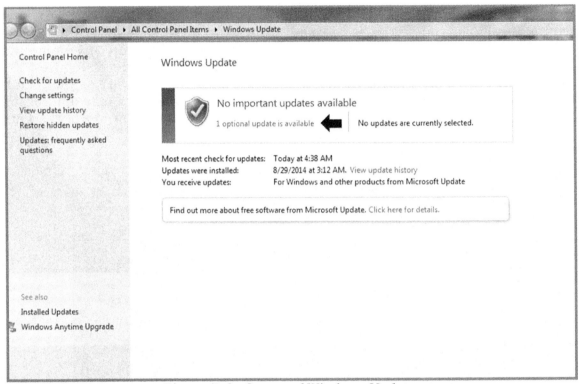

Figure 7.4: Status of Windows Update

When you click on that link, the system enumerates what updates are needed as shown in Figure 7.5. This screen will explain what is affected by the update, how critical it is, and even how the system is likely to respond. You can select the options and press "OK" and the system will be updated. Remember *always* to select those updates noted to be "critical," because they are critical to keeping your computer functioning well.

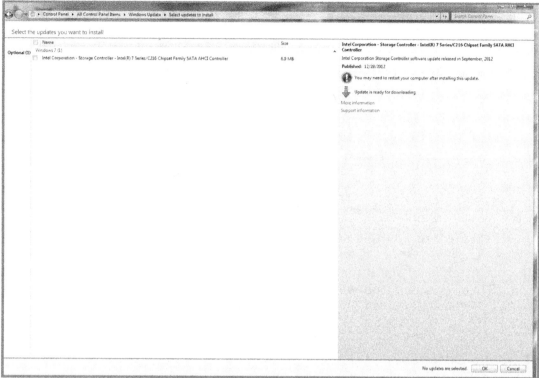

Figure 7.5: Windows Update Choices

version of that software you have. Different software and different versions of software require different patches because they are broken in different ways. Using the knitting analogy shown earlier, one version of the operating system may be broken as shown in Figure 7.2, while another is broken as is shown in Figure 7.66. Clearly the stitches have been dropped in different places and in different ways. The kind of fix should be different as well.

In addition, sometimes there is an order in which the patches must be applied. If a newer patch fixes something that was not quite fixed in the original patch, then the first patch must be installed before the second patch makes sense. Windows will share the order in which the patches must be made when it tells you what patches to install.

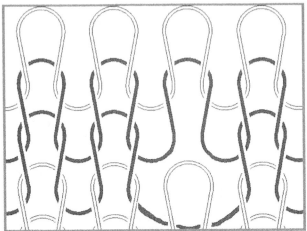

Figure 7.6: Knitting Schematic with a Different Dropped Stich

If your computer is a Macintosh or Android, you will follow similar steps as required. These systems too will inform you of updates and the importance of them.

What Needs Patches?

OK, you have patched your operating system and perhaps your browser and office suite, but you might not be finished. Every program on your machine may have the same problem. Your word processing program, your music program, even your genealogy program will probably need to be patched from time to time. Each of them provides a different way for someone to enter your system. This means, that each of them is like a window that you leave unlocked: it is a way for a stranger to enter the system, steal important information, and do damage to the data that remain. Even if you do not store any data on your machine, you still leave yourself vulnerable to having your machine "hijacked" to do things about which you are not aware, or to copy information you simply type into your machine.

Most programs today have some kind of automatic updating feature. That is, when you run a program, it automatically checks to see if a patch is available and to bring that fact to your attention. If they do not have such a feature, usually the company will email its subscribers with information that the patch is available and give you directions on how to download it.

When you get the information, generally you should act upon it -- cautiously, of course. I have several friends who, when they get messages about software, they delete them because they do not understand them or because they are afraid it might be an attempt to infect the computer. Of course, caution is important. Generally if the request to patch the system comes when you are starting a program, it is authentic. However, if you are not sure, you can always go to the website associated with the software product to learn if the request is legitimate. If the product really needs to be patched, the websites will have information. If it does not have information about the patch, you should probably ignore the request.

An Apple a Day is Not Enough

We have all know about flu season and cold and cough season. Those of us who have chronic problems that increase the likelihood of catching the flu get shots to help reduce our vulnerability. We all know to wash our hands more frequently, not share glasses and to protect ourselves from those coughing and sneezing during cold season. The reason we do these things is to keep our bodies healthy because when we are healthy, it is easier to accomplish both necessary and desirable tasks.

The same is true for our computers, but for them, it is always flu season! Unless you never attach your computer to the Internet and never use a disk in your computer that has ever been used in another computer, your machine is vulnerable to viruses.

What is a Virus?

A virus is an unwanted software program that attaches itself to your computer without your knowledge. It attempts to reproduce itself under specific circumstances. For example, it might replicate each time a particular program is run or each time someone logs into the system. Then, when some signal is sent, such as each time a specific day of the month is encountered, or even when a specific date is reached, the virus begins to do its damage. Some viruses do nothing but reproduce themselves. Some perform trivial extras like beeping the keyboard, or forcing the file to be saved in a specific format. Some are more destructive and attempt to rename or erase files or destroy the hard drive. Others simply copy selected information from your computer to another computer.

One particularly annoying kind of virus is a "macro" virus. Macro viruses are programming code, created by hackers or unethical programmers, which is either annoying, prankish or harmful. The macros are written to attach themselves to the default document of a software package such as Word or Excel. When an unsuspecting user opens a document containing a macro virus, the virus attaches itself to the default document. Each time a document is created or edited from this time forward, the virus attaches itself to that document. The problem escalates as the document is passed on to other computers by file sharing or e-mail. The virus continues to spread until it is removed.

The virus may do nothing but propagate itself and then allow the program to run normally. Usually, however, after propagating silently for a while, it starts doing its damage or mischief.

Viruses are *not* microorganisms that exist "in the wild." Rather they are programs that someone must sit down and program and distribute. The people who write them study vulnerabilities in other programs and how to take advantage of them. Virus writers also study the best ways to avoid detection and to accomplish the desired kinds of damage.

Similarly, there are groups of computer detectives who study viruses. In particular, they identify patterns in the computer virus programs and how those patterns change over time. This activity is similar to the approach that medical researchers take when trying to understand viral and bacterial infections in humans and animals. Once they understand the patterns that are associated with a given virus, these computer detectives can write software to identify when a specific virus is on a computer. This is one task that virus protection software performs. This is only a first step, however. In addition to identifying that the virus exists, the computer detectives would like to eliminate the virus or at least contain the extent of its impact on a computer. By understanding what and how the virus acts, the computer detectives can write another program that prevents the virus from doing damage, and perhaps even erase the virus.

Obviously, these virus protection programs only work *if* the virus on your computer was created before the virus protection program was put on your machine. For this reason, virus protection programs have updates that they offer every week (sometimes more frequently). The updates, generally called "virus pattern updates," include information about new viruses that have been identified and the way to combat them, as well as better ways to combat already identified viruses. It is imperative, therefore, that you keep your virus patterns up to date.

Some virus protection programs will update themselves automatically each week, while others require the user's action to get the update. It is important to know which kind of updating your program requires and take action if necessary. Virus protection is not very useful if it is not updated regularly.

Even that is not sufficient, however. The practice of comparing a known pattern to specific software only works if a pattern has already been identified. There are unknown viruses existing on the Internet and you might "catch" one of these; you want your software to protect your computer even if a specific virus has not yet been identified. For this reason, most virus protection programs have components called heuristics that look for behavior in software that is similar to what families of viruses do and thus is suspicious. The heuristics will evaluate whether the suspicious software are likely to be doing damage and, if so, to contain or delete the code just in case.

Regardless of whether it is a pattern comparison or an heuristic, virus protection programs only work if you keep them running all the time; we refer to this as being "resident" on the computer. Most of the programs will ask if you wish to have them running resident. The answer should be "yes" so that the virus protection can always be looking for the patterns they can identify. The alternative to running resident is to have regular scans of your computer to identify virus patterns. It is good to run such scans as extra protection. It is not good, however, to rely upon them alone to catch the viruses. You want to eliminate or contain the virus as early as possible to eliminate or at least minimize potential damage to your machine.

In addition to running virus protection software, there are other things you can do to reduce the impact of viruses. First, when downloading programs from the internet, only do so from reputable sites. If the site is not "known" and you are not sure about the software, do not download it because the risk is too high. You are better off obtaining software from known vendors even if that means you need to pay for it. Second, when running programs on websites, such as playing games, be aware of what modifications they want to make to your system to allow you to play the game. Again, go to reputable sites and do not take chances. Be careful opening your email. In a previous chapter, we discussed that attachments to email might include viruses or malware (to be discussed in a moment) that once opened will run and infect your computer. Never open an attachment from someone you do not know; even if you know the person, do not open it if the attachment is not expected or explained in the email.

You should always have backups or copies of files that are important to you. These backups should be on a floppy disk, thumb drive, CD, or DVD and kept away from the computer. Therefore if your system is attacked, you can still recover the information that is important. Some operating systems as well as security programs have system restore capabilities that take a snap shot of critical files at regular intervals to fix damage caused by viruses.

The first step is to install virus protection on your computer and always run it. The three most common are MacAfee, Symantec (Norton), and AVG. It does not matter which of these you select since all three are fairly effective in keeping viruses from attacking your system. Regardless of which you select, it is *critical* that you update your virus patterns weekly. You can think of the virus patterns like flu shots.

Malware is Not a Bad Outfit Day

Viruses are not the only kinds of pests that can cause problems with your computer. There is another kind of program that people distribute (unknown to the computer user) that can damage the computer, "malware." The term is short for malicious software (which makes more sense), and refers to intrusive software that is intended to change how the computer operates or steal data from the computer.

One kind of malware takes control of the computer and use it without the user's knowledge. It might be used, for example, to send spam or other messages to other unsuspecting users. Or, it might host data, such as child pornography or stolen credit card numbers; in this case, users in search of such data are directed to your computer to access the data. These uses might be schemes to make money for the writers of the malware, to provide access for illegal data, or to form the basis for extortion from companies or even countries. This hurts the computer user in two ways. First, you are, albeit unknowingly, helping support illegal activity. Second, if the computer is being used for these other functions, there is less memory and less storage available for your use. Hence you may find your computer slowing down, storage room unavailable or even unusable.

A second kind of malware is called "spyware." As the name suggests, spyware watches your usage of the computer. It may, for example, monitor your web browsing to determine what products and services are of interest, and then provide unsolicited, but targeted advertisements. Or, the spyware could monitor your keystrokes when you browse the web as you enter passwords or credit card numbers to steal them. Spyware can also monitor your non-browsing behavior to determine where you store financial or other personal or sensitive information on your computer enabling other programs to steal the data.

Regardless of the form of the malware, it is undesirable, and users must protect their computers. Fortunately, malware protection, similar to virus protection, is available to users. There are many different kinds available, but do your research first. Remember, a malware program might disguise itself as a protection program just to get you to install it on your machine!

The three products I use (and yes, I really do have all three running on my machine) are: Ad-aware, Spybot and Pest Patrol. Why do I run three programs? From my observation, each of the programs seems to find different malware programs and so I get better protection with all three.

Personal copies of Adaware can be run for free on your computer, however you get more features if your purchase the complete version. Spybot is "shareware," meaning the vendor asks for a donation. Each can be downloaded from and, where relevant, purchased over the internet. These products are at:

Ad-Aware (from LavaSoft): http://www.download.com/Ad-Aware-SE-Personal-Edition/3000-8022_4-10045910.html?part=dl-ad-aware&subj=dl&tag=top5

Spybot: http://www.spybot.info/en/mirrors/index.html

Pest Patrol: http://www.ca.com/products/pestpatrol/

These programs work in a fashion that is similar the virus protection programs described earlier. Some malware is blocked and incapacitated. Other malware must be deleted completely from your computer. The programs know the best way to isolate and destroy the malware.

You must install the program *and* update it regularly (at least weekly). Unlike the virus protection, most malware programs require you to update them regularly (weekly). In addition, since most malware programs do not run resident (i.e., all the time), you must also scan your computer regularly. This will allow the protection software to find the malware and disable it before much damage can be done.

Pop Goes the Weasel

I am sure by now you have seen "popup windows" (generally referred to as "popups") when you are surfing the web. Popups are simply new windows (generally smaller than your main window) that suddenly appear on your monitor. They are similar to "pop unders" that also generate new windows, but they appear only after you close your browser because they were opened "under" the browser window. Neither popups nor popunders appear magically as they seem. Rather the webpage you have requested includes instructions to open new windows and display the contents.

Popups can provide useful functions at some sites. They are used to provide greater explanation of options, to provide forms to complete, or to display progress in downloading requested software. However, they generally simply provide advertisements as shown in Figure 9. They are often annoying because they disturb your ability to read the web page you requested. Sometimes the advertisements cause other popup advertising and soon you can have your whole screen with nothing but popup ads. Not only is this distracting, it can cause your computer to run more slowly as you surf the web. Worse yet, the popups often include innocuous-looking buttons that, when selected, can cause malware to be installed to your system without your knowledge.

To protect your security, and avoid the annoyance, set your browser to turn popups off.

Turn off your "popups" on your browser. This will provide less annoyance when you surf too! In Firefox (which, btw, I think is the better and more secure browser) go to TOOLS (on your menu) ---> OPTIONS (the last in the menu) ----> CONTENT (the second tab) ...put a check next to "block popup windows". If you are using Internet Explorer (which I do not recommend), TOOLS (on your menu) ---> INTERNET OPTIONS (the last in the menu) ----> PRIVACY (the third tab) ... you can check block popups at the bottom.

Fire Drill!

Most municipalities that have codes regarding the construction of private and public buildings have some requirements of protection of those buildings from fire. For example, early requirements for bricks in the wall to protect the building's occupants from fire. Today's code generally calls for concrete or other non-combustible materials to be included in the walls for the same reason. These walls are referred to as "Firewalls." The purpose of these reinforced walls is to protect those in the building from the elements outside the building.

Today's computers also need a "firewall" to protect it from elements on the Internet that can cause harm to your computer. There are hardware firewalls that may be running at your ISP, or in a modem or router in your home. There are also software firewalls that operate on your computer like any other piece of software. Sometimes these firewalls are built into the operating system, such as with later versions of Windows, or they can be provided by additional software that you can purchase, such as the products from Norton (Symantec), MacAfee, or ADV. They supplement the protection provided by the antivirus and malware software discussed earlier.

The idea behind a computer firewall is to identify those things that you trust completely, in which you lack any trust, and those about which you are not sure. If you trust a site, or a function or a user completely, then you will allow any interaction with your computer and that site, function or user. If you lack any trust, then you will always block interaction between your computer, and that site, function or user. As you might guess, those in between must be decided on a case by case basis.

We discussed in an earlier section the case of automatic updates to software. These software messages always come from a particular vendor. You can always allow those vendors access to their software so they can patch appropriately by establishing that you "trust" them. On the other hand, if another company, that you do not know, and which has no credentials tries to patch the software, you would not trust them, so you do not let those messages (and programs embedded in the messages) onto your computer. Similarly, if you believe that it is acceptable to use an instant messaging client on your computer, then you can "trust" that function, regardless of who might respond on the instant messenger client.

In today's market, the firewalls generally are configured to ask the user if he or she would like to allow access by a particular company (or individual) when requests are received, and if the user really intended to use services, such as an instant messenger client, when software is engaged. In this way, the user can configure preferences over time so the firewall knows how to protect the user. However, sometimes the firewall does not work that way, and simply prevents a user from running desired software. In those circumstances, it is important to launch your firewall configuration program and, using appropriate menus available with your individual product, state your preferences.

For example, consider Figure 7; this is the first menu available for the Windows XP firewall. It simply allows you to turn the firewall on or off and to control the level of absolute control the firewall has (by blocking exceptions).

If, however, you go to the second tab, labeled "exceptions," as shown in Figure 11, you will see that you can specify particular functions and sites that you trust. So, you do not need to wait until the software or function is needed, you can customize the firewall to recognize it from the beginning.

Finally, you can, by selecting the "advanced" tab, as shown in Figure 12, even specify certain networks, such as your home LAN, as trusted and therefore can use the computer completely.

Of course, if you are not sure what you are doing, then you should not edit your firewall settings directly. Instead, wait until the firewall asks *you* about allowing a particular function or user.

Everyday, Every Time

There are some basic rules that apply for all of the protection types covered in this chapter. Provide yourself the peace of mind that comes with a protected computer. Not only will this protect you from identity theft, it will keep you from inadvertently allowing nefarious individuals from using your computer for crime or mischief. Second, whatever product(s) you select, make sure you keep them up to date. This holds both for the applications software on your computer as well as the security software on your computer. Applications software often needs to be "patched" to keep those who would exploit mistakes to gain access to your computer. Virus patterns and malware patterns need updating to keep you secure. Third, wherever possible, get security software that runs "resident" (or all the time). This is real-time security which keeps things off of your computer; if it never gets on, it can never do damage. If you need to scan and correct problems with your software, do it frequently. Problems only get worse as they embedded. Finally, be vigilant in the choices you make and be persnickety about to whom you give your personal data. While these suggestions will not guarantee you will not have problems, they will certainly reduce the likelihood that you will have problems with your computer.[3]

You can think about these updates similarly to flu shots. During flu season, many people get a flu shot to help protect them from getting the illness. Every year the doctors provide a new flu shot because the kind of flu virus changes

---

3 You can think about these updates similarly to flu shots. During flu season, many people get a flu shot to help protect them from getting the illness. Every year the doctors provide a new flu shot because the kind of flu virus changes over time. The primary strains are Influenza A and B. Over time, the virus changes in small ways so that even if you have immunity to that strain, your immune system might not recognize it. Or, sometimes Influenza strain A will change abruptly. As those changed versions of the strains become more prevalent and become more of a risk to the population, manufacturers add the newer strains to help the populace keep protected.

over time. The primary strains are Influenza A and B. Over time, the virus changes in small ways so that even if you have immunity to that strain, your immune system might not recognize it. Or, sometimes Influenza strain A will change abruptly. As those changed versions of the strains become more prevalent and become more of a risk to the population, manufacturers add the newer strains to help the populace keep protected.

Likewise virus strains on your computer change over time. Some viruses are changed just a little by a programmer to avoid detection. Other times a programmer creates an entirely new program (virus) that no one has seen before. The influenza virus must mutate naturally, thereby taking some time to change enough that our antibodies will not recognize it. Computer viruses, on the other hand, are changed by humans, and so can change rapidly if someone is trying to cause mischief. Hence while the cycle for flu shots is a year, the cycle for virus updates on a computer is much shorter, usually about a week. Therefore you need to give your computer a new virus shot each week by updating your virus patterns.

Index

CPSIA information can be obtained at www.ICGtesting.com
Printed in the USA
LVOW03s1340151015

458405LV00006B/201/P

9 781506 163857